A catalogue record for this book is available from the British Library.

First Edition 2016
Published by NR Publishing

For recordings and other publications by Nick Roach Teachings, please visit the website: www.nickroach.uk

© **2016 Nick Roach Teachings**
www.nickroach.uk
Website demystifying the experience of Enlightenment

A Dream It May Be, But the Dream Goes On!

A Spiritual Autobiography

Nick Roach

Foreword

This book describes a journey of struggle, pain, despair and ultimate sacrifice, with the reward of fulfilment, happiness, love and peace. Nick's journey will make you laugh, cry, gasp and cheer as you follow and feel his every moment, and his total dedication towards finding the 'truth' and 'waking up'.

Nick's honesty is as refreshing as it is sad. To read about someone's life and the struggles and the difficulties they faced (perhaps particularly for me, in relation to someone I care so deeply for), does not make for comfortable reading. But the joy, love and peace he finds in the end can bring hope to so many of us who ask the big questions, 'What is life all about?' and 'Why am I having so many problems?' To know there is an end, and to know it is within my own power to do something about it, is the greatest thing about this book. Many spiritual teachings say one must surrender, give up trying. But giving up is not something that comes easily to many of us. Nick shows us it is the only way if we really want to end suffering; but more so that this is only possible after one has suffered enough, has fought valiantly enough and endured long enough, so that one has nothing left to give but to give up and surrender.

This story takes you through to the life we now have together: a life of love, peace and total joy, every day. A reward received for a heavy price paid, but a price so willingly paid that the end was perhaps inevitable. I am honoured to be a part of his journey, as his dedication to the truth paved the way for me to have an easy life.

I therefore suggest (hope, even) that if you are able to read this book with an open heart and mind, you too will see the value of his life, words and experiences to the ultimate depth of his knowledge, and ultimately, that you may be able to see how some of the lessons he learnt relate to your own life, and can benefit from what is shared here. This book is about life, love, truth and waking up.

By Sally-Ann Powell

Barry Long

As you read this book you will
find the above name referred to
a great many times. Barry Long
was a spiritual teacher and
described himself as a Western
Spiritual Master, having been
born in Australia in 1926 where
he grew up. He later spent a
number of years working in
London. He explained that the
Western mind is different from those of the East, and as such
the beautiful and simple teachings of the East cannot truly
penetrate the 'clever' Western mind. For that you need an
Enlightened mind which is not only familiar with, but actually
integrated into, the culture of the West.

He did not follow a spiritual path or visit other known
teachers, though he read the works of some, such as J
Krishnamurti. He therefore regarded his own teachings to be
unique and original, partly due to his background, but
predominantly due to the way in which truth, or the spiritual
life, entered him.

In 1964 Barry left his career and family for India. He
spent several months in the foothills of the Himalayas where
he experienced what he described as a mystic death, his
'realisation of immortality'. Four years later, in London, he
underwent an intense spiritual crisis and described the
outcome as his 'transcendental realisation'. His teachings on
love and relationships were developed through his love of
woman and particularly by his vision of the 'divine woman' in
and behind every woman, which he referred to as the
bhagavati (a Hindu term meaning 'Goddess in female form').
As a result, the driving force for him was his need to bring an

end to unhappiness, especially between men and women in their relationships, and to introduce them to a more real love. When his second wife died in 1982 he realised that he was united with her in love to such an extent that his love transcended death, so that even in death they were not separated.

He returned to Australia in 1986. By this time his teaching was becoming more widely spread, and he regularly made the long journey back to England to hold seminars, teaching those present how to free themselves of unhappiness, as well as speaking about love and truth, and personal and sexual relationships. By the early 1990s he was visiting many countries, holding one-day talks as well as residential seminars. Then, from 1993 to 2002 he held an annual 'Master Session' in Australia, which ran for sixteen days, drawing people from all over the world.

He died at the end of 2003 aged seventy-seven, having published more than sixteen books and leaving many audio recordings and videos of his teachings. His work has been translated into more than eleven languages.

Contents

Introduction

Introduction

As I write this introduction at the end of August 2016, the rest of the book is finished – in draft form at least. This has been an amazing journey for me, not just in the sense of my physical life but in creating this book. It began as an idea in my early twenties when I was having some rather extreme spiritual experiences, and the thought occurred that I should probably write them down in the hope that one day they would make it into a book. The intention was for a book exactly like this to be written at the end of my journey, when I was Enlightened. It would describe in detail all the insights and experiences which I knew I would never be able to remember if I was to look back years later. I just didn't know at the time that I was looking twenty years ahead!

The notepads became full. Random pieces of paper were stuffed inside these when new items were recorded away from home. The plastic bags which contained them were replaced with a large heavy-duty bag, and the whole lot would move house with me every time I relocated, growing with each move. But when was I going to be able to write this book? When would it be 'right'? Every time I looked over those years, I knew it was not time yet. And now here it is!

And what a book; what a journey! I'm half expecting people not to believe it, but there is too much description, too many supporting factors for it not to be believed. So perhaps the question is whether or not it will be liked. The journey, after all, is what it is.

And I would say it is everybody's journey. This book is about Nick Roach, but it actually describes every single person's journey through this emotional existence. Everybody struggles; everybody has to fight, in one way or another. No-one really gets away with it. If the book is read with this perspective in mind, it becomes a book not about an individual person, but about every person. The names, locations, and specific circumstances will vary infinitely, but the story is the same.

So here it is, approximately the same length as our previous two books put together. And as I read it back, it is as if I am drawing a thick black line under my life before this point, with this book as the physical representation of this underlining for all to see. With everything written, everything recorded up to now, up to this moment (though some of the names have been changed), I may never have to think about anything from this era, this lifetime, again. This book is my life, my journey, my story; and here it is, finished – complete.

Nick Roach

(Note: This book consists almost entirely of my notes and essays as I wrote them, and I have included dates for the entries where I recorded them at the time. Everything has been presented in chronological order (unless stated otherwise), but where there is no date, please take it that the entry occurred on the same day as, or very soon after, the previous entry.)

The early years

Apparently, from day one I was getting letters such as B and D mixed up when speaking. I was two years and one week old when my sister was born, and I'm told it was soon after this my stammer started.

We had a big house in the country in Essex. My father was a solicitor, and my mother was involved with the fur trade advertising for a magazine. Whether caused by my stammer, or just another symptom of a wider situation, I was extremely shy. I loved animals and soon was at my most contented when with a dog (of which we had two) or almost any animal. I would go with my parents to a friend of theirs and would always ask on the way, 'Do they have any pets?', and on arrival would head straight for the nearest furry creature and stay there for the entire visit if possible. On occasion the host would say, 'Stay away from the dog, he doesn't like children,' and would then display his amazement when I and the animal would be happily seated together. It was thought I would grow up to be a vet if it wasn't for having to put animals to sleep. This, it was decided, I wouldn't be able to do. When I was asked, 'What do you want to do when you grow up?' I never had an answer, but as I got a little older and life got a little harder I knew what I wanted to do: I wanted to be able to talk without stammering.

I was often in fights at school, even at a very early age. It was found out after a while that whenever I saw anyone being bullied, I would rush in to help and usually end up the one in trouble. My school work was not a great success, and I was often in trouble with my teachers for this as well. With the punishments for fighting and poor schooling I didn't enjoy school at all. At home my sister and I were also always fighting, apparently to the extent of driving our mother to the brink of a nervous breakdown.

To try to help my stammer, I was taken to a speech therapist, and I also attended a few courses in London at group therapy. The strange thing was that I could be

3

stammering up to the moment that my dad would tell me we were going to the therapist that day, and suddenly it would stop; I would be able to speak fine. On any day, my dad might say to me, 'You're speaking well today,' or 'Your stammer's bad today; why's that?', and to both I'd reply, 'I don't know. It just happens.'

As a child the one thing I do remember, possibly because I was often in trouble with somebody, was how angry people would get. Even those who announced their love for me would get so angry that there seemed to be no hint of love in them anywhere (during the time that they were angry). Whether or not I felt I deserved it, people would shout and scream and hit me and make all sorts of threats. Faces would go red and eyes would pop out and noses would turn into a sort of snarl. The hand would come across and land on my backside and this probably hurt, but not as much as the anger and seeming hatred that came with it. This was what scared me and I'm sure went some way towards instilling a distrust of people and confirming my love and my need for animals. They were always honest with me. There was no hatred there. They either came to me or they didn't.

I don't recall how much children at school teased me before the age of nine, but then things changed. It was during the summer holidays: I had my ninth birthday party and a friend stayed that night after everybody went home. I hadn't seen him for quite a while because he'd been at boarding school for a year. My parents had opened my school report, and I'm told my mum was in tears because of what was in it. (Apparently it said, or at least implied, that I would never amount to much.) Drastic times called for drastic measures, and something had to be done. My parents had noticed an immense change in my friend after just this one year and wondered if they could afford to send me there as well. A word with my current headmaster who agreed I needed something and boarding school may be it, led to those school fees for the remainder of the year being waived. A few weeks later I was all packed, dressed and off to my new home.

***

The headmaster of the new school said in our very first meeting that they would get rid of my stammer. I was intrigued to know how.

The school seemed huge, and I felt as if I was a small fish in a very big pond. I got to know a few people straight away. However, it wasn't long before I was alienated by my stammer, and it seemed very much a situation where survival of the fittest was the routine. Unfortunately, the sheer size of the place and number of people knocked any confidence I still had out of me. I was almost like a scared rabbit fighting for its life in a strange environment. There was a big divide between people only one year apart, and it had always been drummed into me to respect my elders. My elders teased and let me know my place. I in turn bullied others. There was no escape.

I was often in trouble, not just for fighting but for talking and playing when I shouldn't, for being in the wrong place at the wrong time, and of course I struggled with school work. We learnt French, and actually I was quite good at it. The problem was, of course, my stammer, and it was my constant dread that I would be asked to read out loud – not just in the French class, but in others too. Unfortunately, this often happened. It was not long before I became so afraid of stammering that during one of my visits home I scared my dad by pointing and making hand gestures instead of trying to speak.

***

The end of the first term was the Christmas holidays. Things had changed while I'd been away. That evening when I got home, my dad told me that he and mum were getting a divorce. I didn't understand the full implications of this, but my dad said it in a very solemn way implying it was serious, so I responded accordingly by getting a little upset. As it turned out, one of the worst consequences of this for me was that we had to re-home one of the dogs.

However, the benefits of having divorced parents at this boarding school were quite good. As a 'full boarder' I was only allowed out of school to visit my parents every other Sunday. However, if your parents were divorced you were allowed out every Sunday, alternating between parents, and as my parents both lived in the same town, one would collect me and the other would take me back.

What I was learning though, was it was the older children, the teachers, my parents and in fact anyone in authority who would tell me what to do and try to control me. Children my own age would tease me if I didn't get into a fight with them first. People had bad moods, got angry, were mean and cruel, and I was liking people less and less all the time. When I went home on visits I would head straight for one of a couple of friends who lived in my town, but very rarely chose to spend time with either of my parents. I needed the freedom to do my own thing and be my own person with people who wouldn't tease me or try to control me.

***

Every Christmas at the end of term a general knowledge quiz was handed out to the whole school with the answers attached. The following term everyone would have to sit the same quiz to see how much general knowledge they had. And it appeared I had none, literally! I started off in year three (of six), and in my first quiz I found I was amongst the bottom three boys in the entire school! I sort of assumed it was because I was new and still quite young, but I don't think I ever got out of the bottom four in any of the subsequent years. It was supposed to be 'just for fun', but I didn't find it fun. By the time I was in year six, I was still at the very bottom

6

of the list of results, which was pinned to the corridor wall – everyone could see that I was at the very bottom of the list out of the entire school, even in sixth form!

***

We were allowed to have caged pets at school, and I had a hamster. This was my constant friend and companion. Whenever possible I would spend time caring for it, and for those belonging to perhaps younger boys who weren't really able to look after them properly. My first hamster soon developed a tumour and died. During my time at this school (about four years) I had several pets, including a couple of gerbils which were killed by one of the boys squirting trumpet valve oil over them. I was holding the lovely black female as she died.

One half term my dad had to go on a trip for the second part of my stay, during which I went to watch a film at the cinema: *Tarzan of Greystoke*. It was about a boy brought up by apes. When he is found and taken to stay with his 'real' family, he cannot cope with all the stresses of 'civilised' life and the complexities and pains that go with it, caused partly by the lack of love and compassion in the people around him. He soon gives it all up – the large estate and possessions and title – to return to the forest where he felt he belonged. To join his ape family who always loved him. Things were simpler there and he knew where he stood. Not necessarily easier, but definitely simpler.

Obviously, I could relate to this. A couple of days later I got myself thrown out of my Latin class (which incidentally I was only in because I cheated in an earlier exam since I couldn't answer any questions, only to find out afterwards that those who passed the exam were to keep learning it. The others had extra English.) and whilst sitting on the concrete path outside on my own thinking about the film, I longed to be Tarzan with the choice of running off to be with the animals. I wanted to leave all human beings behind, and at that moment, missing my dog tremendously, I decided I'd had enough. I got up and went to the room where my hamster was kept; sneaking in and collecting her along with a bottle of water and some food, I went down to the basement where my sailing gear was kept. This included jeans, a shirt, a jersey and jacket. I put these on and, avoiding people emerging from various sides, made my way to the back entrance and then on foot along the road. My hamster was in one pocket, and its food and water in the other. It was as if a huge weight was lifted from me as I left the school gates, and I was filled with a sense of freedom which I had not experienced for a very long time. I was doing something for me, and it felt like I had achieved something already.

I walked for a few hours along the dual carriageway before a friend of a parent at the school picked me up, realising I had probably come from there – a ten-year-old walking alone on the main road a few miles from a large boarding school!

My dad collected me from the woman's house. It took some explaining to my dad and the headmaster that I had run away because I missed my dog and wanted to talk to the animals. It wasn't fully appreciated and I was fortunate not to be in real trouble. Things were never the same after that episode, and although I had no intention of running away again, I had experienced the feeling of freedom that came with it. And possibly the knowledge that it was always there, if there was no other way out, may have been why things seemed a little easier after that.

***

A new problem soon developed in my final year at the school. The school was an all-boys boarding school, and at twelve years old I was beginning to realise I needed female company. The only way I could get this was to spend time with the matrons, who were mostly quite young and according to my memory fairly attractive. The only way I knew to do this was to offer to help them in my spare time. I spent the majority of my free time upstairs on my own in a large cupboard or washroom tidying sheets, towels and blankets, and making beds, etc. I would knock on the office door or call at one of their flats and literally ask for a job.

This seemed to be working for quite a while. I got teased a little about this, but as I was on my own, no-one really knew how much time I spent up there or what I was doing.

One morning I came downstairs for breakfast, walking past two of the matrons who I often helped. A few minutes later two classmates a couple of minutes apart approached me and told me something I probably wouldn't have believed had it not come from them both, and neither were the sort of people to make things up. They said just after I'd walked past the matrons they heard one imitating me stammering badly whilst asking for a job, and the other laughing loudly.

The bottom fell out of whatever faith in human nature I had left, and never again did I go and offer to help them. A few weeks later my tutor approached me and asked if there was a reason why I hadn't been up to help the matrons as they were concerned. I said I'd got too much hassle for helping them, and since I'd stopped so had the hassle.

Later I was made an 'apprentice' which was one under prefect. This meant if anyone teased me I could send them to my tutor for him to deal with and not have to contend with it myself. This reduced the amount of trouble I got into enormously.

***

I was nearly thirteen years old when the school arranged for us school leavers to visit various trades, to give us some sort of idea as to what we may like to do when older. There was, amongst many others, an art studio, a leather factory, a sweet factory and a pig farm. The problem with the latter was the farmer had arranged for us to visit a closed abattoir situated next door, which wasn't actually closed that day at all. So there was a group of about ten thirteen-year-olds wandering around this factory watching many pigs being hung by their hind legs, throats slit and going along their way, legs often still twitching towards their next encounter. I cried throughout the tour, overwhelmed mostly by the sheer scale of it all. I turned vegetarian after this (as much as I could whilst at a boarding school, at least).

***

My new school (where my cousin had been School Captain several years earlier) was a public school on the South Downs in Sussex, and I was looking forward to all the space and freedom available in the school's three hundred and sixty acres.

The problems started all over again though. My stammer separated me again, and being back at the beginning there was nothing I could do about it. Everything was too big and I was out of my depth. An example of this was on the rugby field where, at the previous school, I'd had a well-deserved reputation for being an awesome tackler, and now I found I was too scared to tackle people. I don't know what in particular I was scared of. I'd just lost my confidence again.

I had a couple of black- and white-hooded rats as pets which were kept in the biology lab. I spent a lot of my spare time with them. There were a few people I spent time with, but mostly only because for whatever reason they were not part of the mainstream either. I had no space to move and grow as I had hoped; in fact, it seemed as though almost all our time was organised or spoken for in some way. People

10

teased me more and more. I had always been told 'If you ignore them, they'll get bored and stop!' Well it didn't work. I let it go for several weeks and had people much smaller than me approaching me and enjoying 'taking the Michael' just because they could. It was getting out of control and I couldn't take any more. One day in the dormitory, a boy who could have been one of the least offensive up to that point began to imitate my stammer right to my face. That was enough for me. I don't know if he fell on to the bed or I pushed him, but once there I hit him a few times in the side and stomach. He got up and stood in a boxing pose. My fist went out and landed squarely on his nose. He shouted out and made for the washroom, trailing blood through his fingers.

That was the beginning of a new life. I practised karate at the school and kept fit with a lot of press-ups, sit-ups and some weight training. If anyone teased me, they would (and did) get similar treatment. Each incident terrified me as I still had not regained my confidence really, but this was a way to cope. It made life a little easier, and I gained some respect as well. People in other houses in higher years would say to me, 'Are you Roach, that hard-nut in the fourth year?' Now I was known for something other than my stammer.

***

However, I was still alone and still had the stammer. I had to read out loud in class, and this was so painful – and probably was for those listening as well. I approached the English teacher and he agreed not to ask me again. I don't know exactly why, but I never felt I could approach the French teacher in the same way. Life wasn't fun and the situation was getting critical. I had no-one to talk to and nowhere to go. This was my lot!

***

My reputation for being a 'hard-nut' quickly spread to the sixth-formers. One in particular used to enjoy hitting and kicking me (at the top of the legs and side of my body) in front of all the people in my dormitory. It was like a game. He was trying to make out he was tough, and it was known amongst his own year he was a wimp so probably had something to prove. I took a sort of twisted pleasure in standing there and not flinching or making a sound to prove he couldn't hurt me. This earned me a respect from those in my class and from him. I don't think he ever did hurt me. However, despite my enjoying it on one level, on another I was too scared to move or flinch in case it got worse. And yet at the same time I enjoyed the attention. In a way it was a form of respect from this senior (who continued to treat me this way even after he became School Captain), a little excitement to break up the feeling of isolation and even depression.

***

One evening during my first term at the school, once I had finished my prep (homework at school) and was seated at my desk, I got out a pen and my A4 pad and began to write how I felt and why. I wrote approximately two sides, and when I had finished I read it through. It felt as though reading it helped put everything in some sort of order, and the whole situation became clearer. I could feel the pressure leaving me as I read my own words. And once I'd finished reading I screwed the pieces of paper up and threw them in the bin. It felt as if I'd thrown the problems away with it. I continued this practice for the next few years.

***

My academic abilities in class didn't improve. I had been put in the second set (group) out of five sets for maths (set one being the highest). I got zero out of twenty for every prep or test we had. The amazing thing was the teacher didn't seem to mind at all. After several weeks of doing no more than just taking up space in her classroom and getting more and more frustrated about it, I approached her. I asked her why I was in her set when anyone could see I couldn't cope, and I knew my Common Entrance exam results had also been very poor. She told me to go and see the headmaster's wife as she had placed people into the sets.

The headmaster's wife retrieved my details and sat with me in her living room. A quick scan through the notes and she had the answer. Apparently, my results in the IQ test I had taken during my interview had been so high it was felt I should be able to cope in a higher set. I stressed to her I couldn't and she eventually allowed me to drop down to set three.

I was more at home there, in the third set. I still couldn't answer any of the questions, but then neither could quite a few of the other students. Not the ideal situation, but a compromise for now.

***

I'd been at the school for a year and a half and was now aged fourteen. I was returning to the school with my mum and stepdad after half term. I sat in the back as usual, but made no attempt to make conversation, which was not usual for a journey back to school, and had them a little worried. (My stammer would not be present all the time, and when it was not a problem, when travelling back to school, I could talk almost constantly). The reason for my being so quiet was that I had made up my mind I was leaving one way or the other!

That evening I walked up the corridor in the building, purposely getting in the way of the sixth-formers who usually hit me. I knew I had to have a good reason to run away from school again or I would end up back there. When at home, I was living with my dad, and I had decided if he was to send me back there again, I would run away again but to my mum's house. If she sent me back, I would run away and live rough on the streets. It couldn't be worse than what I was currently going through. Different maybe. No doubt extremely difficult and uncomfortable. But I thought at least I'd feel I was alive and in control of my life. No more having every single day mapped out entirely from getting up to going to bed. And no more feeling trapped with a lot of people teasing me and bullying me.

The sixth-formers in question, perhaps for the first time in a long time, seemed to be leaving me alone. I would even intentionally stand in their path, fully expecting them to push me out of the way; but they just walked around me! I needed a reason to take to my dad, and being bullied was the best I could think of. I had enough money for the train and clothes to wear. I managed to obtain accurate directions to the nearest station, apparently three hours' walk away. (One of the other boys in the dormitory said that's how long it took him, some time before.) Now I just needed an excuse to go.

I saw someone else in the class using a pencil sharpener blade to cut his forearm, showing how tough he was. I immediately unscrewed mine and proceeded to copy and surpass him. The suggestion again was to show how tough I was, but obviously it was a loud shout for help. *Look, I'm so unhappy I am cutting up my forearm and the back of my hand to show you all how unhappy I am.* Of course there was no-one to hear, and for a couple of days this continued.

Then, one lunch time I was told by a group of sixth-formers to do press-ups on my knuckles in the hallway. This I often did in karate training so it was easy. I had been timed a few months earlier doing normal press-ups, and had done seventy-three press-ups in fifty-five seconds. (It was supposed to be a minute, but it was all I could do to hold myself up for the last five seconds.) One of them put a large bell under my middle to prevent me from lowering myself and told me to see how long I could hold myself up. I opened up

14

my hands at one point to make them flat. Another person took out a penknife and tossed it in the vicinity of my hand to encourage me to return to my knuckles. By this time there were quite a few spectators.

When the situation was over, and as usual no harm had really been done, I had a little think to myself. *Was this serious enough to justify running away?* I decided it would have to be and made plans for that night.

The dormitories had been recently refurbished, and the large six-foot long by four-foot high vertical pieces of wood between each bed had now been replaced with 'Captain's Bunks' (a top bunk with a cupboard, drawers and desk with light underneath). I had my clothes ready in my cupboard and the directions and money with them. I lay on my back when time for bed, knowing I sleep very poorly on my back. I hoped to leave soon after one in the morning but hadn't an alarm to set, not that I could have safely used one anyway.

I woke at about half past eleven and leaned over the three-foot gap to the person in the next bunk, who I got on all right with. I asked quietly if he was still awake. He was. I told him I wasn't feeling well, and if I wasn't here in the morning I'd be in the sanatorium.

I awoke at quarter to five. *Damn, a little late!* I climbed down from the bunk, switched on the small light under the bed and got dressed. The adrenalin was pumping through me with exhilaration of the prospect of what I was actually doing. I was nearly ready to go when I heard the footsteps people had been talking about. It is said that a Roman Centurion patrols up and down the dormitory most nights, and people have been hearing it regularly for years. One of the people I did spend some time with slept just across the room. He was a very light sleeper and claimed he heard the footsteps often. A couple of weeks earlier he'd said he'd woken to find the next bed empty, and the head of a Roman Centurion in the helmet and straps looking at him over the top of the bunk. A few seconds later it was gone and the person was back in the bed. He swears he knows he was awake.

I continued getting ready whilst what sounded like slow, precise, heavy footsteps walked past the end of my bed and towards the changing room at one end of the dormitory. By the time I was ready to go, the 'footsteps' had gone back past my bed the other way and towards the main door. I now had a minor dilemma as to how to get out. The two options were either to walk over these 'footsteps' to the main door, or go out through the changing room which was currently being decorated; and no-one was supposed to go through there. The painters had stuck tape over the door, and although the seal had been broken, it could well make a noise as I was going out that way.

I decided that knowingly walking on top of 'ghostly footsteps' may be pushing my luck a little far, and headed out the back way.

It was extremely dark. The time was now just after 5.00 in the morning, and it was only a few weeks after the big hurricane of 1987. There were still the remains of large trees scattered across the grounds, and as I made my way across the large expanse of grass towards the main gates, I had to detour around sprawled-out trees. I saw the glow of a cigarette and could make out the crouched shapes of two people amongst the branches of one such tree. I knew they weren't supposed to be out here either, but I gave them a wide berth to avoid complications, and they didn't see me.

I left the school gates at around half past five and began a speed-walk. While I felt the elation of freedom, I knew in a couple of hours the teachers would be driving to the school, and meeting one of them would be a disaster.

Carefully followed directions and determination led me to arrive at Pulborough train station at half past seven. I'd knocked an hour off the time I'd been told it should take. I

16

caught the first train out and arrived back home a few hours later.

Shortly after arriving home the telephone rang and I picked it up as I always did. It was my dad.

He'd had a call from the school, who'd just noticed I'd gone. Apparently, a boy from my house had gone to the sanatorium that night and they assumed it was me. My dad said to stay at home and he'd see me later.

When he arrived home that evening, my friend and I were in our swimming pool. There was no pressure from my dad at this time. First, he wanted to know why I'd done it. I didn't know what reason to give, as I was scared he'd say I was making a lot of fuss about nothing and should go back. But on hearing my story regarding the press-ups on the knuckles and the penknife, he said, 'No son of mine is going to be treated like that!' He rang the school and I never went back.

He tried to get to the bottom of the cuts on my hand, thinking possibly the person with the knife had done it. How could I tell him I'd done it myself?

***

After a few weeks at home looking for a new school, my mum and stepdad, who were living in London in a rented flat in the famous Barbican centre, found a small school in London. It was an ex-cramming college, now a tutorial college with classes of only eight people. It would mean going to live with my mum, which was no doubt a big issue for both my parents, but for me was just a base to work from.

The school was very personal, being so small. Although my stammer was still quite obvious, for whatever reason people there didn't tease me. There were a couple of nice girls in my class who I got on with very well, but I lacked both experience and confidence to take it beyond friendship. In hindsight one may well have wanted to try being more than just friends, but as it was so new, and I was enjoying the interaction on a friendship level so much, I really didn't want to risk losing it.

I dropped back a year to try to catch up with my schooling. Again I was asked to read out loud in French. Although people there didn't tease me, it was still painfully embarrassing and frustrating, and after a few occasions I approached the teacher and asked if I could avoid reading in class. She said that was fine. (I hadn't volunteered for English literature for the same reason.)

The good news was that I got on very well with the maths teacher, and amazingly I soon found I was doing well in class too! During a parent's evening he told my mum that whenever I couldn't do something, he'd found it was because I was looking at it in a different way to everybody else. All he had to do was try to see what angle I was approaching it from and then he could explain it in my way. Often I would be nearly there on my own, but via a completely different method – all of my own making! He very quickly enabled me to learn and understand everything which had been a blank to me the last couple of years, and soon I was amongst the top two out of two combined classes.

My French teacher still asked me to read out loud in class. When I questioned her about this she said, 'I didn't realise you didn't want to read at all!' I suggested to her that I give up French due to the stammer and she immediately agreed it was for the best as it would cause me problems. No Shit! She gave up quicker than I did!

Life was better, but it was still far from easy, and far from enjoyable. My cry for help here consisted of standing on the window ledge outside the fourth floor overlooking Gloucester Road in London, going so far as to walk the few feet along to the next window.

Soon I began to wonder why life is so hard. With sayings such as 'Life's a bitch, and then you die!', 'That's

Life!' and 'Life's unfair!', I began to wonder seriously what the idea behind it all was. It seemed to me the fact that these phrases exist suggests someone else may have noticed how hard life can be, but I hadn't come across anyone yet who seriously wanted to know 'WHY?'

It was as if everyone around me was going blindly on, battling through all the emotional pain and upset we go through without giving any serious consideration as to why this had to be the case. The need to know continued to grow in me over several weeks. Every time I got stuck on a word and couldn't speak, the question would rise in me: 'WHY...? WHY...? WHY...?'

The several weeks of carrying this question around with me brought up an answer: Having been born, I could indeed continue to endure all this pain for the next sixty years or so and then die – but if I was to die now, at almost fifteen, not only would I find out quicker whether life had a purpose or not, but I'd also avoid the rest of the pain I would have had.

However, I also knew I had the strength within me to continue in this seemingly nightmare of a situation if only I knew there was a purpose to it all. It would prove useful therefore if I was to find out if there was a reason before doing anything too drastic.

One of the girls in the class developed an interest in the Ouija board. This got me thinking that if anyone knew whether there was a purpose to life or not it should be psychics, because they were supposed to be in touch with dead people; and if you didn't find out the truth when you died, I didn't know when you would.

I began buying almost every book I could find relating to psychic phenomena and the paranormal, etc. Often I would do little more than flick through them before adding them to the shelf with all the others. Some of the books were about psychic powers and mentioned meditation as a way to develop them. I therefore bought several books on

19

meditation, as they provided a route to finding some reasons for myself, through reading and practising the techniques. One such book was by an Eastern yogi named Patanjali called *Patanjali's Yoga Aphorisms*. He described all sorts of powers that a 'Spiritual Master' can attain through various practices in meditation, from levitation to disappearing and appearing at will. He mentioned the drug lysergic acid (LSD) as having similar effects as extended meditation, and spoke about the different types of yoga and the different powers they produce.

We soon moved from London to Surrey, and we celebrated my fifteenth birthday whilst decorating the house. For another year I read books on meditation and psychic powers. I had a little altar in the corner of my bedroom on which sat a four-inch high Buddha surrounded by candles. I would sit in the dark with all the lights out just staring at a candle. I practised concentrating on my breathing which was referred to in the books as hatha yoga, and repeated a manta (word or phrase) over and over as described in raja yoga.

I looked for answers and some hint of purpose everywhere I could think of. I bought rune stones, practised with tarot cards, had books on palm reading, face reading, astral projection. I bought a crystal ball with the hope of receiving some sort of sign that all is not in vain. I looked everywhere and began to come to the conclusion that no-one actually knows what life is or whether all this pain is for a reason.

Whilst out one night in Surrey, I met a few people a little older than myself. I visited one at his home a few times because he only lived ten minutes' walk from my mum's. Although he was a nice chap, he and his mates would often hop on the train and go to the next town for a sort of gang fight with the kids there, and when they went out to clubs in the evening would take drugs such as LSD and marijuana. He described the experience of LSD as opening up a portion of

20

the brain not usually used. Although I was invited to join them, the idea of all this scared me, and I always declined so we soon lost touch. I would stay at home on my own, usually doing exercises with the set of weights I'd bought.

At this time there was a lot of publicity on the television about the ivory trade and the plight of the elephants. I felt I would like to go over to help the park wardens defend the elephants from the poachers. I knew this would give my life purpose, and my death too if the worst was to happen. I would be living and dying for something I believed in.

Left school...

I left the London school having acquired only four 'C' grades, a 'D' and an 'E' in my GCSE exams. I had hoped to do better than this, especially as the 'E' was in biology and it was my best subject; in the mock exam I had attained over ninety per cent. Questions were being asked as to why my results were so low.

I didn't know what to do next, and it was suggested I did a BTEC National Diploma course in leisure management at the local college of technology. The idea was that management was such a broad subject I should find something to interest me later on, once I had the qualification.

The first week went fine. We each had to give a speech in front of the whole group of about thirty people. I spent the entire previous evening practising by reading into a tape recorder. By the next day, although I was very nervous, I did it. I had a word with the tutor quietly afterwards, about my stammer. He was amazed that he hadn't noticed, and said he's usually good at picking up things like that.

As always seemed to happen, everybody began to congregate in little groups of like-minded people, and I was not a like-minded person. I got on acceptably with the majority, but not enough to call any of them friends. It wasn't long before my guard slipped and people noticed my stammer. A couple made comments and others just seemed to have nothing at all to say to me. Again I was isolated.

I didn't enjoy the college at all and looked for a way to leave. My parents said I should not do so until I had something else lined up. After a little consideration I thought that the army would offer a way out and an opportunity for doing what I was good at: physical training. I applied and again my IQ scores were high, and when my stepdad rang up the recruitment office, he was told my scores were in the top ten per cent in the country and I could take almost any position I wanted. I told them my collarbone had been dislocated a while ago. (About eighteen months earlier I had been showing off at a party and had picked up a friend who was standing, and lifted him over my head. The grass was wet and we were on a slope, and I slipped. The full weight of both of us fell on my elbow and it damaged my shoulder.) I was told I'd need to have that X-rayed first, and the wait would be about six months.

I worked for a few weeks for my mum's boss on his grounds, and continued to return to Essex to visit my dad and my friends at weekends. On one such visit, whilst in the local 'New Age' shop looking for any new books which may hold the answers to all the mysteries in the universe – or at least a few of them – I noticed a leaflet advertising a college in London called the College of Psychic Studies. The lady in the shop said her friend worked there, and that it was very good. I went home and rang them, and made an appointment in a week's time to have a session with one of their psychics. This was it. I knew that after all the books and being none the wiser, if a real psychic didn't have the answers then I couldn't think of anybody else who would.

***

I felt sorry for anyone I ever saw upset, even if I didn't know them. I assumed it was because I had had so much pain I knew what they were going through. *Home Alone* was on at the cinema, and I went to see it with a few of my friends in Essex. There is a scene where the old man speaks to Macaulay Culkin in the church. Watching this I suddenly felt a dragging feeling inside me as if I were really upset and depressed. It was pulling at me from inside. I was sure I had nothing to be depressed about watching this film, but there it was. I was feeling it. I examined this feeling for perhaps a minute in all trying to puzzle out why I felt so awful. I looked to my friend on my left, and then to the girl on my right. She had tears coming down the side of her face!

Admittedly this scared me. I had read about this sort of thing, but this was too big. How do you explain it, and who can you tell?

Outside, I was walking my friend home. He was a very scientific person: if you can't measure it, it doesn't exist! As we walked the long straight up the road in the dark to his house, after a little internal debate with myself, I decided to share my experience with him. As I was completing the story I felt a hot sensation shoot up my spine. It was impossible to ignore as it too was a little frightening. After only a few seconds of internal questioning I thought I knew where it had come from. 'John,' I said, 'Are you angry?' He didn't answer the question.

About forty-five minutes later we were in his kitchen having a cup of tea, talking. He explained he had indeed been annoyed at my suggestion that I had sensed the girl's unhappiness as he didn't believe it was possible. Me asking if he was angry had scared him as he prided himself at being able to hide his feelings really well. We talked for a while and then sat quietly watching the television, when suddenly the hot sensation rose up my spine again. I looked at John who was just sitting across the room saying nothing. 'Are you angry again, John?' I asked. He turned to me, eyes wide in disbelief. (He confirmed he had indeed just been thinking about it again.)

***

As the time grew nearer and I could think of little else but my approaching hour-long session with a real psychic, the knowledge dawned on me that this was my last point of call. I had nowhere else to look and no-one else to ask. I knew also that if this psychic couldn't tell me that life had a genuine purpose and that there was a reason behind it all, then my search was over. I would make a social call on my friends and family, and then end my futile existence. I hadn't even decided how I was going to do it. It didn't matter. There are so many different ways that I knew when it was time, I would do one of them.

The day came and I made my way up on the train to South Kensington to the college. The walls of the hallway around the entrance were filled with notice boards advertising various classes and meetings being held at the college, including 'spiritual healing' and 'becoming a medium'. The reception was like a library with walls of bookcases stretching from the floor to the very high ceiling. I checked in at reception, accepted the offer of a tape recorder and went as directed up the flights of stairs to one of the highest floors.

The psychic was a man in maybe his thirties, quite short, thin, and perhaps most noticeably, entirely bald and spoke with a very soft voice. He met me at the door. I tried to introduce myself but my stammer was very bad. He invited me to sit down in one of two large armchairs by the window, and he sat in the other. He explained it was his first day there (I popped in again some years later and he was still there, with several books he'd written for sale on the shelves), and after I fumbled for a short while with the tape recorder, he began.

First, he said my aura was extremely strong, and I had very strong energy. As he was talking, I could feel a pressure beginning in my stomach, almost trying to escape, and I struggled to hold it down. He said several times that I had 'such clarity' due to meditation in past lives and had the ability to see above problems. He explained he would now go up on to a higher plane, and closed his eyes. He then said the spirits are always very pleased when someone of my level takes an interest in the spiritual path, and I would develop very quickly if I chose to go that way.

I felt like I was going to explode. Energy was surging in my stomach area and I wanted to laugh out loud to release and express the feeling. But I continued to fight it, with just little bursts forcing their way out every so often.

He added, whilst still on this 'higher plane', 'You don't have to follow the spiritual path.'

I said, 'Yes I do!'

He said, 'No you don't.'

I said again, 'Yes I do!'

He went on to say I was already quite a few rungs up the ladder towards spiritual Enlightenment. (This is what I'd been reading about in all these books on Yoga.) He said, 'If you do follow the spiritual path, you will reach a very high level in the next five years, and have many followers!'

He went on to say that my stammer was due to my being unable to control all the energy within me. Through the practice of meditation, I would learn to control it and would probably wake up one morning and it would be gone. My stammer was awful; I could hardly speak, and I was struggling to contain the impulse to laugh. It was like a huge release. I now had a reason for my stammer and a purpose and aim in life!

He suggested I enrol in a spiritual awareness course for the next term at the college, as the current term had already started. He said, in the meantime, to continue to practise meditating as much as possible. (A real sceptic may suggest the whole routine was designed to get people to enrol in a course at the college, but I had experienced enough up to that point to feel a lot of what he said made sense. Besides, I had no choice; it was either devoting the next five years to becoming an 'Enlightened Master' or death!)

The college advertised a policy that it didn't take any students under the age of twenty-one. I was now seventeen. Apparently in my case it wouldn't be a problem.

I returned to the college that evening to attend a talk/meeting held by the psychics and mediums and healers at the college every Thursday. There was a television set on the table at the front of the hall. A video was put on, showing four of the psychics each placing a hand on each of the legs of an upturned table, and it lilting up. The chap who I'd had the session with earlier also explained, when holding a séance on a regular basis as the group had been doing, there had been a lot of 'automatic writing'. They left a pen and paper in the middle of the table with the light off, and when the light was turned back on again there would be a message on the pad. One time the pen disappeared and later the 'entity' explained it had given it to another spiritual group.

On the pad on the table several pieces of information were shared, such as 'A falling tree makes no sound at all when there is no-one there to hear it.' And 'When psychics speak with or channel souls who have passed, they are actually speaking with the one Being that is behind all beings.' The psychic said they intended to explore further exactly what was meant by these statements, and would share any new information at the weekly meetings.

***

Whilst working for my mum's boss on his grounds I continued to try to practise meditating as had been suggested. The trouble was I had read about several different types or ways to meditate and I wasn't sure I knew quite what to do.

***

I was still waiting to go into the army. I passed my driving test and went to live in my dad's empty house in Essex. It was up for sale as he'd followed his work down to the West Country. I was seventeen and had the house all to myself.

One evening I was at the fair in the next village with a couple of friends, when one returned from speaking to a few people he knew and said, 'Hey Nick, how do you fancy trying some LSD?'

30

I had heard three things about LSD. For one, it was highly illegal. Second, people had become mentally unhinged taking it and three, it was mentioned in some detail in Patanjali's book, where it was described as being tried by a few yogis and included their different reactions to it. A friend had previously described it as opening up a part of the brain not usually used.

I was cautious, but eager to do almost anything to find a greater reality, and if yogis had willingly tried it, why shouldn't I?

It was a small square piece of paper like blotting paper, possibly six millimetres squared. It had a purple design on it and was apparently called a Purple Ohm (a spiritual reference).

He said to us both, as it was our first time and we only had the one, he would have half and we would each have a quarter. I took the tiny piece of paper and wandered around for quite a while with it laid on my tongue, repeating to him, 'So when is it going to start then...? What's going to happen...? So when is it going to start then...?'

The three of us began the long walk along the road home in the dark, and nothing had happened. I began to think it was a waste of time or that the tiny piece we'd each had wasn't enough. Then a car passed us trailing its lights behind it. WOW! It had started! The whole feeling was so strange.

When drinking alcohol, the experience was that it seemed it was me that would change if I'd had too much to drink, with symptoms including not being able to stand up properly or walk straight. I'd be clumsy and bump into things and knock things over. I'd not be able to think straight, let alone make sense in anything I did say. The surroundings would as a rule remain the same and I would *know* it was me and the alcohol doing this.

With this LSD, the opposite was true. I was entirely aware and conscious – if anything even more than usual.

31

What had changed was the world around me, or at least my perception of it. I was noticing things I'd never noticed before, seeing things a different way. Thoughts and ideas occurred, and the three of us laughed as we shared our ideas. Mine was 'Time's relative!', and I spent the next couple of hours saying this every ten minutes or so. The reason was that it was almost as if there was no time. Whatever happened, happened 'now', and what occurred to me was that time only exists because we use our minds to link a number of occurrences together. I was experiencing what had been described in the books as the 'timeless'. One effect of the drug is it only allows you to focus on one thing at a time, thus preventing the mind jumping ahead or behind in the imagination to link situations together. This meant everything that happened, happened NOW. The next moment, or the last, didn't exist as we weren't thinking about it. This made life for that period seem ever so simple.

One little trick he taught us was to lie down on the grass and look up at the sky. He said, 'Right, now imagine you're stuck to the ceiling...'

'WOW!' Just that new way of looking at what had been taken for granted for my whole life changed the whole experience. It really felt as though we were pinned to the ceiling by this stuff called gravity, and if it was to let go we would all go plummeting down towards the clouds and the stars.

We spent the rest of the night in the dark living room with the music on, either staring at the shadows on the ceiling or lying with our eyes closed. The idea of going to sleep was entirely beyond possibility. The experience was of being alive and alert, and yet it was easy to relax. It was truly amazing, and I really felt I had benefited from the experience.

***

The spiritual awareness course at the College of Psychic Studies was one morning a week for eleven weeks, with a week off in the middle for half term. I'd had to go up a few weeks earlier for an interview with the psychic/medium taking the course to ensure all concerned had the ability to benefit from a class in spiritual awareness. All went well.

On the first day, there were about eight people with the tutor, and we sat in a circle on the plastic chairs provided. After introducing ourselves in turn, we were asked to close our eyes and focus on our breathing. We were then to visualise a closed door. I immediately saw the door of that room. We were to open the door and look inside. (It was explained afterwards that what we found in there was to mean something to the individual with regards to their current spiritual position and what was to come through attending the course.) I turned the handle and pushed open the door. What I saw confused me. I thought I must be doing something wrong or that it wasn't working. I was the second to last in the circle to describe my experience. People had been describing a nice comfortable room which they were familiar with, or a map or something equally tangible. I told them, a little apologetically, what happened to me: I had pushed the door open and gone to walk in, but couldn't. There had been no floor, no walls, no ceiling – in fact, nothing at all except complete blackness.

The tutor smiled. 'It's all right,' she said. 'All that means is for you anything is possible.'

***

I went home that afternoon really feeling I had a purpose now. I was going to practise as much as I could. My friends had not broken up for their summer holidays, so I had until about 4.00 p.m. every day on my own. I spent most mornings walking alone on the seawall near where I lived, across the fields and through the trees. I would sit against a tree in the middle of the field just feeling my breathing and enjoying the simplicity of it all. Enjoying the idea that now I was doing something with a purpose. I was going to be an Enlightened Master. The psychic had said so!

I found a bench around the side of the small country church and spent an hour at a time sitting there. I found who held the keys for the big church and would go and ask to be let in. I wasn't religious but I was spiritual. I got some pleasure from being in the church, if only from the idea of not being able to do any more than I was currently doing to attain 'true spirituality'.

When sitting in meditation (which to me only meant feeling my breathing go in and out, in and out...), on occasions I would become aware of my head being fixed facing forward. I would be unable to move it without added effort. It was as if an energy had filled my head and was holding me rigid. It was an odd sensation, but in a strange way reassuring as well.

I had three main friends: one Roman Catholic who, although not really practising the values, still preached them and defended them and their philosophies; another, a hardened scientist, the one with whom I had had the hot sensation up my spine. And the third was Church of England, though studying various other religions and other spiritual philosophies. The four of us as you perhaps can imagine used to have some quite long and in-depth discussions.

***

Part of the college teaching was to make a note of any dreams as they can give important clues as to what needs to be done or is being done. For a couple of weeks, I would wake up every half hour or so with another dream to write down. I soon grew tired of this. However, one small dream I do remember was of being outside in the garden and seeing a garter snake curled up on the path.

34

I had kept a couple while at school so knew they were harmless. However, as much as I tried in the dream, I couldn't find the courage to pick it up. Whenever I went near it, it would withdraw as if taking up a striking pose. I was even too scared to put a jersey over it to catch it. On waking I interpreted this as just demonstrating that I had a long way to go (to overcome fear).

***

I continued to practise meditating whenever possible and felt incredible feelings of what I can only describe as love, which would come and go and lasted for several weeks. The tutor explained it was the heart chakra opening up. Each week we had a different visualisation exercise and a discussion afterwards. One was to imagine an area of woodland, and we were to make our way through it. What was relevant was the density of the trees in the wood, and the path, if any.

I had a really thick, black forest as dark as you could get with a winding, glowing golden path running through it. This was interpreted as symbolising possibly quite a hard life with many potential obstacles, but never any real danger as the path was clear and well-lit so I could see where I was going.

***

Another quite uncomfortable visualisation for me was of a lighthouse. We were to go into the building and up the stairs. There would be six floors, and we were to see which floor we felt most comfortable on and any other experiences. The lighthouse of course represented the spinal column, and each floor was a Chakra.

As I approached the outside of the building, I began to float up. I used concentration to hold myself down, and struggled through the doorway, feet way off the ground. Once in, I began floating straight up towards the top, through the floors. I struggled and fought to stay down, having to open my eyes on a couple of occasions to bring me back into the classroom in an effort to gain some control. But in vain – the instant I closed my eyes again, there I was floating up again through the floors. Again the tutor smiled at this. 'We really do need to get you earthed!'

***

A friend in Essex was regularly attending a t'ai chi class and invited me to attend one evening. I didn't seem to get much out of it, partly because (perhaps like any new person) there seemed to be a lot of learning required to get the moves exactly right, and I wasn't all that good at learning.

At the end of the evening we spoke with the teacher. He was an older gentleman who had been practising t'ai chi for many years. I shared with him that I was looking for Enlightenment, and he said, 'One cannot be Enlightened until they are able to squeeze and relax the muscles in the anus independently of each other.' He continued, 'There is not one, but two muscles there, and until a person can control these separately, they are not ready to handle the energy of Enlightenment.' (This seemed a little bizarre to me, and was not something I'd heard before nor have I since.)

***

I had my eighteenth birthday during the course at the College of Psychic Studies. While it was nice to now have a purpose and a goal, I still had my stammer (though I did seem a little more in control now), and I was still isolated, except for this handful of friends in Essex. But I was finding it harder to talk to anyone about my experiences. This was even a little much for my closest friends to understand.

I continued to experiment with LSD occasionally. It was a lot cheaper than alcohol, the effects lasted longer, and I seemed to glean new experiences from it. I would always do my best to meditate whilst taking it to increase my awareness and ability to receive new ideas and insights.

***

I had spent long enough out of a restricted environment to know the army was not for me. (I had by now had the X-ray on my shoulder. I had spent an entire day at the hospital's assessment centre. The X-ray had been in the morning, and I had to wait till 5.00 p.m., sitting at the end of an extremely long queue in a corridor waiting to see the surgeon. When I finally got to see him, he commented on how amazingly low my blood pressure was. And when looking at my body and shoulder he said I was in the best physical shape of anyone he had seen all day (and it had been a long day). He said most of the guys were just too big. With regards to my collarbone, he said he had seen a lot worse. The collarbone was indeed out of its socket, but he would have to break the bone to put it back, and this would result in problems as I got older. He said I could continue fine as it was.)

So now I was not going into the army, but it had served its purpose in getting me out of the leisure management course at the college. Now I had to decide what I was going to do. I had discovered the 'guilt' I felt of being aware of other peoples' emotions and decided it may be put to a good use as a counsellor. I was also starting to see that this 'gift' was also contributing to my stammer: when the person or people around me were impatient or worked up in some way, it would affect me and I would stammer. That, in hindsight, was probably why some days my stammer was non-existent and others terrible. I could pick up the 'vibrations' from my parents, and my own state of mind was affected accordingly.

I applied for and got into the local sixth form college in Surrey to retake a couple of GCSEs and take psychology and sociology A-Levels. The idea was for the A-levels to provide an opening to get into counselling while at the same time giving me a greater understanding of how the mind works.

It was about this time I was lent a book by Scott Peck, *The Road Less Travelled*. The book describes how Scott Peck, an American psychiatrist, believes God's intention in giving us difficulties is for us to learn from them with the aim of being like him in our emotional state. This can be achieved by consciously watching and analysing one's actions and thoughts and feelings, tracing them back to their origin. A lot like what I'd been taught at the College of Psychic Studies but to a much greater extent. It was like a chain effect: 'I thought "this" because I saw "that", which reminded me of "that" which I didn't like because such-and-such happened, which did that and that.' It was quite a long process, but I loved it. It was the best book I'd ever read, and it was absolutely fantastic. It hit every point in my body that it needed to, and I followed every instruction to the letter.

My aim to learn in my psychology class about the mind was a bit of a failure. It seemed none of the psychologists we studied actually knew how the mind worked. It consisted of a lot of theories and opposing theories, all of which have been proven and disproven on several occasions by different psychologists, and it was my job as a student to learn all the information, and be little or no wiser at the end of it. Instead, I was learning about my own mental processes by reading and following the exercises in this wonderful book.

I finished the book after a couple of weeks, and for the next few weeks barely a thought entered my head without being pounced on and dissected.

One afternoon I got home after college and sat on the sofa, as I did every day, and waited for the next thought so I could analyse it. I sat there and sat there, and suddenly the knowledge came to me that I'd got as far as I could with this teaching. I was seated on the sofa, alone in the house with no noise coming from anywhere. And I surprised myself as I opened my mouth and said out loud to the four walls, 'I need a Master!'

At that exact moment I remembered a book I'd bought about a year earlier that I'd never actually opened. It had caught my attention when scanning the shelves of a book shop for hints of a greater reality. I got up and ran to my bedroom. For some reason I knew exactly where it was and I knelt down to my bottom drawer where a lot of the books had been put due to a lack of space on the shelf. I removed a couple from the top to reveal a completely white paperback book with the words 'Stillness Is the Way' on the front cover in black letters across the middle. I returned to the sofa and began reading.

Stillness is the way

The book was a manuscript of a short course in meditation between the teacher, a man called Barry Long, and perhaps five students. He had only just begun holding sessions and was using a friend's attic as a meeting place.

He stated clearly they were not to try to remember what he said. He explained that The Truth is energetic, and you will realise bits of it for yourself as time goes on. Then it will become a part of you, and it becomes your truth and not only what you've heard or read. If the words are learnt and remembered, they are only words and hold no truth for you, so mean nothing.

He suggested an exercise of first focussing on the breathing and using the diaphragm as much as possible rather than the chest, which calms the mind. Then he said to feel your feet. There is a slight tingling there if the person is relaxed enough. This can be followed up the legs and over the entire body. It may take a little while, but it is there.

The book was fantastic. It described how to practise feeling inside your whole body. I sat and read for a few hours, and when I got up to make a cup of tea, the sensation was similar to that of being on LSD. I was completely conscious, and it was so relaxing that my mind was completely still and focussed on nothing but making the tea. For a while the merry-go-round of the mind and its goings-on had ceased, and so had the analysing and questioning that went with it.

This was the way to go! Why had I not read this book earlier?

I knew why. I hadn't been ready, and it wouldn't have meant anything. I was beginning to understand what was meant by the saying that there is a right time for everything, and nothing happens until the right time.

***

My A-level studies at the college in psychology and sociology went downhill from there as I quickly lost interest. They seemed in some way unimportant compared with what I was doing. It seemed to me that this man knew what the psychologists were all trying to find out. He described himself as a Spiritual Master, and from what I was experiencing I had no reason to doubt him.

Life seemed simpler somehow now. I became even more withdrawn than I had been before, feeling I no longer needed people, as opposed to earlier when I felt dejected. All I wanted was the feeling I got from sitting quietly and focussing on my body – not concentrating, as that implies effort. This was an open, continuous (as much as possible) awareness of wherever my body was at that particular moment, and of whatever was going on inside as well as around me. Meditation before had seemed to be concentrating on one thing to the exclusion of all else. This was very different, almost the opposite. This was being aware of my body and wherever it was at that moment. Be it on a chair, or even walking along whilst remaining constantly aware of the trees, the birds, the clouds, even the buildings, cars and people. And I at the same time would feel and watch 'within' for any feeling or sensation. I was practising being completely conscious.

Whereas I used to spend a little time in the vicinity of people and enjoyed watching television, now I spent every spare moment, whether at college or at home, walking in the nearby woods and playing fields at school and the large boarding school near us. There was also a golf course and a public footpath that ran out of sight around the outside of the course. The school and grounds were on top of a hill, and the surrounding path had quite a lovely view across the valley to the fields and hills opposite. There was a bench situated in an excellent position to enjoy the peace and scenery, and I would spend a little while on every walk seated there looking out across the valley of trees and fields before continuing my circuit.

***

I soon found it easier to remain conscious and aware without thinking of completely unrelated things (such as what I did yesterday and who said what) by walking slowly. On one occasion I took this to the extreme by challenging myself: I was going to walk my usual walk, which was normally about an hour to an hour and a half, with steps so small that the back of one foot had to touch the toe of the first foot. This was quite a challenge, and thankfully there were few people around, so initially no-one paid any attention to me. It was on the way back when I walked (more like crept) past the groundsman's portacabin as usual that he noticed me walking at a snail's pace across the courtyard and came out. He approached me and put his arm around me. 'Are you all right?' he asked.

I had to think quickly of an explanation for this somewhat bizarre behaviour. 'I'm just doing an experiment,' I explained.

He asked again, 'So you're sure you're all right?'

'Yes,' I replied. 'Thank you,' and carried on, making a conscious effort not to allow this episode to disturb me and encourage me to speed up. I eventually made it home but never again went to the extreme of telling myself to walk that slowly. I had done it once and that was enough for me.

***

In the book was a card with the address and telephone number of The Barry Long Foundation based in Somerset, for obtaining details of other publications. I rang the number and asked for a list. From this list of several books and a number of tapes, I ordered a cassette which arrived three days later. It was called 'What is Enlightenment?' and was the recording of a talk Barry had given more recently to an audience in Bristol.

Again I was amazed at the simplicity of it all. The talk explained that the word Enlightenment simply means unburdened: 'To be free of problems and worries and to be made lighter and therefore Enlightened, just as to put a light on something makes it clearer is also "Enlightening". While we allow the mind to remain cluttered and burdened we will always feel unenlightened.'

The tape explained 'to *be* the Master' means only to be the master of your own mind, and to think when you choose to and not when it wants to. Barry claimed this was the state of the Buddha and others. The idea is that if the mind is not involved with its daydreaming and imaginings and instead focuses on what is going on around it, then you are better able to cope with whatever situation is at hand, and don't spend time worrying about situations that cannot be changed. The logic of this I thought was wonderful, yet I heard people on the tape from the audience asking questions and seeming to have difficulty with the concept.

Another logical teaching was on an A3-size poster which came with the cassette. It was a piece of writing by Barry, and the contents were to get me into many arguments and disagreements, especially with members of my family. It described how we all expect to be loved all the time, even when we are in a foul mood over something. It said moods are entirely selfish, and we must give up our 'right' to have moods. It explained that when something happens or someone does something, we feel we have a 'right' to feel a certain way. A loved one could ask us to let go of it and we would argue the point that we are entitled to feel that way because 'this' happened, or 'they did that'. In this way we actually *choose* our moods and will fight for our right to keep them.

I could see the obvious truth in these simple words, yet seemed unable to find anyone else who was either willing or able to see this. I was eager to share what I could with my family in order to try to save them from their emotional plight. I would get responses such as 'It's natural to get unhappy, and

46

angry and frightened; it's all part of being human!' And these discussions could get a little stressed. On occasion I used the following in response if I felt I could get away with it:

> That is great. Just try to remember next time you do feel like that, it's because you chose it and don't blame anybody else for it!

This was not perhaps the best way to gently encourage people round to my way of thinking.

(Note: Barry taught that emotion cannot survive in conscious awareness: a problem happens in the world and the emotion connected to it rises as a disturbance, and immediately the imagination begins re-living the problem over and over. This, Barry explained, is actually feeding and strengthening the emotion within, and the person unknowingly becomes increasingly emotional with each and every situation, growing and solidifying over their lifetime (though much of the time it may be lurking beneath the surface, so cannot always be felt).

However, the more the person can stop the mind, cease the endless churning of the imagination and instead hold on to the knowledge of the problem, but not actually think ABOUT it, perhaps incredibly the emotion begins to be dissolved (though this can take anything from a few seconds to several weeks each time, depending on the situation and the strength of emotion attached to it). As one faces the emotion, it can feel like a death within, which Barry described as the death of the emotional self. Thus the person becomes less emotional and more conscious (self-aware) with each difficult situation (instead of less so). (Barry further described this as 'returning through the hell of one's self', as one must face and consciously endure the past emotion so as to be free of it.)

The other half of the equation, and what made Barry's teaching so practical, is the need to take action when required; to avoid doing so, for whatever reason, would only prolong the situation and would also further feed the emotion.

I also learnt over time that often the intention to take action can be enough; sometimes the action decided upon later turns out to no longer be required, but only once the mental step had been made.)

***

A more positive conversation took place when visiting a friend and speaking with his mum. She was known to be quite emotional (as many people are) and became somewhat defensive when I was explaining what I was doing. She said, 'Getting upset and grieving is an important part of the process! What if you have an accident in your car and you've got no money to fix it?'

I replied, 'OK, imagine there were two people: both have had car accidents and they've got no money. One sits at the side of the road, looking at their damaged car, sobbing at how desperate the situation is.

'In the meantime, the other walks home, gets out the local paper that was recently delivered and goes straight to the jobs page. Within an hour he's circled a few jobs, made a few phone calls and lined up interviews for the next day. By the end of the week he's got a job and can get some money to fix his car. The other chap is by this time sitting at home, staring at the walls in desperation at what he's going to do!'

They looked at each other, my friend and his mum, neither of them speaking for a few seconds, and suddenly my friend said to her, 'Well, he's made a monkey out of you, hasn't he?' and she agreed.

***

I had a couple of dreams two nights apart which were very vivid, and in a way quite similar. The first was that I was with a woman whom I loved with everything I had. (I actually didn't have a girlfriend at this time; in fact, I hadn't had a great deal of experience at all with regards to relationships, which perhaps makes this all the more intriguing.) She was worth more than life itself to me. I would have done literally anything for her, and that was going to be put to the test: there was a very good reason for it (the details of which weren't entirely clear at the time), but she asked me to help her to die. She really needed to die and for some reason needed me to do it for her.

In the next scene, I was walking with one of my friends from Essex confiding in him my predicament and looking for advice. He stated strongly that she shouldn't have asked me, and if she wanted to die she should do it herself and I wasn't to get involved!

In the final scene, I was back with her, sitting, holding her. I gave her a drink from a glass knowing it was going to kill her. She knew too. As the life slipped out of her, she looked deep into my eyes and said softly, 'It's all right. It's all right.' She was so unbelievably sweet that I hurt inside as I heard those words and looked back into her eyes. I would have willingly died for the love I felt from her at that moment. But I wasn't the one dying, she was, and I had helped her. I knew it was the right thing to do and I really had no choice, but still it hurt. I held her for a while after she had gone.

***

The next night I had another dream. I was walking with my girlfriend across a park and her friends were walking a few yards behind as they always had, and I had wondered why they were always with us. We were getting serious about each other, and it was time to lay all the cards on the table.

49

That night in bed (and I think it was to be our first night together), she explained to me what she and her friends were: she said they were vampires, and as much as she loved me, if she woke in the night hungry, she may kill and attempt to eat me without being aware of what she was doing. She was giving me a chance to get out because she loved me and didn't want to hurt me.

I thought for a moment about this. I didn't want to die, but I certainly didn't want to lose her. I soon decided I would stay with her. If it so happened that one night, being her natural self, she was to kill and begin to eat me, then so be it. I hoped that as our love for each other was so strong it would protect me, but I knew the most important thing was that we were honest with each other above all else. I was prepared to let her kill me rather than lose her.

***

On waking I wrote down these dreams straight away. I knew as they were so vivid there would be some meaning to them, but at that time they simply displayed the lengths I would go to in my search for the truth, and for love. The truth included being true to myself and to whatever I knew to be right, however outrageous or painful it may be. (Even if it included killing the person I loved, or dying myself, when necessary.) There were to be no limits, and the dreams demonstrated this.

The full meaning behind them would not become apparent until much later.

***

I went to stay with my dad and stepmum in Somerset, and spent the majority of the time sitting in a large armchair staring out of the French doors, much to their disapproval. Practising feeling my body and the chair beneath it whilst watching and listening to the goings-on had definitely become

50

the most important task for me above all else. Not only was it going to cure me of my stammer – my life's ambition – but it was also going to make me into an Enlightened Master with many followers, if the psychic was to be believed.

There was a local man in Somerset who, amongst other things, owned a strawberry field, and my sister had worked for him during her school holidays picking strawberries. He had told her he was Enlightened and even had a little meditation retreat up in the hills. On hearing about me he had agreed to meet with me. I drove to his place one dark evening and was invited into the large kitchen and offered a seat on a sofa. The man explained he was in several groups and was an elder in a local Buddhist group. He had raised the Kundalini energy twice and now felt he had got wherever there was to go.

The Kundalini energy is that energy that travels up the spine to the top of the head, through the chakras or energy centres that I was taught about at the college. Raising the Kundalini, as I understand it, is when a lot of energy rises at one time giving the individual an extremely heightened sense of awareness, and colours and sounds amongst other things can become much more vivid.

We sat on the sofa, and the idea was for him to give me some pointers to help me on my path. He looked around the good-sized kitchen. There was a large wooden table in the middle of the room, and on it were a collection of plates and cups and other utensils, seemingly from the meals of that day. He looked at me and asked, 'What is wrong with this room?' I wasn't sure what he meant. I fumbled for an answer, and he asked again, 'Is there anything in this room as it shouldn't be?'

I felt inside my body to find the peace and stillness as I'd been taught. I then looked at the pile of dirty plates and pots, the kitchen looking as if it needed a really good clean, and felt at the same time everything was just as it was meant to be. 'No,' I replied. 'Everything is as it should be.'

He smiled. 'That is very good,' he said. 'I've only met a handful of people in my whole life who know that everything is actually perfect, no matter how it looks.'

He then asked, 'What is stopping you from being Enlightened?'

Again I fumbled for an answer. 'The emotions?' I suggested.

He asked again, 'What is it that is getting in the way of your Enlightenment?'

'My thoughts and imagination?' I suggested, trying hard to understand what he was getting at.

This went on for a few minutes. 'Your mind!' he said eventually. I felt I knew that. I had been more specific than he needed, that's all.

He went on to draw a diagram representing me, then a space and then Enlightenment. He pointed out all that was between me and Enlightenment was my mind. He went on to say that through meditation a person can reach a state of 'no mind', therefore eliminating the separation between them and Enlightenment.

He later said to be sceptical of anyone who claims they are Enlightened because he said even he wouldn't claim that, as he wasn't even sure what it was. This I found slightly confusing as my sister had had conversations with him, and she had told me of some of his experiences of being Enlightened, namely that of raising the Kundalini as he had told her. I took it that he possibly calls his experiences 'Enlightenment' when speaking with anyone uninitiated, but with someone who was already following the teachings of an 'Enlightened Master' and who was studying the process for themselves, he would have to be more careful with his words. Although there was no doubt he had some rare knowledge, he seemed to lack the energy and the power in his words that

52

Barry Long had. I didn't feel the same 'ring of truth' or recognition as I did when I heard Barry talking. The time spent with him was more an exercise in seeing what I knew, and seeing which bits he confirmed and which bits he didn't.

As we finished our conversation he said to me, 'You remind me of what I was like when I was your age. Anytime you want to pop in again, feel free.' This felt a little odd to me, because he seemed to be in his forties, and had said I was like him at my age. I hoped this didn't mean I would only get as far as he had: in my forties and still not sure if I knew what Enlightenment was. I felt I wasn't that far behind him now. No; although I was grateful for the time he had spent with me and the help he had attempted to give me, I didn't feel there was much more I could learn from him and didn't expect to be back in the near future.

***

During the same visit I telephoned The Barry Long Foundation to order another cassette. The foundation's office was based in Somerset not far from where my dad lived. (This was the UK centre from which the books and cassettes were distributed, and meetings were arranged.) I hoped they would permit me to drive by and pick it up in person rather than them posting it (as I wanted to listen to it whilst I was staying in the area). It seemed no-one had ever done this before (perhaps not least of all because the location was quite remote), and it took a little persuasion. Eventually it was agreed, but it was made clear to me that the staff were not there to discuss Barry's teaching nor answer any questions. I would simply arrive, remain outside, and someone would bring the item out and collect the payment from me.

While I waited outside for someone to come out with the cassette, a man and woman did come out of the building and walked past me. We acknowledged each other and I made eye contact with the man. He had thick brown hair and

53

a full beard, but what struck me were his eyes. They were also brown, but the energy I saw (felt) from them was incredible. They were 'full'; of what, I could not be sure, but they were amazing. There was no effort behind them; no trying to 'do' or 'be' anything. It was just how they were – 'full'. I had never seen this before and I knew that I wanted to have eyes like that one day.

***

I spent the remainder of my stay with my dad and stepmum, still sitting in the armchair staring out into the garden. I had learnt at Barry's suggestion on one of the tapes that one way to save energy, making it easier to remain conscious of your body and surroundings, was to stop talking about the past or the future unless absolutely necessary. This also didn't make me particularly popular with family. My stepmum attempted to listen to Barry's 'What is Enlightenment?' tape, but wasn't impressed. She said although he may be right, she didn't like having it rammed down her throat that her moods are hers alone and no-one else is responsible for how she may be feeling.

That wasn't a move forward at all. Although she wasn't saying he was wrong, she was saying, 'I don't want to hear that because I don't want to do anything about it.' And she didn't. They also didn't like the way I was changing, the way I was withdrawing emotionally, and it was not long before my dad began referring to Barry Long as 'Larry Bong', and did so from then on.

One aspect of my withdrawing emotionally (as they saw it – to me, I was working very hard to dissolve all the emotional pain within, so as to be able to keep going), was to let go of my past, and this included anything and everything I cared about. I had a little trophy shield awarded to me for my achievement in karate whilst taking classes at my last boarding school. (I was only first belt, but had worked very

54

hard to be as good as possible.) When having a clear-out of my room, I threw this away. It was of the past! Another item was my lock-pick set; I had become intrigued by this subject, had bought this set and had been practising (as a hobby). But this too, as I was attached to it, was thrown away.

A couple of items I did not feel I could throw away were a Chinese wooden puzzle box that my dad had given me many years earlier, and a little leather photograph holder with two photographs of our dog, which I had had with me at school. So both of these items I gave back to my dad. To me, I was doing the right thing. These few items were too 'good' to throw away, but I had a lot of work to do on myself, and holding on to anything emotionally would mean I would continue to suffer with emotional pain, and that I could not stand. But this further contributed to my family's dislike and distrust of what I was doing.

(Note: Another statement that Barry repeated on many occasions during his talks is 'Love is not a feeling!', and this would invariably cause some disturbance in people (my own family included). He would go on to explain that love is the stillness, the presence, the sense of being complete which is always behind the emotions. Love – 'true love' – never leaves and never dies. And it is this that he was guiding people through his teaching to not only connect with, but to realise as their own nature. But it was not easy for everyone to accept.

With regards to 'feeling' love, Barry taught that when one person loves another, what is happening is that the other person is reflecting to them a part of themselves, a bit of their inner 'being' they are not currently in touch with. Therefore, when they are with the person they feel whole, but when they are not with them they feel incomplete, as if a piece of their self is missing. It turns out there is; they have let go of it!

Barry explained that instead of thinking ABOUT a loved one (which only serves to further strengthen the

55

emotions), if one remains conscious and connects 'within',
they find they are still in touch with the very love that the
person reflected. Thus they do not 'miss' the person; at least
not in the same way – they can know they miss the person's
presence, but they themselves do not feel incomplete.)

***

I still didn't know what I was going to do with my life career-wise. I had now left the college a year early, having retaken the two GCSEs and obtained two more 'C' grades (bringing my total up to six 'C' grades), but only completed the first year of the A-level courses. There had seemed to me to be too much learning and not enough progress being made (in the sense of growing in self-knowledge).

On one occasion at the dinner table with my dad, stepmum and sister, it was said I could never do what my sister did (working in the old people's homes). I said I didn't know, but it wasn't something I wanted to do. 'Oh come on!' they said. 'You know you couldn't!'

I went home to Surrey and spent a few weeks considering some religious future. I certainly had enough spiritual knowledge and ability to succeed whatever the religious tradition may be. Whilst walking through the local town one afternoon, a young chap in an orange robe and shaved head handed me a large book about the size of a bible. I gave a him a couple of pounds and went on my way. On the cover of the book were the words 'Bhagavad Gita'.

It was the book of Krishna, and the chap had been a devotee from a Hare Krishna temple in Soho. The book had seven hundred pages, comprising Sanskrit (the ancient text) and the English translation under each paragraph. The book said inside the back cover that the public were welcome to visit their temple on a Sunday afternoon. It was now Saturday; my aim was to have read all seven hundred pages before next weekend, demonstrating I was sincere, and then speak with the Enlightened Masters there. It would also give me more chance of understanding what they would be talking about if they referred to the teachings in the book. I read a hundred pages a day. In essence it was the same as Barry taught, stilling the mind through certain exercises and becoming fully conscious. I went up to Soho as planned.

It turned out the time I had been given to be there was inaccurate and I was a couple of hours too early. Despite this, I was taken into the temple and shown round. I removed my shoes as directed, leaving these outside the door, and was taken in to see the altars. A great deal of work had been put into them, with pictures of Krishna, and flowers and other ornaments, and they looked impressive. But I felt uncomfortable. It felt unnatural to me to go through all this, and certainly unnecessary. Kneeling at an altar and repeating 'Hare Krishna, Hare Krishna, Hare Rama, Hare Rama', and clutching the beads, moving to a new bead at every completion of the verse, wearing robes and shaving one's head; there were just too many rules for me.

I was taken downstairs to have some food. The women devotees had to sit at a separate table from the men and seemed to be seen as lower class.

I was told I would have to work for my food as I was early and was led to the washing-up sink. This I did quite willingly.

I had a few conversations with some of the devotees, and having read the whole Bhagavad Gita, could see the idea behind it all. Krishna was supposed to be the incarnation of 'God' himself. The book claims there is no difference between Krishna (God) and his name. Therefore, in order to get to know Krishna, repeating his name over and over, hundreds of times a day, will advance a person's spirituality and bring them closer to him (Krishna/God).

All the traditions, though, I saw as being just that: traditions. The idea behind this was devotional service to

Krishna. And to do anything in Krishna's name is to bring the person that bit closer to knowing him. It also said that via this method one would realise the Supreme Personality within oneself that exists within all things, but I didn't see why it had to have all the rules. It was like being back at boarding school. And having heard Barry say that traditions are just the mind holding on to its past and its own mental structures, and having had pointed out in both the Bible and the Bhagavad Gita that in each case it is taught to 'abandon all dharmas' and let go of all beliefs and opinions, praying to an altar and following these traditions seemed to be going against their own teachings.

***

Later, back in Surrey, I increased my investigation and visited a Buddhist monastery. Again people were walking around in robes and shaved heads, with their own traditions. I did not wish to restrict myself. I was looking to grow spiritually but felt this would suffocate me. I read a little from a few of the books they had on the shelves. Again the idea was the same as with the Hare Krishnas in the sense that they were looking for union with the great intelligence behind all things, and everything I read whilst there confirmed what I was doing anyway, except I wasn't restricted by ancient traditions from another country.

My only rule was to do whatever I felt to be right at that particular moment as often as possible. Sometimes this could be scary, because I would know inside I have to do a thing and I don't want to do it. I was well aware, though, that I didn't really have a choice and if I had to do it, it was because I had something to learn. Not doing it would deprive me of that experience, and I would have to face a similar situation another day in order to grow. There was no escape.

***

I then found a Franciscan friary not that far from where we lived, and decided to investigate. Not surprisingly I found the same situation. The basic aim was to get closer to God, but again it was so smothered in ancient traditions that no-one seemed to know anything other than that. This was to be my last point of call in organised religion. Anyway, even speaking with people who were within these 'proper religions', I had not found anyone yet who seemed to know what Barry Long knew (or the other Masters I'd read about); but then he had spent time criticising organised religions exactly for these reasons. They are too bound in tradition to know anything about love, truth and honesty.

***

I looked in the jobcentre for a job to earn some money for the time being. It just so happened that on this day one of the only positions available not requiring experience was as a care assistant in an old people's home. It certainly wasn't what I wanted, but my sister seemed to enjoy it, so I'd give it a go.

I was given directions to a small semi-detached house on the outskirts of town and had a very brief interview with the owner. I was then asked to follow her to the next town in my car. I had a little Fiat 126 at the time.

We pulled into the driveway of a large white house with old wooden windows and large, double wooden doors. We went into the large square hallway with wooden panelling around the walls and up the very wide wooden staircase opposite. A glass chandelier hung above the centre of the hallway and another over the stairs lighting the deep red patterned carpet beneath.

The first thing I noticed was a thin woman with long fine grey hair in a bun, wearing what looked like a cleaner's apron, walking towards me. Her eyes and her mouth were wide open, displaying a pained and somewhat terrified

59

expression. Saliva was drooling from her mouth, joining the expanding wet area on her chest. She then emitted a blood curdling shriek, making me jump. Her arms outstretched in a Frankenstein pose, she began to circle the room, murmuring and whining as she went.

My God, I thought, *do I really have to do this?* The answer was strong in me. *Yes, I do have to do it!* There was a knowledge inside telling me I needed what this was going to teach me. I didn't like it, but I felt I didn't really have a choice.

The woman interviewing returned from the office and invited me in.

It was a privately run home for the elderly and mentally ill, and was run with the owners and staff cutting as many corners as possible. This included paying any unreasonable wage and not employing any qualified staff for the thirty-four patients living there. I was nineteen years old and it was 1992. I was to be at work to assist with getting the residents up at 5.00 on the Monday morning of the following week, for the grand sum of two pounds and seventy pence an hour. I was terrified, but had been out of work for about three months now and something had to change. Obviously it was going to be me.

That evening I told my stepdad I'd got myself a job. He said, 'Great, what is it?'

'In an old people's home,' I told him.

'But you don't even like old people?' he exclaimed, more than a little confused.

I knew he was right. I had very little time for anyone really, but especially saw nothing particularly thrilling in the elderly. But I needed a job, and this was it. It felt a little like a leap of faith. (It would also prove whether my dad and stepmum were right about me when they said I couldn't work with the elderly as my sister had.)

60

Start work

61

It was quite an amazing experience, working in a home for the elderly and mentally ill, and it took a lot of getting used to. One of the hardest things was that I had been brought up to respect my elders, to do as I'm told and not to answer back. Now I was telling elderly people what to do and had to develop a sense of authority over them. (I ended up staying at this home for two years, leaving as a senior member of staff, solely responsible for the smooth running of the home when on duty.)

***

Soon after starting at the home I ordered another Barry Long tape called 'How to stop thinking'. Again it was so simple and down-to-earth. The idea was that all our problems and worries are due to our thinking. It is thinking about a situation that creates the emotion that we associate with it, the happy or sad feelings, and the emotion turns a situation into a problem when the feelings are negative ones. The tape provided instructions on how to gain enough energy to be able to halt the thinking mind when it tries to get its teeth into a situation. The mind enjoys the imaginings of a situation, usually imagining the worst. Giving the person mental pictures of a situation is a little like watching a scary movie and hiding behind a cushion whilst peering round the corner. The person may not like what they're watching, but they often keep watching anyway. It is very hard to let it go.

The mind creates this film in the person's imagination, and when finished, plays it again and again, sometimes getting worse and more graphic every time; all the time the emotion is growing inside the person and getting stronger and stronger. You are now locked in your imagination, unable to escape, destined to relive the scenario – or one similar – time and time again until the emotional energy has had its fill. At this time, it calms down leaving the person feeling exhausted. It's not long though before it rises again to absorb more energy.

The tape explained that we need to learn to use the energy ourselves and not allow the emotion to take over. You've heard sayings like 'I don't know what came over me!' Well, the emotion did – that's what!

The tape suggested exercises such as not fidgeting, as this is the emotion ticking over, entertaining itself because it likes to keep moving. Another is not to talk about the past unnecessarily because this encourages the emotion to go into this memory with you and give you some sensation related to it – then it's got you again. Another powerful exercise (but maybe the hardest and least popular) is not to allow happy or exciting thoughts or memories to take over. What happens is when imagining or remembering a lovely or pleasurable experience – which at the very least would seem to be a harmless, if not a truly beneficial thing to do – the emotion becomes stronger. As we are enjoying the feeling we don't notice it, but the next time we for any reason think of a negative experience, whether it be a problem or a painful memory, we find it that much harder to prevent the emotion from taking over.

This 'taking over' was quite close to my heart because I had found I could sense others' feelings and sometimes found them hard to handle. If I was with someone who was angry or upset, I would feel it and want to help. If the feeling was anger and aimed at me, it really scared me. I could never understand before how someone who loved me a moment earlier could have so much hatred towards me. Now I knew: it wasn't actually their hatred; they had 'lost control', allowing the emotional 'entity' to control them.

That's why people say things they don't mean. The reason, as it turns out, is that they aren't saying it; it's the emotion that says and does awful things. It is responsible for all the hurtful things you've said that you didn't mean, as with

64

every other human being on the planet. If we are not completely conscious every moment – and that means 'aware of our body and surroundings, and therefore not lost in thought' – then in the moments when we are daydreaming and in our own private world, we are susceptible to any emotion that the daydreaming (i.e. images) may stimulate. These are sometimes pleasurable but often not, but it (the emotion) doesn't actually care. It gets energy from our imaginings whether they are pleasurable or extremely painful.

And therein lies the bottom line behind the path I was following and the bit that disturbed my family particularly. The path involved stilling the pendulum of emotions. I was reminded time after time that 'you can't stop having negative emotions, because you need the negative ones to have the positive ones'. And that is of course true, but I had decided the negative feelings were so painful that I was willing to give up the positive feelings in order to be free. This is the state of mind or attitude it seems a person needs to progress with any sort of speed with this: not necessarily being suicidal, but having had enough emotional pain that the person is willing to begin giving up their quest for excitement to replace it with peace and purpose, and even understanding. We've all had lots of emotional pain, so I was surprised at my family and friends arguing that it is natural to get upset and angry, and that I was wrong to endeavour to live without it. The old saying 'We just want you to be happy' may be true, but only to a point. They didn't want me to be free of unhappiness. It was preferable to them that everyone, themselves and me included, have moments of happiness and excitement and others of despair and anger, riddled with problems and worries, rather than to be in a constant state of equilibrium. Not very exciting I admit, but at least I was learning to be free of unhappiness.

***

I progressed very quickly, grasping the concept enough to argue the point in quite a persuasive manner. I was still learning though that I couldn't even share this wondrous new way of living with my closest family, and it was a long time before I gave up completely.

Somehow I got it into my head that being honest meant telling the truth. I upset several members of my family by stating I didn't want to see them as I wanted to be somewhere else, and other similar lines. I now had people trying to convince me that I should lie, to save people's feelings. But I didn't see their feelings as being my problem; as long as I was honest with them, surely that's the most anyone can expect. Why would people want me to lie to them?

One day the health and safety registration officer came round the nursing home. He saw that one of the old ladies who was eating her lunch had a large chair with a table fixed to it. He asked me whether the table fixed to her chair was on only whilst she was eating, or was it there all the time? The owner of the home was there and she answered, saying it was only there for meal times, and the man looked at me...

The truth was that it was there all the time. And that was because on the occasions we had forgotten to replace it after taking her to the toilet, she would slide down out of the chair, and being unable to walk, would edge along on her behind across the floor. Not only was this a hazard to other residents, but her incontinence pad would come away as she slid herself, sometimes leaving a trail of faeces across the carpet.

I had only a couple of seconds to consider my options: tell the truth, lose my job, and it wouldn't help the old lady in the slightest because it seemed she needed some sort of restraint for her own good. Or lie and carry on as usual. It went against the stand I had made, but it felt like the right thing to do, so I lied. And I had learnt that sometimes lying was necessary.

***

I had a friend at work with whom I spent a lot of time and I talked to him a little about what I was doing. He could follow it up to a point, but didn't have the drive to actively pursue it. We had both experimented with low-level drugs in the past and managed to get hold of some 'microdots' which were the new LSD out at that time. We had a green one which we split between us as we had heard they were very strong. We then went for a walk in the park near where he lived.

It was certainly stronger than any I'd had before, even with only taking half of it. We sat on a park bench in the dimming evening light, and as usual I practised staying as aware and conscious as possible, feeling my breathing and my body whilst consciously looking around me.

Suddenly everything froze. The whole atmosphere was intense and full, yet it felt and looked so still, as if nothing had ever or was ever going to move again. It took my breath away and was actually quite frightening at first. I really felt as if it belonged on another 'frozen' planet and could be like this forever now.

Later back at his flat we were sitting in the living room with two other friends: one who hadn't taken anything and the other who'd had the edge of one. I got up from where I was seated on the floor with my back to the wall, and made my way to the toilet. Whilst sitting there in the bathroom I had the sensation that I wasn't really on the toilet at all, and actually could still be in the living room, trousers round my ankles, squatting on the floor. This was quite worrying and put me in the position of having to make a decision. I either had to carry on as I normally would when visiting the toilet – and that involved wiping myself in the next minute and standing up to pull up my clothes, possibly with those in the living room watching the whole procedure – or I could stay exactly where I was until morning when the effects would have worn off enough for me to know what was real and what was not.

Of course, if I did the latter – if I was really on the toilet and it was real – it wouldn't be long before someone noticed I'd been gone a long time and came looking for me. This could prove equally embarrassing, and I decided therefore to take another leap of faith, thinking that if I could see it and touch it, that's all I had to go on. It was a strange experience, but it really felt as if the whole room and everything in it wasn't real at all.

Once out of the bathroom and sitting in an armchair, I looked around the room. I felt that I was no longer just sitting in the chair, but that I was now the room itself and everything in it. It could not be said where I began or ended. I and the room were indeed 'one'. This experience lasted for several minutes.

Later, exchanging experiences with my friend who'd taken the other half, before I had a chance to get into my toilet story, he jumped in with his own experience: whilst standing at the lavatory urinating, it occurred to him that he could actually still be in the living room urinating on the coffee table! He also came to the conclusion that it was better to continue as normal. He explained as well that whilst lying on his bed later, he could feel a spinning, spiralling sensation which was sucking him in. He said it felt as though were he to let go and allow himself to be pulled in, he would disappear and never come out again. Frightened, he'd fought it for as long as it lasted – he really felt he could disappear if he wasn't careful.

***

The Barry Long Foundation sent me information about a seminar Barry was holding in Earl's Court in London. It was only for a weekend, and at fifty pounds a day I paid only for the Sunday. I didn't know what to expect when meeting a real live Spiritual Master; I had read much about Indian Masters and the amazing things they could do.

I sat near the centre of the auditorium. The theatre was full of a lot of ordinary people. One or two were dressed in hippy/New Age style clothes, but the other three hundred or so looked like anybody on the street.

Already seated on a chair on the stage was an elderly gentleman, dressed in a dark suit with (I think) a purple shirt and colour-coordinated tie. He had grey hair in a middle-parting and a neat, full beard. He looked very stern as he gazed around the audience – almost scary, with a severe gaze.

I wondered what mystical powers he would have as a Master. I had read so much about Masters walking on water, appearing and disappearing, that I didn't even know if once a person was 'at one with the universe', if they still needed transport, or whether a single thought would materialise them wherever they wished to be. He looked ordinary enough, but then that was an important part of his teaching. That is, that he was nothing special, as it is every man and woman's right to be in that state.

I don't remember much of that day, but before I left I did book into the five-day seminar at Leicester University beginning two weeks later.

***

A few days later, I left my friend's flat having taken possession of the last microdot, a red one. He had decided he wouldn't want any more after the last time. I was willing to do almost anything to experience the mystical or paranormal in an attempt to find the truth, and went back to my mum's house where I was still living to take it.

It was late and they were already asleep. I crept downstairs to where my bedroom was situated in the

69

maisonette. I popped the entire tiny round pill in my mouth, and once I was changed and ready for bed, switched off the lights and lay in the dark silence, listening and watching.

After a while the effects started. Usually I would at least have the music on, and I had never taken it on my own before. I don't know why I did this time, but it was an experience which I will possibly never forget...

A couple of weeks earlier I had had half of a green microdot which brought the sensation of becoming the room. This time, possibly due to me lying down in the dark, I not only became the room again, but seemed to lose my body and all personal relation to it. I now knew I was the whole universe. My consciousness was everywhere and everything at once. I knew what it meant to be 'at one with the universe', and suddenly at one memorable point actually felt myself 'click' back into place *as I had done so many times before*. I wasn't entirely sure what the 'as I had done so many times before' actually meant, but that is what came to me as it happened. It occurred to me it may refer to previous lives, when I was separated from the 'Universal Mind' or God, and on death was reunited. But this was just me looking for explanations for the powerful experience.

I was now at one with God or the Cosmic Consciousness (as it is also sometimes called) and thought it a little strange that the purpose of life was to take some LSD to realise the truth. If I'd known, I would have taken it earlier and then avoided it all these years.

Lying there, I wanted to run and tell everyone what I'd realised. Everything felt like a big dream, and I even wondered if everyone was in on it except me. I questioned what my mum and stepdad would say if I ran into their bedroom now. Would they say something like, 'Well done, you know now!'?

Then I was reminded of what the psychic at the College of Psychic Studies had channelled through, about a falling tree making no sound when no-one is there to hear it. I had the terrifying thought, *What if they're not there at all? What if there's nothing there?* If everything is just a dream, then perhaps there is currently nothing at all outside these four walls, just as when in bed dreaming and the mind creates the dream. And all that exists is whatever you are looking at in a particular moment. I saw then that I really am all alone. So is this what it is like to be God, or at one with God? There is no-one to talk with, and nowhere to go and nothing to do. I am just here, being me! That is all I can do.

I thought maybe there were other 'Gods' around to talk to, but no, I was alone...

Now that I knew all this, I saw that there was no need for the rest of existence, and I was to spend the rest of eternity within these four dark walls. Why couldn't I have realised this whilst abroad on a beach? At least I would have had people to watch and the warm sun to enjoy. Now I was to look at these dark walls, where I could just make out the shapes of the drawers and sink unit. I had no-one to talk with and nothing to do. This was going to be the rest of my eternity. This was my forever!

I thought perhaps, as the Universal Mind, I could create another 'Being' to talk to, but then saw that there was really no point as it wouldn't be real anyway. I saw that even if I had someone to talk with, or a nice, sunny golden beach to enjoy, none of it would be real so I'd be living a lie. No, I'd stay here; though I wondered why, if I was now united with the Cosmic Consciousness, I didn't have the ability to just create a beach at will. I did try but it didn't work.

I remembered my friend from years back describing to me how the Buddha's final test was to leap into the jaws of the Dragon, which he explained symbolised death itself. This was the Buddha's last test – was it now mine? I was experiencing being God or Life itself, and to be true to this knowledge, should I perhaps let go of my physical life, break my attachment to it? There was a sensation of breathing that would have been in my chest and stomach area if I had one. As it was, I was actually no more than an 'intelligent space' with no body at all, and focussing on this I found I could actually stop the sensation with no effort or pain – actually stop breathing. There was no feeling as such, only knowledge of what was there. Was this the right thing to do? To be true to life and what I now knew, would the right thing be to stop breathing now and let go of the physical existence altogether? After all, it's not real anyway. It's just a dream, referred to as *maya* (as I recalled in one religion), meaning illusion.

Maybe this was the whole purpose of life: to realise that existence isn't actually real at all and to 'take the bull by the horns', having the courage of one's convictions in stepping off the precipice into the unknown. Was the purpose to end one's own life, not through emotion and pain, but through realising the truth that it is all an illusion?

I began to wonder what would happen when my mum and stepdad came in the next day and found me dead. Then I saw that as everything's only a dream, if I died it would be like waking from a dream and it would end. The dream would disappear. They wouldn't find me because they wouldn't exist anymore. They only existed now in my imagination, and to die I would wake up from this dream, and it would all end.

I stopped breathing for several seconds, just relaxing into it. It was so easy. I knew I could go all the way without effort. Then I was hit with a great sense of loss for the whole of nature, with the trees and wildlife, all the mountains and clouds. Everything was so perfect, and in my death I was going to take it all with me. I would be consciously destroying the whole of life itself: every animal, the beautiful sunset and all the flowers. The idea hurt too much, and after several attempts I gave up. I would see what happened in the morning, assuming there was still an 'out there' and people still existed. I half expected strangers and family alike to approach me, congratulating me on realising the truth. Maybe I would see clearer in the morning that to end my physical life was the right thing to do. I didn't see the logic of continuing now that I knew none of life was real. To continue would be living a lie and would not be true to what I knew. If the worst came to the worst, I was due to see Barry at Leicester in one week. I didn't intend to stick around that long, but if I was still alive then, he'd know what to do.

***

I woke the next morning as usual. I went upstairs to see my mum and stepdad and still didn't know what to expect. Actually nothing happened out of the ordinary. They were exactly the same as they always were. The huge experience from the night before was quickly wearing off, leaving behind only the memory and now even bigger doubts. Last night everything seemed so simple, and I was so sure I knew what was real and what wasn't. Now I didn't know at all, and I was in a state of utter confusion. I began to feel scared and longed for the coming week of the five-day seminar so I could ask Barry what to do.

Later that day at work I told my friend of my experience. I knew I could trust him, so I asked him whether he was real, or just a part of my dream.

He said he was real. For a moment everything seemed a little easier until he went on to say, smiling, 'But then, I may just be someone in your dream saying they're real!' That didn't help. I would have to wait for the coming seminar if I didn't find out anything beforehand.

Dying for love

Once at the seminar in Leicester, I collected my room key, and as we were at the university we were actually using the students' rooms and other facilities. There was time to put my bag in my room and have a walk around the grounds before the seminar started.

I followed a group of people out of the entrance and across the road. I had seen the sign opposite when I had arrived marking the University Botanic Gardens. The flower beds and shrubs and bushes were absolutely fantastic, and all were marked with individual plaques. I came across a large raised pond containing huge koi carp and lots of lilies. It was wonderful. I would come back here later, but now it was time to make my way to the seminar hall.

There were over three hundred people seated in the hall for the talk. I was desperate to find out what I was to do. I still had the memory of that night and didn't know what was real or what was the right thing to do. The memory from that night of realising nothing is actually real still raised the question that perhaps the honest and proper thing to do was to end the dream in order to face reality: death; and this frightened me.

There were a couple of people I recognised from the Earls Court seminar, but a lot I didn't. I don't remember much of what was said, but then again Barry's teaching is that you are not supposed to remember what is said anyway. Just hear the words, and it is either true for you at that time or not. What I do remember is he got on to the subject of what is real and what isn't. I listened carefully, looking towards the small stage that had been erected for Barry. There was a table next to Barry's chair holding vases of wonderful flowers alongside a glass with a bottle of water. I was halfway towards the back of the hall, seated near the aisle. I had left it too late to get a seat near the front.

Then Barry stated that our surroundings and everything physical are not real.

This sent a shock through me. What did he mean? Was everything I had seen that night true? Was this all a dream and I was all alone here?

I put up my hand quickly, without thinking. He pointed at me to proceed. 'Does that mean everybody else isn't real either?' I asked out loud, amazing myself.

'That's right,' he said simply, and went on to answer a question from another member of the audience. With problem questions, where a person was describing a difficulty in their lives, he would ask the person to look at him and try not to look away, explaining that his energy helps them not to think, so they speak directly from their consciousness without the emotions getting in the way. With me, he answered quickly and moved on.

I sat there for the rest of the session, not really listening at all, just trying to understand what had happened. Had he just told me that no-one and no-thing actually exists, and I really am all alone here, in one big elaborate dream created by my own imagination?

The hall cleared at the end of the session, and I remained in my seat. I was fighting to hold back the tears, quivering all over, possibly in shock. *What now? Do I now have to end my life? Is that the 'right' thing to do to be true to the spiritual path?*

After several minutes I stood up and made my way out into the lobby. Barry's assistant, or right-hand man, came out of a side door. I looked at him, eyes filled with tears. 'Can I see Barry please?' I asked. He seemed to hesitate, so I continued, 'I asked a question and would like some more information.' He asked what my question was and went back through the door. A few seconds later he returned and led me through into a large room behind the hall.

At the far end of the room Barry was sitting in a large armchair. He got up as I entered the room. His assistant introduced me. 'Sit down, Nick,' Barry said as he pointed to a chair opposite his. His partner pulled up a chair next to mine, so she and I were both facing him.

As we sat down he said, 'Don't worry, it scares people sometimes.' I barely had time to wonder what he was talking about as I sat and looked up. I looked straight at him, and my mind froze. His eyes, looking right at me, were blue-grey. It was as if something was coming from him, and the whole atmosphere was energised with an intense stillness. For a moment I felt I was in shock. It was absolutely incredible, terrifyingly still. I was fixed. I felt I had nowhere to go. An amazing aspect was that the whole experience was exactly the same as that night in the park when I felt I was on another planet, where nothing ever moved, not even me. It was as if my mind was frozen. I recalled him telling people in the audience to look at him because it would help them to stop thinking, and how hard they had seemed to find it not to look away. Now I knew why. I had no doubt I would not have been able to look at him had I not faced the experience several weeks earlier in the park. It was still hard, and I had to force myself not to look away.

I repeated to him my question from the session, and he could see I was upset by his previous answer. I tried to think of another way to phrase the question. I said, 'Are other people trying to reach Enlightenment as well, or is everyone just a part of my dream and not real at all?' I went on to explain, 'I was hoping to become a teacher one day, and if they're not real, then there's no-one to teach?'

He looked at me silently for a couple of seconds, and then said smiling, 'They think they are.'

This seemed to satisfy that question in me. Now for the other big one. I wasn't exactly stammering when talking, but my chest seemed to be shaking and I was having to force the words out. Barry noticed and said, 'Don't worry, it's the energy making it hard for you to speak.'

I said, 'If life and everything isn't real, is the purpose of life to realise this and "take the bull by the horns" and end it?'

He replied, 'You don't have to do anything you don't want to do.'

In hindsight, he had not exactly answered either of my questions, but what he had done was put my mind to rest. He had convinced me everything was all right, and now I was to carry on as before. The rest of the seminar as I remember went without incident.

***

Shortly after returning to work, I began part-time in another nursing home. I became involved with a thirty-eight-year-old woman. I was still only nineteen years old. It was never serious, but we spent a lot of time together for a few weeks, both no doubt gaining from the experience. A major part of Barry's teaching covered making love. The idea was that if the man remains conscious and as much as possible feels every movement and puts the entire focus on aiming to please the woman rather than his own end, then it helps both parties grow in consciousness and energy as opposed to growing in excitement and emotionality. I didn't know whether this was the case or not. However, it was certainly true that by not allowing myself to get excited about the idea of orgasm and instead putting all the attention on to pleasing her (to the extent of ceasing all movement, and if necessary, withdrawing momentarily should the feelings get too strong that the 'end' seem inevitable), then in this situation the whole experience was entirely different from the usual 'sex-love' people seem to get used to. Of course I had not much experience of 'normal sex', but knew that being able to go on for several hours without stopping was not the norm, and my new partner expressed her amazement about that; and even more so regarding what she was feeling by constantly

80

repeating, 'You're only nineteen! How can you do this, you're only nineteen?' I felt though that she wouldn't be interested enough for me really to explain where it came from, so I just smiled when she asked.

I'm not sure if it was due to me not introducing her to my mum and friends (as she said she felt a little like I was hiding her) or whether it was due to my making the mistake of telling her I loved her (Actually I wasn't emotionally attached. I just loved being with her and the whole experience, and thought the right thing to do was to express that to her; I saw the expression on her face when I said it: almost shock), but a few days later she cancelled a bowling evening with me and all my work colleagues whom she was going to meet for the first time, at short notice. When she didn't call me back later as agreed I thought it was over. A few weeks later she rang me and told me she was moving house (I forget where to). On two occasions over the next couple of years she rang and left a message with my mum or stepdad to say she'd rung. I called her back and spoke with her twelve-year-old son once, and the next time didn't bother ringing at all. It was over.

***

I later became involved with another woman from work. This time nearer my own age, and it was serious on both sides, although initially she was already in a formal relationship. The love that developed between us in only a couple of days served to emphasise the failings in her current relationship; the proposed marriage already having severe doubts cast over it, our feelings served to seal its fate. She moved out of their joint home into her parents' house, and it was awkward at first because the only time we had together in private was when we stayed at a friend's flat. Fortunately, a couple of weeks later she was given a flat by the council due to sharing her bedroom with her young daughter at her parent's home.

81

The feelings we had for each other were powerful, and I really loved her. As Barry had instructed, I told her at the beginning what I was doing. That is, to endeavour to grow in love and consciousness through the practice of not thinking, and making love rightly, thus eliminating problems and negativity. She listened and said she would try. The idea was that we were to help each other remain conscious. I was able to describe how, when we are together in a room and one of us is imagining being somewhere else, then it is as if that person is not really in the room at all. Their body is there, but their mind is elsewhere. In order to be completely honest with each other (and ourselves) it is necessary, as much as possible, to keep your mind where your body is. She could just about follow this and agreed to point out to me when she noticed I had 'drifted off', and I would her.

Two weeks later she told me she felt she didn't have enough desire to give up excitement, and I said it was best we went our separate ways. It was really hard, but Barry had said a relationship with someone who was not looking to grow in love with someone who is cannot work, and therefore should end. This was the right thing to do. I was giving up a person I really loved, to do the 'right thing', and it hurt.

***

That afternoon I went on my usual walk around the school grounds and to 'my' bench. I hadn't been there for a couple of weeks. The pressure to think about her was overpowering; her image and the memories of where we'd been and what we'd done kept blasting into my mind. After a little while of being lost in thought I would notice and return my attention to the trees, the grass, the sounds and all that was around me as I had practised over the last two years, at the same time being aware of the pressure pressing down on me to make me think. Even when I wasn't actually thinking of her and was holding on to what I could physically see and feel, I was very aware of what was wrong. There was no forgetting her even when not thinking about her. It was as if the knowledge was there without the image. I would be fully conscious and aware, and yet could feel the emotional pressure to think about her pressing in on me.

Whilst I 'kept a close eye' on the knowledge of the problem – that is whilst I walked along being aware of the trees and birds, possibly feeling my breathing, keeping a hold on the feeling inside that I was hurting but not allowing myself to think about why – I had learnt that I was actually 'dissolving' the emotion. To go into the memories and think about her would give the emotion more strength. Not only would it hurt more and drain me, making me feel tired and worn out, but when it was satisfied it would settle down for a while, only to come up again later. It was my duty now to use this experience to get rid of this little piece of emotion for good.

It would be very crafty at times. I would be feeling my body, my arms and legs, feeling my breathing and enjoying the scene, when slowly a thought would slide in which would seem entirely innocent. It could be of where I had seen a similarly shaped tree, or what I was going to have for tea. My mind was looking out for any thoughts of her and would not notice this sleight of hand. Suddenly the thought would switch to her again, but by then it was too late. I was already in the thought and being swept away by it, only to be brought back a few minutes later, back to my senses. By seemingly depriving myself of memories of her and how much I loved her and wanted to be with her, I was depriving the emotion of a feast. I was exercising my strength over the emotion's strength to make me think. By not giving in I was becoming stronger, and thus its hold over me weaker. It was very hard, and I loved and missed her so much that this process went on for nearly a week.

By this time it was a lot easier not to get sucked into thoughts about her, though I had to be careful. The following weekend, a few of us from work went to a nightclub. I had been told she would be there with her new boyfriend. It didn't hurt as much as perhaps it ought to have; I even went with everyone back to her new flat for a drink. Several of us sat in the living room together. The flat was only around the corner from the friend's flat where we had stayed together on occasions, and he and his lodger had helped her move in that week. She was making the most of having her own home, enjoying having visitors, and obviously they had been there most of the week.

Late that same evening when I had arrived home to my parents', the phone rang. It was her. She had decided she really wanted me back and she was determined to make a go of it, including practising not thinking and reducing excitement. I asked if she was sure. She was.

I was overjoyed, but had learnt that with excitement 'what goes up must come down', and I was to remain calm if I was not going to set myself up for some more heartache later. I got in my car and drove straight over to her place.

The next few days we didn't see each other a great deal due to my working nights. She was busy with other things during the day, so I would go back to my parents' for a sleep and see her in the afternoon. Later in the week I was at work on a night shift. It was the early hours of the morning and I was sitting in an armchair in the living room trying to get a little sleep. I had rung her up that afternoon to go round and see her, but she'd had things to do.

Suddenly, I was enveloped by the knowledge that she was with the lodger who had helped her move in. I knew he had been spending time round there, but it hadn't occurred to me something could be developing. It was as if the entire room was filled with this energy, the knowledge that at that moment she was with him.

84

I tried to tell myself I was just allowing my emotions to use my imagination. I stood up and made my way over to sit at the dining room table, holding on to the room with my senses and mentally gripping my breathing in an attempt to dispel the idea. But it didn't work. The energetic knowledge was still there, as strong as ever. It was undeniable, and quite frightening. It was almost as if I were being given the opportunity to get used to the idea, and I spent the rest of the night carrying the feeling around with me, and yet at the same time denying myself the suicidal luxury of imagining her – both with or without him. I was getting stronger, and the emotion weaker.

By the next morning I had accepted the idea that she was with him, and now I just had to wait and see what would happen. Before I left work I rang her to ask if I could see her that morning instead of going to bed. She said, 'No', she 'was busy'. I wasn't surprised and went home to bed.

I had only been in bed for about an hour but knew what I had to do. I couldn't go to sleep with this. I got up and went into the other room. I was alone in the house. I dialled her telephone number and she answered. I said, 'I know you said you were busy this morning; can I see you this afternoon?'

'No,' she said. 'I'm still busy!' This was it. I had to take the bull by the horns again.

'Is Terry there?' I asked.

As she answered I felt her voice change. 'Yes. Why?'

I said, 'I was at work last night and I knew he was there.'

'How did you know?' she asked, sounding a little scared, perhaps even shocked.

'I just knew. The knowledge filled the whole room and I couldn't get rid of it. Are we finished then?' I asked.

'I don't know!'

'You need to decide who you want to be with: me or him.'

'I don't know!' she said again.

'Well, I'll decide for you,' I said. 'You can be with him. Tell Terry that I don't blame him, and I love you both. Everything happens for a reason and it's no-one's fault. I love you both!' With that I hung up and went back to bed.

I was later told by the friend (who had also helped her move in) that she had spoken with about him liking both Terry and I, but in different ways. The friend had told her it wasn't fair on me and she should tell me. I knew Terry was more exciting and liked a laugh. I don't think she was planning for it to turn out that way.

Again, I had to get over her. But it was much easier now. After all, I had done it twice already in the last two weeks, but I still had some work to do. The emotion was still coming up; memories of her were still strong and the emotion hurt when it was allowed to fill my mind. But each time got shorter, and it was easier to let go and return to my senses.

***

(Note: There were two other dreams I had around this time: in the first, I was outside in the grounds at the home of my mum's boss. Suddenly an elevator landed on the grass not far from where I was standing and out of it stepped an alien; he was extremely tall and not unlike the giant in the Roald Dahl story The BFG. He came straight over to me, picked me up, threw me over his shoulder and returned to the elevator. For a few moments I struggled, but quickly saw that there was nothing I could do. And with that thought I noticed I relaxed completely and accepted the situation without any fear at all. As the elevator doors closed and we were about to shoot up into space, with me still over his shoulder, I saw out into the garden for what could be the last time ever, and felt totally at peace.

In the second dream, I was in my gran's flat and there was a man with a pistol shooting people. I turned and headed for the front door, but as I did so he aimed at me and shot me in the back.

I fell to the ground, still alive, and began to crawl towards the door, still hoping to get away. The man followed me, and then stood over me with the gun pointed at my head.

Before I knew what I was doing I heard myself say, 'I'm sorry!' and immediately regretted saying it. Why was I apologising? And why was I apologising to someone who was going to kill me anyway? They didn't deserve my apology, not that I had anything to apologise for, and I wished I could take it back.

BANG! He fired, and the bullet went into my head.

As I lay there, still alive and with my head still supported by my arm, I knew death was inevitable. It would happen as soon as I let my head fall to the carpet.

I had a few moments to consider this and accept what was going to happen. And then I carefully and gently lowered my head to the floor, and everything went black.

By way of interpretation, it is clear these dreams refer to my accepting of life, or more precisely the challenging situations of life, however distressing they could potentially be.

One could perhaps go into them further, interpreting the giant alien as perhaps symbolising a higher aspect of myself, and the elevator was taking me 'home'.

Being shot and dying could simply symbolise my accepting death, in whatever form, but especially when there is nothing else that can be done. Regretting pleading for my life is an interesting aspect, and I'm not totally sure what it means. As I look now, it was as if I didn't want to give his emotions any pleasure, any satisfaction. So perhaps that is what it means: I do not wish to give in to, or feed, my own emotions, let alone someone else's. And this is even the case when faced with my own demise.)

Master Session
1993

I continued to buy and enjoy Barry's books and tapes, and by now had developed quite a collection.

I went to the Leicester seminar the following year and found I was hearing fewer and fewer things that I didn't already know for myself. I could be walking or working, or almost anywhere when an idea or an understanding would suddenly come to me, and I would remember Barry saying the same thing in a certain tape or meeting. But now I knew it as well, as my own inner knowledge and not just something I'd heard.

Any new knowledge would quickly be absorbed, and the feeling of elation at having seen something new quickly wore off leaving me for a moment looking to repeat the experience for confirmation that it was real. Of course it didn't happen again for the same piece of knowledge; it was already a part of me.

At the end of that Leicester seminar, after Barry had finished talking, a member of his staff told everyone about the introduction of The Master Session. It would be an annual sixteen-day teaching event to be held during late October that year, at Cabarita Beach on the Gold Coast in northern New South Wales, Australia. It would be held in a campsite in a forest, and would last over three and a half weeks in total, with one or two two-hour sessions on most of the days.

This would be a dream come true if I could afford it. It looked like a wonderful experience. Then I heard it would be two thousand pounds. I had saved up just over that amount by working sixty hours a week in the nursing homes. I wasn't entirely sure about using all my money, but knew I had to go. My boss at work agreed to let me have the time off, and once all the arrangements had been made and the Australian staff had been kind enough to arrange the hire of a tent for me (the literature offered this facility, but I was the only one who took them up on the offer), I was off.

***

Barry's 'right-hand man', Ian, met the coach on the way to the campsite. His beard was shaved in a way that made him look like a gnome, accentuating his already broad smile, and again there was the energy in the eyes. I knew if I was to get the most of this time I would have to get in with him and any others who were seriously living the teaching.

I had made so much progress with my own internal realisations and developments that I really felt that this may be the last time I needed to be with Barry. He had said in the past the aim is for the individual to become their own Master, so they won't need him anymore. And I felt a little resentment (probably towards myself) for still being there, even at that time.

For some reason I did seem to feel different from those also there for the seminar. I was staying with quite a few others on the campsite (the talks were to be in a marquee onsite). We would acknowledge each other, say hello, and maybe even smile, but I had nothing to say to them, nor it would seem they to me. Listening to them, they were talking about everything but the teachings and the seminar. It was like being back at school where I knew everyone but didn't actually have any friends.

There was one Indian chap from America whom I did get on well with, Sanjay, perhaps in his thirties, who it seemed also had made quite a bit of progress. In a discussion he confided that he too thought this may be his last time with Barry, and was really here just to make sure he didn't need to come back again.

When the marquee arrived, I gladly offered my services helping with the setting up, arranging of the three hundred plus chairs and the straw bales designed to act as a sound and wind barrier.

I continued to offer my help to Ian where I could, and soon became regarded as a member of staff. One great experience was of having to do exactly what I was asked to do, and not what I thought was wanted. If the instructions were wrong, it was not my responsibility, but it was my responsibility to make sure I understood exactly what was being asked of me. (This was a valuable lesson, but tricky to grasp at first.)

Spending time with Ian as well as being in the sessions was increasing my ability and strength to remain conscious and alert, and it was amazing.

At one point when I was seated at the back of the marquee (as I did throughout the meetings, in case I was required to get up for something) and looking at Barry on the blue stage and background that I'd painted, I felt a connection. It actually felt for a moment to me as if we were like brothers. This came about as a result of being 'still' and conscious enough to feel that I had some idea of where he was coming from.

Between sessions when not with Ian or carrying out a task delegated by him, I would follow my usual practice of going off for walks on my own in the surrounding (manmade) rain forest. The other people would mostly be in the campsite or elsewhere enjoying chatting and doing what people do. I now had at least some feeling of belonging, as a member of staff, but while this was extremely beneficial to my progress, I still ultimately felt alone.

***

On days when there were no talks, trips out had been arranged for those who wanted to go. I had opted to travel up to a nearby mountain with a real rain forest. Once there we were to explore the mountain paths in pairs. I was paired up with a woman, Sophie (also thirty-eight years old it turned out), who was staying on the site, and I had spoken to her that morning before leaving.

Once alone she plucked up the courage to tell me that following our conversation that morning, as soon as I had gone she found she was unable to stop crying. She said I had touched something inside of her and she had no control over it. Nothing like that had ever happened to her before and it scared her. Sanjay, the Indian chap I had met and got on well with, was with us at the time, and was a friend of Sophie's. He had told her the stillness and love (i.e. consciousness) within me was what had touched her. She said she knew she had to be with me, and asked if I would kiss her.

This was all happening too fast for me, and perhaps surprisingly I declined, explaining that it was not the right time. She was obviously disappointed, but we carried on with the day.

That evening we were sitting on the beach across the road from the campsite. We were alone. It was dark, and we could only just make out the crest of the surf as the small waves broke on the shore.

She was still following her feelings and knowledge that she needed to be with me. She lay on her back on the sand. 'Kiss me,' she said. I hesitated again. This was not something I was used to. 'If you were a real man of love you would kiss me!' she said.

This all seemed very strange to me. She was certainly attractive. What was my problem? It didn't feel right, that's what!

She told me to lie down on my back, and then leaned over and kissed me. Instead of the earth moving, all I was concerned about was the intense pressure she was putting on my mouth, and I was trying to sink into the sand beneath as a method of escape. It was far from comfortable, and if anything almost frightening. This was not fun!

Once allowed up for air and having checked for any injuries, I said as carefully as possible that I would like to show her something. I knew I was not prepared to go through that again so told her I would kiss her now. I leaned over and kissed her gently but fully for several seconds. It was a lovely kiss, full of energy, and yet tender. It was amazing to both of us, the difference.

On the way back to the site she displayed an interest in taking things further that night. Again I felt this was not right, if only due to her pushiness. Once more she said if I was a proper man of love I would do it. I said that may be so, but it didn't feel right to me at that time. We parted for the evening, with Sophie not exactly pleased with me.

The next day we met again. She actually said she had realised later that night that I was right not to allow things to go further at that point. She had seen that I was a man of love as I had not jumped straight into bed at the earliest opportunity. Everything was all right now, and she was grateful to me.

***

The next three weeks were like a roller coaster ride. Barry had said it is the man's job to tell the woman he's with about life and the universe. He explained that the Enlightenment of men and women are different. Men come to understand more about the mechanics of things (with their scientific questioning minds), and women with their openness become pure love, with nothing to work out or understand. Quickly, concepts which before would have been laughable to the majority of people became logical and undeniable truths to me as I went deeper and deeper into my own consciousness.

I had some experience of this process now, and Sophie and I spent a lot of time together during which I would explain bits about the mind, emotions and aspects of life as I had realised it. I was soon talking to her about things I never knew that I knew!

There was certainly some pride or jealousy from me with regards to Sophie still saying she would like to speak personally with Barry. I thought, 'Why should she need him, when I can tell her everything she needs to know?'

***

When together, the aim is to be especially present, not allowing oneself to imagine being elsewhere. As Barry had explained, it was for the man and the woman to help each other in this, by pointing out to each other any times when one felt the other may have drifted off and become lost in thought. This of course can put big pressure on things, and that's exactly what happened.

We had a lifetime together in those three weeks, splitting up and later getting back together several times. Each time when we split up, I would go for a walk through the woods, having an internal battle to hold back the enormous urge to think about her. I would feel my breathing first, and after a few breaths would feel most of my body and look at the trees and wildlife as I walked. I would catch myself thinking and go through the process again, feeling the agonising tearing of the emotion all the time. Each time it took about a whole day to get to the point when I did not have to fight as hard and it didn't hurt as much. And then each time we got back together again.

During one of the good times I was sitting alone on the low wooden barrier that surrounded the campsite. My eyes were closed and I was enjoying feeling the warmth of the sun. Slowly I became aware of some movement of my head. It was beginning to nod. After a few seconds it was quite definite. It was a strange and yet enjoyable sensation, just feeling the smooth movement of my head back and forth, and it felt as if in some way a greater power had taken over. A couple of minutes later I opened my eyes to see Sanjay walking towards me. I told him of my experience and he said years ago the Masters used to nod their heads in meditation, and the students used to copy them in an attempt to experience the wonder.

96

***

Watching people and listening to them, it seemed I had made progress quicker than most. I had spent quite a lot of time with the man who ran the campsite, Derek ('Deek' to his friends). He commented that he had noticed my eyes seemed deeper than when I had arrived, and knowing nothing about what we were doing, he was concerned. (He had been given a cassette of Barry's so he would have some idea and know it was not a cult; but he had yet to listen to it.)

***

I asked and was allowed to have a private talk with Barry himself between a couple of the sessions. I attempted to demonstrate where I had got to, explaining I felt I had given up trying. I described that for the few years since seeing the psychic I had been aiming to become a teacher one day, and asked Barry whether this was knowledge of where I was going, or if it was just another belief to be given up.

He said it was a belief. And to give it up.

I also said I had seen Ian playing table tennis and trying to win, and could not understand this. Barry had taught that you should just do what you do, and do your best, but don't try to do (or win) anything.

He smiled. 'It may be your turn to try to win one day!' he said.

Two days later, swimming in the local lake, I was with another woman from the site. 'I'll race you over there!' she said, and off she went.

I paused for a moment, preferring just to enjoy the relaxing, leisurely breaststroke and neither wanting to exert myself particularly nor actually wanting to beat her either.

The next moment I found myself doing my best attempt at a front-crawl, and trying to beat her. As I was swimming alongside her, I remembered Barry's words, 'It may be your turn to try to win one day!'

***

A couple of days before the end of the teachings Sophie and I split up again. I spent the rest of the day as usual locked in battle with my emotions as they were trying to make me think about her. That evening it was dark, and I made my way out of the campsite and across the road onto the beach. As I got there the feelings changed from one of pain to one of giving up. Suddenly I was filled with the knowledge that my insides were literally trying to die. My emotions were unable to take any more and felt as if they were trying to commit suicide internally. The strange thing was, I was actually fine throughout the experience, able only to sit it out, watching as the emotions went through what they had to. Again this was an amazing experience and one that I have vividly remembered, the feeling of an emotional entity inside me surrendering, giving up, and actually wanting to die. And of course, as had become the routine, the next day we were back together.

***

The sessions ended, and all those from America had to leave the very next day as part of their package. (Apparently they had shorter holidays.) The rest of us were to stay there for another three days. I had attempted to avoid thinking about this day, trusting – or probably hoping – that an easy solution would present itself. It didn't. The situation was as planned. Sophie would return to America and we would keep in touch, possibly with a view to me going out there, but there was a lot to be arranged before that happened.

We held each other as the coach pulled into the car park. She asked that once she was on the coach I didn't look at her. She said it made it much harder for her when people waved her off. I agreed.

As the coach turned and began to pull away I turned and looked up towards the windows. I had to at least try to

98

see her one last time. I did. She was sitting halfway back by the window looking at me. Our eyes met for a moment as the coach moved towards the entrance. I let it go, making no attempt to walk alongside to catch another glimpse. This was it. The woman I would have willingly died for – and it could be said that emotionally I had died many times during the three weeks – was now leaving my life, if not forever then at least for a while until things could be arranged.

I turned and began to walk through the campsite as I had many times, but this time was different. All those breakups must have gone some way towards preparing me for this, but that was little consolation for the way I felt. The sun didn't seem to be shining as bright and the trees and plants seemed to have lost some of their colour. The site was pretty empty now, and I was walking through where tents had been only hours before, and where Sophie's tent had been only hours before. The experience could possibly be likened to being the only one left behind after the best and most wonderful party you have ever had or been to. All the people you love in the world had been there and you'd had the time of your life. You would have given up absolutely anything for them to stay, but now they were gone and you know you may never see any of them again. All that is left as a reminder is a few empty bottles and glasses, and furniture that had been moved... soon everything would be back into its rightful place, thus eliminating all evidence of the wonderful time you've had... gone forever.

As I walked, the pressure to remember what we had together was unbelievable: the things that had been said and done. As I had done so many times before, I focussed on my breathing as I walked, then felt my body whilst consciously looking at the trees and dusty ground beneath. The knowledge that she wasn't with me was still there as strong as ever, but at least I wasn't feeding the emotion by thinking about her. Suddenly she was back with me, in my thoughts. I loved her more than anything and I would have died to be with her. Again I brought my attention back to what was real – back to my body and to what I could see and hear from the trees and woodland around me. And suddenly, as I pushed the thought aside of us together, there was a terrible voice crying out from the depths of me, or the knowledge of such as voice. It was a sorrowful pleading voice, full of pain and despair, and it cried out:

But it's all I've got left of her!

Experiencing this was a powerful realisation that drummed home to me why we as human beings are so reluctant to stop thinking about a person we miss. We know the thought is not the actual person, but the memories are indeed all we've got left. To let go of those is like losing the person again, and to purposefully deny oneself the thoughts is to deny yourself of being with the person that you miss with all your heart. It was as if I was pushing her away, and at the same time longing to be with her.

It wasn't going to beat me. It may well have been all I had left of her, but it wasn't *her*! I was not going to spend any part of my life having a relationship with an imaginary person, as that's what she was now. The physical body had left me, and if I was to be true to myself, not to mention life, I had to face this fact!

Each time, the past separations had taken a day to come to terms with and for the related emotion to be dissolved. The next three days I spent alone, walking and sitting, struggling with this powerful genie within pretending to be the woman I loved. I was determined not to fall for it. I did continuously, but I fought with everything I had.

***

There was another woman who had shown an interest in me from the start. I had talked with her during the three weeks as

100

she was struggling with her own emotional genie, fighting for supremacy over her mind. She had made it clear that she wished we could be together, but I had been with Sophie so that hadn't been possible. Now, on the last night, I was seated in her hotel room talking. It got late and she asked that I show her what it was like to be loved by a man of love, by a man with as much conscious energy as I had.

Again I was put on the spot. She had made it clear all along that I stirred something in her as I had with Sophie, and she'd spent the last three weeks struggling with it. Now she wanted me, and I couldn't use Sophie as an excuse anymore.

I didn't do it. I explained as best I could (without being entirely sure myself) that it didn't feel right, and it was better that we just talk.

***

I had quite a few more days, even after returning to the UK, of fighting against the impulse to remember Sophie. We wrote a few times and spoke more about me moving over to America, but things soon died down and we went back to our lives. (I never did see her again.)

***

(Note: Initially when I found Barry's teaching, I was determined to remain conscious and aware all day, and would catch myself during the day, perhaps a handful of times, 'lost' in thought and imagination (daydreaming) and would bring myself back. As time passed I noticed I was catching myself more regularly, and the initial fear was that this meant I was thinking more than I was before. It was now not a handful of times a day; it was every hour. But I quickly saw that whatever was responsible for 'waking me up' and bringing me back to my senses, was just doing so more often.

I recall a period when I was catching myself approximately every ten minutes. And If I had been walking at the time, I would look back along the path and would be able to tell at what point I had drifted off, and on occasion would walk back and make myself walk it again, but this time consciously.)

A Dream it may be,
but the Dream goes on!

One night whilst at work, my friend and I were sitting outside in the garden on the bench having a cup of tea. I said to him, 'If the Christians believe God is everywhere and in everything, then as I am a part of that (as are you), I must be God! If I am not, then God is everything except me, in which case he can't be everything!' We laughed at the logic.

Over the following months I had many different experiences of floating, being larger or smaller, of seeing things from a different perspective. But I could never wilfully repeat each experience and often could not even remember it for long. Each felt amazing at the time, and then was gone.

The hardest thing was still having no-one really to share the experiences with. I could attempt to describe them to my friend, but without him really experiencing the whole thing for himself, it was all a little academic really. I had read in a few other places that other people having similar experiences on the spiritual path also found the isolation factor difficult to cope with. The further I was going into it, the further away from my friends and family I seemed to get.

I longed for someone to share it all with, someone who would experience it all with me. We could help each other, exchange realisations and perceptions. That way I could continue to grow and would no longer feel alone. But it was not to be. (At least, not for quite some time.)

The conversations with my parents continued. The futility of my efforts was slowly becoming evident, with the same discussions going round in the same circles. They would tell me it was natural and part of being human to have the emotional ups and downs. I would say that I didn't want the downs and had found a way not to have them, and to also grow in understanding. They would reply, 'You can't have the ups without the downs!' I'd agree, saying I didn't want the downs at all, so was prepared to give up the highs, the result being a constant state of awareness and peace... not very exciting, I had to admit, but at least I was unhappy less and less. I was reclaiming control.

I would as usual try to make the point with the comment 'It's fine to have the lows. The aim is to remember, when you are feeling hurt or angry or any other negative emotion, that you have chosen to feel that way, and try not to blame anybody or anything else for the way you are feeling.' Of course, this never made any difference.

***

My stammer seemed to be subsiding. It was still there, but didn't seem to be there nearly as much as previously.

I had also learnt that people aren't actually all bad. The problem is their attachment to the emotional rollercoaster ride that is going on within them. People are not prepared to give this up until they have had so much pain that they will do anything to get rid of it, even give up the highs. I know people who have lots of very hard times, but not enough yet to make them want to give up the highs. In fact, these are some of the very people who may argue to me their right to keep both.

***

Another two-day seminar with Barry Long at Earls Court in London. I saw many people I recognised there – no-one I really talked with though. Even here I still felt alone. I felt I was amongst people nearer to what I was doing, but there was still a separation there. Maybe it was simply because those seriously following the teaching with everything they had also kept to themselves, having little to say. The ones wanting to chat though still seemed to be struggling with the basis of the teaching. That is, to be as conscious as possible every moment, and not to speak about the past unless necessary as this helps you to remain focussed in the present.

106

During this session, Barry told the story of a man on trial for murder some time before (elsewhere in the world), who for the duration of one part of his trial sat with his arm in the air, apparently for over an hour. The point was he was exercising 'the will' over his mind. He could have put his arm down any time, but he didn't. Barry then asked all of us to sit still – not to change our pose unnecessarily, just to sit still. I thought this would be easy, but after only a few seconds people were beginning to shuffle and scratch, and Barry again asked that people do their best to relax and stay still: not forcing or repressing. Just knowing you could move if you wanted to, but you didn't.

I did well for a few minutes, then it became hard. The pressure began to build up. I wanted to move my foot slightly, move in my seat and move my shoulders. The idea was that it was the emotion in the mind that wanted to move as it hated sitting still. I had practised sitting still over the last few years, but this was difficult.

It seemed like ages, and I was getting desperate. I was eager to successfully complete the exercise, but by this point it was probably fifteen to twenty minutes we'd been sitting there, maybe more. People were shuffling all around me, but I wanted to show I could achieve this.

Finally, I gave in. I had a little stretch, moved my toes, swapped over my crossed legs, and was ready for another long stint.

The next moment Barry indicated it was lunch time, and everybody moved. I had almost done it.

***

Back at home after the seminar, I tried sitting in the armchair with my arm in the air. What was really clever is that, after the initial few minutes that are quite easy, as soon as the mind drifts off to imagine other places and times, the attention is no longer on keeping the arm in the air and it starts to drop. It

107

was like a sort a barometer, dropping as my consciousness wavered. I managed half an hour on this occasion, but was determined to do the full hour at some point.

It was the following night at work that I tried again. I was sitting in the large hallway in an armchair with the lights off, leaving only the dim lights from the landing above. I had my right arm straight in the air. Again, after a few minutes it began to hurt. After half an hour I had to stay very alert. As time went on, the slightest movement of my mind to anything other than what I was doing and my arm would begin to lower. This would alert me, and I would 'wake up' again.

I completed the hour, with the final few minutes being especially difficult. It was an amazing experience, having a challenge which was every bit as much, if not more so, mental as physical.

***

I had been joined on my night shifts by Elaine, a woman of forty-eight who had worked at the home for ten years. I would drive past her house on the way to work, so gave her a lift in as she didn't drive. I began to enjoy her company. One day, I rang her up mid-afternoon saying I fancied going into town before work. Did she want to come with me? She said yes.

The next day I hesitated, but decided to ask again. Again Elaine accepted. We would just go for a walk along the canal, or at one of the parks nearby. I didn't know where it was leading, and was actually afraid to consider it. I just knew it felt right to be with her at that time.

This continued for several weeks. I turned twenty-one years old in June, and it was soon after this that I asked Elaine if she would like to go to the cinema. Once more this felt right, but still it scared me. I was twenty-one, she was forty-eight. What future could this possibly have? I still didn't know whether or not I even wanted anything to develop. I was just blindly following where life led. That day, before I left to

108

go and pick Elaine up from her house to go to the cinema, I packed an overnight bag. I told my mum and stepdad I would be out for the evening. When asked if I would be back that night, I replied that I didn't know. I was going prepared for all eventualities!

Once back at her house after the film, we were sitting on the sofa talking. I still didn't know what was happening or what I wanted to happen, so was at a loss as to what to do. Eventually I bit the bullet and described to Elaine what I was trying to do with my life. She said she understood and was prepared to try it.

It was now getting late, and we were still sitting on the sofa talking. Elaine offered me the opportunity of staying the night, and I accepted. Sleeping arrangements were not mentioned.

Later, it was time to go up. I followed her upstairs, still not knowing what was going to happen. At the top she turned to me and said, 'You can either have the spare room, or my bed?'

Believe it not, I still wasn't sure what I was being asked. It occurred to me that perhaps she was offering her bed, and she would have the spare room...?

I decided to take a chance. 'Your bed would be friendlier!' I said, and in we went, keeping in mind that at this point we still hadn't even held hands. It all felt a little strange, and I was out of my depth.

Actually, on that night nothing happened. Elaine had suffered with asthma for years, and the stress proved too much for her. However, we were now together, and I stayed there from then on instead of going home to my parents'.

With regards to the asthma, I noticed it was bad when she breathed through her mouth. Whenever the asthma was making her struggle to breathe and she opened her mouth to take a breath, it started her coughing and gasping. I suggested she tried breathing through her nose instead.

Amazingly this was enough to all but cure her. She went from having to use her inhaler when she first woke up in the morning and many times throughout the day, to using it twice in the next two weeks, and not again for the following few years. I had to remind her for a while initially not to open her mouth and to breathe through her nose, but soon she was doing it on her own.

(Note: Many years later I saw a television programme about an American travelling the world teaching people how to cure their asthma. He described an asthma attack as the body thinking it is hyperventilating and closing the airways to address this, and therefore by gasping in more air, one actually exacerbates the problem. His technique was to slow the breathing down (as I recall), ten seconds in, ten seconds out. The medical scientists were appalled at this 'dangerous' approach, but the people who attended the sessions said it worked for them. And I understood why.)

***

It was my first real relationship, and being loved and wanted was everything to me. I needed her to continuously reassure me in order to know I was loved. This was not to be, and life was going to free me of this.

When she would leave the room we were in, I would look up to see if she would turn round to look at me as she left, but no. It felt as though she forgot me as soon as she wasn't looking at me.

Our second night together, on leaving the bathroom I went into the bedroom to join her expecting to find her waiting for me. It was quite a shock to see her facing the wall with her back to me, going to sleep!

Every night when we would be sitting on the sofa together watching television, she would be at the end nearest the screen with her back to me. Again it felt as though it

110

wouldn't make any difference to her at all whether I was there or not. We had only been together for a couple of days before I saw signs of negative emotion in her, seemingly over nothing. She would suddenly not talk to me, and I would struggle to understand what was happening. At times she would refuse to give me a kiss, or hold my hand, or sit with me. This was particularly bad in the evening when we would be sitting together; suddenly I would feel the atmosphere change. It would be as if a wall had come down between us, and it would feel to me as if it no longer mattered to her whether I was there or not. In my need to be loved, I would point this out. She stated emphatically that nothing had changed, and appeared to be oblivious to what I was talking about, and we would argue nearly every night.

We would have big arguments daily, and on many occasions I slept downstairs on the sofa, waking the next day feeling awful. I went to work before she got up and would spend all morning feeling terrible, keeping up a constant fight to remain conscious, trying to dissolve the emotion as I had learnt. I would then return home expecting more of the same, only to find Elaine cheery and acting as if nothing had happened. It was as if she hadn't said all sorts of aggressive things to me, not least of all to 'fuck off out of [her] life'. All was well, until the same time that evening when it would happen all over again. It was a real roller coaster ride.

Not only was this not what I wanted, but it was also too much for me to cope with. Barry taught people to have a loving relationship, where the aim of both parties should be to grow in love and to help each other in this aim. I heard him say on many occasions, particularly to women when it came up, that a person practising his teaching should not be with someone who is not. So what was I doing with Elaine? I talked to her often about the teaching, in the hope that she might see the logic as I did and take responsibility for her moods and outbursts. She listened, and at times seemed to see the sense of it, but not enough to put the energy required into it to make it last.

Three times during the first year I moved out of her house back into my parents'. I couldn't take any more of the ups and downs. I needed love, and this was killing me: being loved one minute and hated the next. Barry described the process of consciously facing emotion as 'returning through the hell of one's self', and I could see why. Each time I moved out though, it felt as if it wasn't really finished, as if I had more to do there. It felt right to be with her even when it was extremely painful. She would promise it wouldn't happen again. So I would move back in, and the very next day it would indeed happen again. Every time I ended up back where I started. I couldn't see what was happening or why. All I knew was that I was in emotional pain and didn't know what to do. After the third time I told myself I wouldn't move out again until I was sure that it was over and that I wouldn't go back again. I just hoped it would not be too long.

***

Slowly I was indeed developing more, and in hindsight I see that all the pain I was going through was bringing up emotion buried within me in order to remain conscious and begin to straighten it or dissolve it.

And certain realisations were becoming more real for me. The experience I'd had that night whilst on the LSD that I had put down to a weird encounter was turning out to be more real all the time. I had the growing knowledge that all existence really is just a dream, or the Buddhist illusion *maya* that I had read about. Nothing is real, not even my own body. I was starting to see that the real reality was the stillness behind the dream, behind my body, behind me. I realised that deep dreamless sleep was possibly the nearest I got to that reality.

112

It was time to ask Barry the question I had tried to ask two years earlier but to which I had not yet been ready to hear the answer.

I sent a letter asking about the 'dream' of life. I had seen that the Bible says, 'Be still and know that I am God' and similar statements. It had been said that there is only one God and that it/he is behind all things, in which case he must be behind me also. If God is everything, then I must be God, or at least a part of it/him as I am a part of that everything. And more to the point, life has been described as a dream, and therefore it must be 'my' dream. My question therefore was whether this was indeed an elaborate dream?

I was fairly sure that what I was asking was going to be confirmed. However, it was still a little shocking when it was. This is what Barry wrote:

> *You are doing alright, Nick. Keep going as you are. Your letter has a humility and straightness that pleases me. The purpose of the dreamer's dream is to wake up. So the dreamer is dreaming for himself, the only one in the dream. The more he can love, serve and give without reacting selfishly and emotionally the more he diminishes himself, the dreamer. When the dreamer himself is diminished sufficiently the dream evaporates and the dreamer wakes up. Keep going.*

> *Barry Long 18.11.94*

So, I was now twenty-one years old. And I had had the insight, which was now confirmed, that life is indeed all a dream, and therefore nothing is real! It was fortunate that for some reason I had no work lined up with the nursing agency for the next few days, because I wasn't going to do any. If life is just a dream, then what is the point in getting up and going to work, if none of it is real anyway? But worse still, there is no escape. If this is all a dream and if, as Barry taught, the emotion had to be faced and dissolved here whilst alive in a body – if my life were to end before I had dissolved all the emotion, all the pain – it would just come back again in another dream. I was trapped in my own nightmare!

The next day I got up late and made my way downstairs to the sofa where I sat in my dressing gown, not even bothering to get dressed. I faced the situation like this for the next three days, processing the information and facing and dissolving the powerful emotion: the feeling of sheer despair and isolation. The inner knowledge was not only knowing that nothing is real, but also that I was all alone as nothing and no-one actually exist either!

So what now? I kept asking myself. I seemed more lost than I was before. It was strange that I knew these things and yet nothing had changed. I was still here and still had to eat, sleep and do all the normal everyday things. There seemed to be no escape!

On the third afternoon of doing little else but sitting on the sofa in my dressing gown, looking at the walls, a phrase came to me as if from the depths that put it all into perspective. That phrase has stayed with me ever since.

A Dream it maybe, but the Dream goes on!

What I was being shown was that whether this existence is real or not is almost by the way, as there is still no escape. Everyday duties still have to be carried out. Bills still have to be paid.

With that thought I got up and got dressed – just in time, as it happened, for a shift at work later that day.

(Note: I recall wondering whether Barry really had realised it was my dream, or had he realised it was his dream and was just saying it was mine? But of course it didn't really matter. I knew I was real, in the sense of being self-aware. Therefore, I

114

knew I was here, and that meant it was my dream. And even if, for Barry, this was his dream and I was an aspect of that, that would only be according to a character in my dream.)

Seeing the Truth

(Note: I was moved to write a few articles of my own from the insights I had received. The following were handwritten on folded bits of paper during my coffee breaks at the residential nursing home for people with epilepsy and learning difficulties.

As I read it now, some twenty years later, I notice the content feels quite direct (blunt, even), but reflects and demonstrates a little of what I was seeing and going through at that time.)

***

(13.03.95) The Adventure of Life and Living

The purpose of my being here is, now at least, for me to return to my original state of Being, behind and before the world existed.

Being a return journey, I won't know exactly why it began until I reach the beginning again. I am developing into a fully conscious being with a knowing of oneness with all things. Whether I lost it when the dream of living began, or whether I have emerged out of ignorance, I don't know.

I do know that as a child I was a lot like a little ball in a pinball machine, rebounding off the problems and obstacles, each knock giving me a little more pain, all contributing towards waking me up. At first each hurt made me more withdrawn from the world and my surroundings. I was living in an emotional shell which would react to each new situation from that position.

Having reached a point of knowing enough is enough, I decided there must be more to this living business than pain and death (which to me seemed like a way to escape the pain).

I began to become more intelligent, more real, aware and perceptive, questioning what others accepted as normal and reasonable and yet seemed to me to be quite unreasonable but nonetheless normal!

I followed various avenues hoping to find logical answers and eventually found them. I had learnt that if I stop thinking about what has been and what might be, all my energy goes into where I am now and I therefore come to know what I am now.

The more energy I put into this moment, the more I know what this moment really is. I become conscious of a stillness, a nothingness, yet a completeness behind all that exists for me in this moment and every moment, which is always _now_.

Fear comes from thinking ahead and therefore separating myself from the stillness, from the knowing that all is in fact as it should be.

Once alone in my imagination, thinking and worrying, hoping and fearing, that pressure at times verges on the unbearable.

The isolation from the love, from the well-being, is terrible and I long to get back there. Yet all I must do is give up my own worries and return to the moment when I am and to where my body actually is, and I know once more that there are no accidents and all is well, despite appearances.

This stillness, love and oneness I have found are mentioned as the ideal in most (if not all) religions, yet no-one has realised − or so it seems − that their own mind or imagination is the problem.

It is the one reliving past hurts and imagining possible terrifying situations. It is the one telling me about vengeance, and judging and criticising, thus preventing me from enjoying the wonder of what is going on around me in any moment. It destroys the sound of the birds singing, the view of the trees and grass all around me, all so often taken for granted; and above all, from feeling the stillness behind and below the feelings of hurt and pain I have put on top.

My own imagination is my only enemy and the one I must conquer. My external situations are always there to

120

stimulate the mind and the resulting emotion shows me any weakness and sets me to work on it.

The emotion is actually designed to be a warning to me that something is not quite right, something is 'out of sync'. And this could be one of two things:

1) Either an action I'm avoiding taking, for any number of reasons.

Or,

2) A situation that is absolutely right at this moment but my imagination combined with the emotions are wishing things were different.

In both cases it is the imagination causing the problem, imagining reasons not to act or projecting into another space and time and therefore separating me from the inner knowledge that actually at this moment all is well.

Returning to the 'here and now' in the midst of a problem, I'm aware of a peacefulness beyond the ache and pressure to think about it, and holding on to the stillness the emotion is actually dissolved. Although the situation may not appear to have changed externally, it no longer feels to be a problem.

However, if I am unable to change the situation physically, the simple process of resigning to it, letting go of the apprehension, seems often to be enough to encourage it to change itself. I have come to see that if I want something to work out, the most I can do is to accept it may not, but feel the energy, the knowledge of it inside my body. The more I do this, the greater the energy with which I am 'in the moment', the more my life runs smoothly and effortlessly along. 'As within, so without' is an old saying and is coming more and more true for me.

The emotion of past hurts is still living on in me and rises at new 'hurdles', but as it does so, instead of allowing it to whisk me off in its imaginary world, I hold on to this one thus informing the loveless space of the stillness and knowledge of the moment. This way I'm growing in love and life, and dying to the past. Whilst in my imagined world I feel vulnerable and isolated, and once connected again with the moment I no longer feel separate. In fact, despite still seeing separate objects, I'm aware of the truth in the saying 'Everything is One'.

Therefore, when a person or object dies or leaves me, although I am no longer able to observe the physical form, as long as I do not get carried away in my imaginary world of pain and sorrow, I feel no loss. I feel nothing has changed: just energy changing form. The love I felt for them remains the same and only goes when I leave it to think about the person or object. When I've finished mourning, the love and stillness is waiting and ready to tell me the truth: that actually there is no such thing as death. There is only the knowledge that 'I am', and the movement of energy around me.

Now, here is where the adventure for me starts. All that has come so far I have learnt from, and the knowledge written down I know is the truth, at least for me.

What comes next, I do not know. I have an understanding beyond my experience. This next section is for me to put on to paper what I understand is coming, and what I don't yet know.

I have realised through logical reasoning and inner knowledge that the whole of existence is in fact a dream: a dream from which the spiritual life is a quest to wake up. (Many religions incidentally recognise the same truth.)

Using the dream analogy, if we have a closer look at our dreams (when asleep in our beds), we can use the nature of them to help us understand the real dream: life!

When deep in the dream, it may be frightening. We not only believe it's real, we are part of the dream and it won't even occur to us to think it's not real. It is happening and that's that!

122

As we begin to wake up from our sleep – becoming more conscious – we may become aware that it is in fact only a dream. Once this is realised fully, the dream is no longer frightening as we know we are in no real danger. If we die in the dream, we just wake up back in our real existence. We then may find we are able to continue the dream consciously, in our own imagination, and alter anything and everything we like; but it isn't as fun or exciting because we know it's not real. We are awake.

So what now?

I will continue to remain as conscious as I can during this dream existence until I am fully 'awake'. What I will wake up to, if anything, I do not know.

The only truth I know greater than what I can see, touch, hear, smell and taste is what I feel inside; and that is only a knowledge of completeness containing everything (which, as you'll remember, is only a dream).

So, I am trapped in my own dream. The dream, to the best of my present knowledge, is all that is; and the more conscious I am, the less absorbed in it and emotional about it I am, and the more I can control the moment. The stiller I can be, the more life seems to be on my side. The dream analogy shows the same thing.

Life or 'God' has been referred to as the Universal Mind. I now know whose mind it is! Whether I will continue to enjoy the external world, or lose interest the more I wake up, I don't know. I must wait to find out, and trust that whatever happens is right and is in some way my own choice!

***

(April 1995) Within a few weeks I wrote another piece:

Now!

There is one simple truth. It is so simple that the world will disregard it as nonsense, or will not understand it. The world

123

screams out for answers to its problems; yet offer it the answers and it will turn away in disgust. But ask it more questions and it revels in the opportunity of another challenge. Everyone is avoiding THE question and instead inventing others, and therefore avoiding the responsibility of having to do something about it.

The question is perhaps 'Why am I unhappy, and what can I do about it?'

So why do we get unhappy?

We can blame any number of reasons within each and every situation for the resulting emotion, and we feel quite justified in feeling that way. In fact, have someone suggest to us we shouldn't feel as we do and we are prepared to have a row with them over our 'right' to keep it.

We will continue to blame the person or situation for our feelings yet are not prepared to give them up. So who's to blame really? Can we give up the feeling if we want to? Yes! (*If* we want to!)

The problem is that despite us swearing blind we don't like feeling angry or unhappy, we actually are not prepared to stop. We are doing it to ourselves. We are unable to see this due to the cleverness of the emotion and the control it has over our mind. The emotion reruns a situation, past or future, over and over, again and again in our imagination. It then tells us to blame the situation for the feeling. Suggest to it that *it* is to blame for making itself unhappy and it will squirm, huff and puff, snatching for excuses.

Please see, if you're able, that the problem is actually in the remembering and not in the happening. Give up remembering, and you give up unhappiness. You cannot have one without the other.

The mind we have is supposed to be a tool with which we are able to operate in the world. Use it for entertainment and it takes over. Be its master and it will be a loyal and (relatively) obedient servant. (It may still try its luck occasionally.)

It seems whatever we are doing, we spend most of our time in our imagination daydreaming, thinking and hoping. Every single problem is derived from thinking. And by 'problem' I am not in this instance talking about the situation itself but the emotion we've put on it. Stop thinking and it ceases to be a problem.

All problems (all emotional problems) are in the past or the future. Be in the present and you'll find there are no problems. (There is only the situation.)

You are reading these words now. Feel the space inside your body, being aware that you exist and are not lost in your imagination. Look at these pages and anything else here and now but do not watch the screen in your head. It is because you spend so much time watching the screen that you can't turn it off. It is the cause of the world's suffering and the state of things today.

Put all your energy into being where you are here and now, and things are very simple. Inside, you won't have any ups and downs: not very exciting, but at least there are no problems.

You may think you want to keep the 'downs' because they make the 'ups' more enjoyable. OK; just don't be bloody irresponsible and blame others for them when they happen!

Do you want to be free of unhappiness or do you want to keep it? It is honestly your choice.

If you want to be free you have to exercise control over your imagination. Practise switching it off, breaking up its momentum. When all is well and it occurs to you that you've been 'away' for a while, in that moment you're back. Hold it for as long as you can. Continue to bring yourself back to your senses as often as you can.

The moment you have a problem is the hardest time to stop and the most important. At this time, look around you and see that the problem isn't where you are. It is in your imagination. That is your problem.

Having made the separation briefly, and if you are able to hold it (if not, don't worry, it does get easier), you will notice the intense pressure of the emotion trying to start up the mental engine again. Withstand this pressure and you take the energy away from the emotion, and it dies. You will actually recognise the sensation of dying inside. Following this, the situation ceases to be a problem. It was the emotion causing the problem all the time.

Can you see this? Can you see that when you no longer think about your worries, you don't have any? And please don't let your mind convince you that you need to think to act. Thinking is AVOIDING taking action. Either do it or don't, but for God's sake don't think about it!

***

I wrote the following straight after:

Where Am I?

Well, the one writing these words is at present sitting in a little room on his own. No problems here. Oh, sure I could probably conjure up any number with very little difficulty. I could turn on the little screen and would very soon be absorbed in it, and the emotion rising from me trying to be in two places at once. But why?

Why do something as futile and soul-destroying (not to mention world-destroying) as trying to be in two places at once? I must be honest and be where I am, or go and be somewhere else. For my body to be in one place and my attention (me) to be somewhere else means I am not operating properly in either place, and this leads to confusion, stress and ultimately problems.

Now, what do we find if we stay in the moment, conscious of our body's surroundings?

126

We find that the external physical world is looking after itself. By us connecting with the 'Now' we become conscious of a greater reality than we ever thought possible. That is that. In fact, all is as it should be. There are no accidents. To shut up the mind and its criticisms, its ideas of how things should be and to see things objectively, we are in touch with the truth: the knowledge behind all things. We are conscious of a knowing, a peacefulness despite whatever may be happening. We don't have to 'believe'. We KNOW all is well.

Nothing is random. Consciousness is creating all that exists. It knows what it's doing. You can either fight it or you can go with it. The same intelligence that is creating your body is creating everything else the senses perceive. Please don't fight it if you can avoid it.

We are like fish longing to get out to the freedom of the sea. We are at present caught in a fast-running stream. We don't know where it's going so we are swimming against it, yet still going backwards downstream. We are absolutely exhausted and scared. Turn around and go with it and you will get where you want to go. Life will take you through many different situations, 'good' and 'bad'. Both are there to be learnt from, so good and bad cease to exist as do right and wrong. All are subjective points of view which diminish as you see things as they are.

For a mind to be allowed to say that things should be different, be it the weather, the starving people or the colour of the flower, it is saying the consciousness governing all existence is wrong and it (the thinking mind) could do a better job. (Do you recognise this story from the Bible? In that instance the critic was called Lucifer or Satan or the devil.)

You are only responsible for your own thoughts and actions. Focus only on those and your life will run smoothly. Try to change or even think about changing anything else, and you're asking for trouble. Even if you succeed you will

127

pay for it with a lot of emotional energy. Do what you do. Don't 'try' to do anything. Work with life and life will work with you – towards making you totally free! Fight against life and you'll find yourself in your own living hell, full of worries and fears, both past and future.

***

And then another a few weeks later:

The Dream of Life

The physical universe is only real for as long as the objects exist; they soon die (if they were living) and are broken down. Is anything so real that it lasts forever? Even the stars, we're told, eventually burn out and 'die'. I say that anything that does not last forever cannot be real. It only has the temporary illusion of being real, and then returns to its original state of nonexistence.

So, is this original state reality? And if so, what is this nonexistence? What is it that makes an object be there, and then not be there?

Assuming it's not all just random chance and coincidence, it has to be an 'intelligent energy' creating and destroying all things. And in order for all things to co-exist as they do, it must be the same intelligence behind all of them. The same intelligence creating your body as is creating all the animals, trees, and even buildings and cars. Everything obeys certain physical laws before disappearing again. 'All is one!' (You may have heard that said before.) I believe religions have called this intelligence 'God' amongst other names. Religions seem to be constantly searching for God, for some sort of union with the creator.

They look all over the place, ranging from churches, temples, mountains and deserts. They even look into space. But very few ever find what they're looking for. And those that do, try to tell the people, who are too busy looking to stop and

128

listen. If God is the intelligence behind all things, then obviously it is also the intelligence behind your body. Behind you! You cannot get closer to any other physical thing than you are to your own body, so why not start there?

If you focus your eyes on an object and don't allow your imagination to intervene and draw your attention away, you may be able to feel a 'space' in your body. Feel your body first, then there is the space inside it.

If you have pain in your body, or maybe are just hungry, or have some other feeling or sensation, you will probably feel this first. But still the space is there.

Do not allow your mind to imagine what is in your body. There is nothing there until there needs to be. At this moment unless you have your stomach open and are physically looking into it, it is all imagination. And imagination is never real. What is real is the space you feel which is the intelligence before it creates an object. That space is the nonexistence. You have no feeling there and you can't see anything there, so there is nothing there. If you're looking for God, look there!

God is just the intelligence behind this temporary reality: your reality, your intelligence. It must be your intelligence or you are making yourself separate from the rest of the universe. You are saying, 'God made the universe, and then there's me!' And that means you created yourself (are you God?), or the God intelligence created you, which makes that your intelligence! Religions such as Buddhism look for a union with this intelligence, which they call Spiritual Enlightenment. This is when you are 'One' with life because you come to realise it's all your own mind anyway, as everything is within the mind of God. That makes your mind the mind of God, even if we are talking in a broad sense. The problem is that the intelligence for its own experience imagined a body for itself, and lots of other bodies to talk to. It then became so involved in its dream that it forgot it wasn't real. It really believes it has arms and legs, and is terrified at the thought of losing them, along with the rest of its body when the dream ends. And instead of realising that everything is part of its own mind, it picks certain objects (living or otherwise) and makes them an extension of itself to the exclusion of all else. The result is that when one of these is lost or broken, The Being feels a part of itself is lost.

The answer is always the same. If The Being was able to remain conscious and aware of the space in its imagined body, the intelligence would communicate to it the knowledge that all is well and absolutely right. It would no longer feel a part of it was lost, because it would be in touch with its own intelligence creating (and destroying) all things. To be conscious at all times is to be free of all emotional upset. You can be aware at any moment of what is going on around you, and still be feeling, or in touch with, the intelligence behind it all. But the moment you let go of this, you are likely to take things out of context and think about being somewhere else. Of course you then won't have (contact with) the intelligence to inform you that all is well, as this is a little secondary world you've made for yourself. And as a result you'll find yourself getting worried, angry, or scared, etc. Stay in your body and not in your secondary imagination and you'll always feel complete because you won't be allowing your imagination to separate you.

This is why you feel sad when someone dies. Not because they're dead, but because you have become far removed from the rest of yourself, and this is why you feel there is a part of you missing. Then we blame the departure of the object or person we are thinking about for the feeling.

Death does not exist anymore than when you are asleep in bed dreaming that someone dies. They are not really dead, perhaps because they were never really alive. Even so, you can go through all the emotional trauma because you believe they were, and now they're gone.

130

The knowledge that it was only a dream would have protected you from this. This physical life is no different from your dreams at night, just a little more substantial (solid). By staying conscious, you wake up in the dream. When you are fully awake (conscious of your whole Being), there is no longer any need for the dream and it evaporates, leaving you as just pure intellect with no objects to reflect upon, so no sense of being.

You experience the essence of this when in deep dreamless sleep: your senses are not communicating anything back to you (no external, nor internal images), so whilst there may be no doubt you're alive, you don't know it. That's death.

You are then 'woken' back into your divided world (divided by the mind, and then the senses) and you may often feel you'd like to go back to sleep. At the very least you might acknowledge it was peaceful and trouble-free. Without sensory information there is no time. This is the real eternity.

Of course we cannot imagine this because we only imagine images. We cannot imagine a state with no images. That state is within you every moment and forever, because it is 'you' before your mind gives you a body. Just to be conscious and alert is to be in this state (or at least, in contact with it).

Making progress

I continued to try to teach Elaine, sharing with her what I knew about life, and specifically in being responsible for one's moods and emotions. But after a year or so I gave up pushing so hard, and just waited for a sign that it I'd learnt what I could and it was time for me to move on. Twice in the initial two years we were together Elaine came to Barry's five-day Leicester residential seminars. Both times (but the second more insistently than the first) she said that Barry had not said anything that I had not already told her, and asked why we were there.

***

(28.07.96) During one session at the recent seminar Barry told of a Master who described that it was as if a rose could be placed inside him, inside his chest for a thousand years, and it would remain intact and perfect forever. (Not literally, of course.)

As Barry said this, I was in that state of mind or experience, and in that moment I felt I understood this perfectly, but later lost it.

I also had a dream on the last night:

There were two Incredible Hulks and two 'Supermen', one real and a fake. (For some reason Superman had blond hair, not black. Also, the Incredible Hulks seemed very small.)

I was walking up a spiral pathway (as opposed to a staircase) in a building and the fake (or so I thought) Hulk was at the bottom with someone else. I turned and taunted the Hulk, and was surprised when he grabbed the bottom of the path and pulled it, ripping the bottom and knocking me over. As he pulled it away from all its fastenings I scrambled to the top. I then saw in my mind's eye Superman pulling his civilian shirt open (as he's famous for) and running to help the Hulk get me.

Then I was in an elevator and pushed 'up'. At the top, I arrived on the roof, stepped out of the elevator and walked swiftly towards the edge of the roof. Without thought or feeling I stepped off the roof towards the street below, with the knowledge in that moment that the only way to get rid of the Hulk and Superman was to end the dream.

My interpretation of this at the time is as follows: Superman represents 'positive' emotions; the Hulk, negative ones (and in the dream he appeared angry or scared). Both of these are strong but fictional characters. It's possible the fake ones represented little emotions I might regard as harmless, hence my taunting of the Hulk who then became the strong destructive one.

The upward spiral path may represent the spiritual path. My going up this path and reaching the top would mean the end of both emotions, Superman and the Hulk, and that's why they tried to get me: to prevent me from reaching the top. I really don't know what the elevator represents, but it could be grace, where life will be doing some of the work for me. And I imagine that my stepping off the building was not only the actual deed to end the dream, to 'kill myself', but it could also be symbolic of throwing all into the hands of life or God: total surrender.

I wrote to Barry today describing my experience, as well as my dream and my interpretation of it.

***

I still listened to Barry's tapes, and the words and their energy were powerful in helping to confirm what I already knew and kept me motivated to continue. But again, I already knew the principle, and more.

Life continued as normal. Occasionally a situation would arise, and I'd see myself getting emotionally involved and pull back.

***

(October 1996) I wrote to Barry again, but this time it was to say that I could not understand why I was with Elaine, struggling emotionally as we were, and this seemed contrary to his teaching of a man and woman being in love and growing in love consciously together. He had always taught that one cannot do it for another; that one should only be with someone else who wants to live in this way. But Elaine did not really appear to want to.

Barry replied a week or two later saying that the relationship was indeed serving us both, and that Elaine's mature female energies would be doing me much good in my process. He finished by saying, '...it's still not easy, and that love doesn't happen the way the idealising mind would imagine it!'

***

I left the nursing homes to become a double glazing salesman. My stammer was now much better, but this was still quite a challenging prospect. I'd occasionally get stuck if I allowed myself to get involved with what I was saying, but I only had to stop for a moment, regain composure and I was again in control.

People's moods no longer bothered me either. It seemed my time with Elaine, fighting to remain conscious in emotionally difficult situations (and being directly affected by feelings in both her and me), was beginning to mean I was now less affected by the feelings of those around me: there would still be the knowledge there, as an intuition of what they were feeling, but much less of the feeling itself.

I still didn't have many friends, but lots of acquaintances.

I had also learnt, as Barry had taught, to pull back from the eyes, to see the whole scene at once.

I sold the double glazing for about six months. I did very well at first, but then learnt that some of the things I was saying were not completely true and I lost heart, and with it apparently the ability to sell, going several weeks with no success (so no income).

***

I then went to work for a sales agency, selling door-to-door the change of gas and electricity supply to Southern Electric Gas. This was another very challenging role, but one I seemed to be quite good at. After all, everyone wants to pay less. The trouble is no-one wanted to change supplier (due largely to a lack of knowledge as to what the word 'supplier' actually meant). This meant one had to be very smooth and hide the truth a little to convince people to sign the agreement, describing the process in detail whilst being sure to avoid the dreaded word (supplier). After a few months I was signing pretty much every household I visited, but the energy and concentration required to do this took its toll. After about a year I was finding it hard to go to work at all. And about six months later I recall sitting in the van at the end of the road of houses I was due to knock that day, ready to go to work but not having the energy to get out of the van.

***

(July 1998) One night whilst driving home in the van, I suddenly felt so at one with my body and the van, that the idea of there being a past or future didn't exist. Not only did the past or future not exist, but the *idea* didn't exist! I 'knew' then that I could spend a lifetime with Barry Long and not be closer to Enlightenment than I was at that moment.

***

Elaine and I got a little King Charles spaniel. I went out walking one evening, through the park, looking at the trees,

138

and I realised I didn't actually exist at all. The objects I was looking at did, but I didn't. *I am just consciousness looking at the objects. I am the objects. Take these away and I am nothing. I won't even have a sense of being. I won't exist at all if there are no objects.*

I wrote to Barry describing my experience.

I also made the following note:

Enlightenment doesn't happen with a flash of light. Our emotions through our imagination run our lives and we are at the mercy of the ups and downs. A still mind is an Enlightened mind. But it's also not very interesting. Entertainment is what we are looking for.

That night I realised that there are no answers, as Barry has said many times. And this reminded me of the story of Jesus on the cross and how he apparently asked why.

***

We were advised by The Barry Long Foundation that Barry would no longer be coming to Europe for teaching sessions. They explained that travelling was taking its toll on him and was now too much.

For a moment I wondered what I was going to do. Getting to Australia would be difficult with Elaine.

***

At work one day I was sitting with a colleague. He was saying he was really interested in spiritual stuff. He'd read a couple of books and one day really hoped to 'get there'.

'Get where?' I asked.

'Get to that state of being completely at one with everything!' he replied.

I said, 'While you look for it, you'll never find it. That state is being here, in this van now. Consciousness is being *here.* Then your body would be here and so would you. Then you are to be at one with it!'

He said, 'Yeah, I'll get there one day!'

I went on (probably enjoying actually speaking with someone who was genuinely interested), 'You can only feel what is not you. You don't feel you. You *are* you! You feel something else! There is one consciousness, one energy, behind everything, including you and me. If you are connected to that energy, you become at one with everything, which means there is no feeling at all. NONE! Something would have to be separate from you for you to feel it. But then you wouldn't be at one with everything, would you? If you, as much as you can, practise bringing your attention back to wherever your body is, that is to be at one. The more you practise, the easier it gets!'

We never spoke about it again.

***

Another time I read an article about a teacher who claimed to be God and instructed his followers to worship him, and yet at the same time told them that they should abandon all beliefs. It was at this point that I decided I should write a book describing what I had realised and how, and in a way that is accessible to everybody. (I began writing by hand the notes which became this book.) The following are the notes I then wrote under the heading 'What is Enlightenment?':

Once there was a space: a space of pure awareness and nothing else. The space made images and objects for it to look at and an image (body) for itself to interact with them. It enjoyed the new feeling of experience, and whilst in the form soon forgot that it was creating the objects and accepted this as being reality. It became scared of some objects and attached to others, all the time enjoying the sense of experience. After a while of this toing and froing it became

140

tired and longed for something reliable, something that would not die or leave it... for some meaning to all this.

It began focussing its attention inwards, on its own awareness and not on the objects. It came to realise again that the objects weren't real, and as long as it remained fully conscious all the time of its own sense of awareness, it was no longer moved by the toing and froing of the objects. Remaining conscious is Enlightenment.

***

I left the door-to-door selling of gas and electricity supply and took a job as an IT recruitment consultant. This was on the back of my sales experience, but I had no experience of IT, nor recruitment. I was also told in the interview that it would be all telephone work. This of course concerned me again as my stammer would still appear occasionally, but I knew I had to try this. It would be great experience if I could do it.

After two weeks, no-one knew that I had a stammer. Every evening after work I would read out loud from a book to help me speak without stammering. It worked.

I also found I could relax inside of the body and again feel like I didn't actually exist. I was just an empty space.

***

I went up to London for a talk by a spiritual teacher of Enlightenment. He was quite famous and well-thought-of at the time. He had published several books and was regarded by many as an authority on the subject. During the interval, as I was getting a cup of tea, one of his members of staff said to me, 'Isn't he great?'

I replied, 'I don't think he's actually said anything. He just keeps repeating the question he's asking. And when anybody asks him a question, he tells them that that's not the question he's looking at and repeats his own question!' (I was less than impressed.) The staff member replied saying this is just his way. But I couldn't help thinking that if this was the type of spiritual teacher people regarded highly, I wasn't sure whether this would make my being able to teach easier or harder. The chap had even announced at the beginning that he was not there to deal with people's emotional problems! And if they had any problems, they should go and see a counsellor or a psychiatrist! To me, and as per Barry Long's teaching, dealing with problems and facing and dissolving emotions are vital parts of the spiritual path and Self-Growth.

***

After being with the IT recruitment company for two weeks and having to practise being as conscious as possible to avoid people finding out I had a stammer, it seemed to be going really well. And I seemed to be conscious a lot of the time. But there were times when it seemed more difficult, as if the energy was less and my body needed a rest from the effort of trying to stay conscious.

I would go for walks every lunchtime across the MoD heathland area, which started at the end of the road, to regain my inner strength. One day, sitting under a tree, the question occurred to me *Could I stay here forever?* – the feeling being that there was no time.

When I got back to the office I went to the loo, and as I sat down the thought occurred to me again *Could I stay here forever, for all eternity?* And the answer came to me as an internal *YES!* But in the same instant an insect scurried beneath the cubicle door and across the floor towards me. I saw that even if I was here for all eternity, with the open window, occasionally an insect may pop in giving me something new to experience and enjoy. It was such a pleasure to see this tiny insect, I wished I could always have this appreciation of the little things like tiny insects.

This experience reminded me of that night in my bedroom when on the LSD. I thought I was going to spend

142

the rest of eternity in that room, except now I didn't seem to mind the idea; even sitting on the loo would be all right.

Occasionally throughout the afternoon, the question occurred to me again, and each time the answer was *Yes, it would be OK!*

That night, when walking our little dog around the block, a thought occurred to me. *I don't need to go any further. I've come so far, and things are so still, I can stop trying and pushing now. I don't need to go any further. I can give up now!*

A moment later the knowledge arose in me that I must push on. *I've come so far, I can't stop now! It would be easy to stop now – I mustn't!*

I had pushed so hard for so long. This 'peak' I seemed to have reached, it would be lovely to be able to sit back, relax and tell myself it was all over. That I've got as far as I want to. *I can take it easy from here on in; forget the spiritual stuff, and just get on with living!*

When getting ready for bed that evening, just as I was standing at the edge of the bed drinking hot chocolate, the thought occurred *What if the physical universe all froze solid right now? What if nothing ever moved again, but I remained completely conscious throughout and forever?*

Just the idea might be enough to terrify some people. But again, I felt I could cope with that; even in the middle of a sip of hot chocolate, it wouldn't matter. I would still be me, and the physical world would still not be real. This showed me my attachment to the physical existence was being broken.

***

(02.06.99) Over the last couple of days, the drive to 'continue' (trying to be more aware) still has not returned. It is almost as if I've reached a pinnacle. There is another one higher, but this one might be high enough.

I awoke this morning following another dream. The dream itself I don't think is important, but one of the characters is. He was in an earlier dream I'd had. He was a very big nightclub bouncer, always smiling, very calm and cool, but enjoyed inflicting severe pain and damage to people. I don't remember if he did it to me in the last dream on not, but I do remember being afraid, and knowing I was powerless to stop him doing whatever he wanted to do to me.

Last night he told me (and my dog?) to leave the club. We did, but he still scared me, made me feel uncomfortable and I wanted to avoid him.

I've been trying like mad to remember where I know him from, because I certainly recognise his face. I kept seeing his face in my head and trying to understand why. This afternoon I realised he looks exactly like the Kraken character in the film *Highlander*. The film is of course famous for the phrase 'There can be only one!', and in the movie this character was the last one the Highlander had to defeat before being 'The One'.

I then remembered I'd heard Barry talk about the 'Gatekeeper' (or something similar): the last piece of ego or self that has to be faced. And I saw that these dreams may symbolise my reluctance to meet and face him, this core of myself – the bit that could be regarded as pure evil (if one takes unconscious or emotional energy to be such). The final battle!

Two days later I wrote the following:

I've been thinking more recently. I saw today that my ego now has a face. This Kraken is my ego. Walking during my break today I had to hold on to the image of his face, or the knowledge of him, to stop 'him' thinking (I would have to take his mind, his head), and then take his power. And then there will be only one!

144

I had a week of being partially deaf in one ear. This made my voice echo in my head, making me very conscious of every word I said.

Then I had toothache the next week, for which I was using TCP mouthwash. This also kept me conscious again.

I wondered what life would have in store for me next week!

***

(20.06.99) I had a talk with a colleague in the IT recruitment office. He told me the manager had asked him what he thought of me. (I knew he wasn't happy.) He also said that the administration lady was frustrated and annoyed with helping me. (I found the technical terminology very confusing and could never tell from a CV whether a person was suitable for a job or not. But then I never got any training either. I was also very new to using a computer, so the most basic of things had to be explained.) He also told me that he knew I stammered. (This was a shame, as I'd tried very hard to hide it, but not unexpected.)

I knew I had one to two weeks to prove myself or I'd be out. I felt, after the second week of being there, that I had achieved what I had set out to achieve: coping with being constantly on the telephone and learning computer skills. Now I would have to see what life had in store for me next.

***

(25.06.99) The manager keeps having a go at me for doing things wrong. I confess I'm getting a little low now. I did apply for another job, but was unsuccessful. Today in the office I 'remembered' that I'm responsible for my own life and feelings. I then remembered something another teacher had said (from one of the many books I had read): 'Change how you feel about a situation, and the situation will change accordingly'. Immediately I found I could raise my energy level to be lighter and easier.

***

(07.07.99) I made my first placement at work today. I've been there seven weeks and this was unexpected for everyone. It's taken the pressure off but I'm still looking to move.

Walking today during the lunch break I felt a strong feeling that all of nature – the trees, grass, soil, etc. – was like my brother; it was a part of me, my closest friend, and it was a very strange but lovely experience.

My computer should arrive tomorrow and I can start typing up the book.

***

(20.07.99) Walking near work through the woods, I again felt the trees and grass and nature were my friends. And a few days later, when again walking, I felt I would like to *be* nature. Just being as life happens to it. Simple!

***

(27.07.99) I feel I am as much a part of the woodland as the trees in it. Today I am a walking tree! But at work, things have got worse. The manager and I will fall out big time if we're not careful, as I'm standing my ground now. But I also had the realisation/reminder to keep everything in perspective: for me to think about anything not happening in this very second is to take it out of perspective. And this will achieve nothing good.

***

(01.08.99) When walking today I felt I could merge with anything: a tree, a bush, a dog, another person... in fact anything physical; I could become one with it. I wondered why I couldn't disappear altogether to become like the air, until I realised I have already 'disappeared' and am like the air. My

146

inside is completely empty and I don't really exist. I am no more my body than I am the walls and the trees around me.

***

(10.08.99) I recently had a dream of a girl I used to work with. We were at a friend's house. She and I were on the sofa and she kept trying to kiss me. I turned my face away each time so she kissed my cheek. It didn't feel right. But after a few attempts from her, I decided it perhaps wouldn't hurt, and we kissed. Her mouth tasted very sweet and it was lovely. Then I woke up. I carried the memory or mental imprint of this experience for a few days, but I was not quite sure what it meant at the time.

Walking through the trees at lunchtime again, I felt I could lie down on the ground and disappear into it. This has been in me now for several days. And I asked myself whether I would really want to disappear, and at first I said yes. But then I felt I would probably want to get up again, as I don't feel I've completed everything yet. I'm not ready to die or for the dream to end.

***

Today at work my manager, during my third appraisal, acknowledged that I have a stammer but added that it's not a problem. He said, 'Yes, you have a stammer, but that's part of you!' I do feel it's not there at all most of the time and when it is, it is not a big deal. This is a big step forward.

***

I am on holiday this week. Quite early on I said to myself, *Right, for the rest of this holiday I am determined to remain as conscious as possible!* In the next moment I saw that there is no need to try any longer. Only time will increase my consciousness. There is nothing else I can do or need to do. I have done all I can!

I feel I could be a famous pop star with many millions of pounds, with everyone wanting to be me, or close to me, and it wouldn't matter. I wouldn't have actually helped anybody. Writing (the notes for) this book even if no-one reads it, is doing more good than being a famous pop star.

***

It occurred to me that I don't want to die until I finish this book. Although I know there'd be no-one to read it once I'm dead (because that is the realisation), it is something I need to do.

***

Today I saw that the book doesn't actually matter at all, as long as I'm conscious.

***

I have been looking for a Yin Yang watch recently, but bought a pendant instead. Funnily, I wanted the person in the shop to ask if I knew what the pendant meant, and I could have shown off what I know: opposites are part of the whole and are inseparable. If you see everything as part of the whole, they are complete. Take them out of context and it's then that problems happen. But of course the lady didn't ask.

***

(14.09.99) I was moved to write the following essay. (It was so important to me at the time that I investigated copyright laws. In the end I phoned the Citizens' Advice Bureau who advised me to send a sealed copy of it to myself in the post and not open it. I still have the letter now.)

The Mind of God

There was a space of pure intelligence. Within it there grew a need for some experience. This need created the illusionary world. The illusion was its own 'Being', its own unconscious

148

mind creating its surroundings every moment. The need for experience was the reason for existence in the first place, so The Being relished in every opportunity. It looked forward to the next experience and this looking forward created a separation between itself and its own unconscious mind.

For a while this was a little uncomfortable as it had let go of the feeling of being complete and whole. However, it knew this would be made up for when the event arrived and it would be able to enjoy it in the moment, thus being complete again. This created a positive edge to the feeling. It knew soon it would be reunited again in the moment, and the feeling would be wonderful. The anticipation of this would grow stronger as the event came nearer.

When something was absent (somebody left it or died, etc.), again it let go of the moment to look back into a secondary imagination, remembering the object. This letting go of its own unconscious again gave it the feeling that something was missing. In its ignorance it thought this was the object, not stopping to realise it was because it had let go of its own truth, its own knowledge that it was behind everything. It felt incomplete because it WAS incomplete!

Through its own unconscious, The Being got what it wanted. It wanted feeling and experience so that was what it got. Situations would happen, people would come and go, just to give it the feelings it sought. The more it enjoyed these feelings, the more it had! The Being was spending all of its time thinking now about past and future, very rarely conscious at all of its missing half, so always feeling incomplete. When remembering something that had gone forever, it felt negative as it knew it would never have the experience of being with that object to make it whole again. When thinking about an upcoming event, it looked forward to it because it knew that would give it the feeling of completeness it required. As soon as it was reunited with its 'Being' again and was complete in the moment, it would quickly find after the initial impact that there was actually no feeling there at all. Unable to stand this for long, off it would go again in its quest for feeling, thinking of other times and places.

There are occasions when The Being gets such a strong feeling from being somewhere or doing something, that it is unable to think about anything else. In these instances, it feels 'free' or 'Enlightened'. During times which require great concentration, especially involving personal risk, again there is no space for the mind to move and The Being feels 'at one'.

The more The Being uses its imagination, the more it is separated from its unconscious and the stronger the feelings get. The unconscious creates situations with the sole purpose of causing a feeling. Treasured items break or get lost; loved ones leave or die; routines are interrupted; fears and insecurities are played out.

After some time of this, The Being may begin to wonder what it is all about. Why are things so painful?

If it is earnest in its desire to no longer have all the ups and downs, its unconscious as usual brings to it what it wants. The Being is taught how to no longer identify with feelings, instead to remain conscious of its own 'Being' in the moment as much as possible. This is of course extremely hard. It seems almost impossible not to get sucked into the feelings which were its constant companion for so many years. With practise and its distaste of negativity becoming stronger, it gets easier, and The Being comes to know again the wonder of being complete. But this time it is a constant state. No coming and going. No ups and downs. Life seems to work out for the best every time. When a situation occurs that would usually provoke a feeling, The Being remains conscious denying the movement. As a result, fewer situations are created as they are no longer required to stimulate The Being's feelings.

150

The Being now knows the truth again, and yet is still within its illusionary existence. It has not yet satisfied its need for experience and continues to enjoy its world in a state of fullness and completeness. It is no longer separated from its knowledge by situations. All are solved quickly and without effort as its physical life continues to unfold every moment.

The Being becomes more and more engrossed in the feeling of being complete and less concerned with the illusion around. Eventually the need for experience will have been satisfied and the illusion will end. The complete Being once again settling into a state of just pure intelligence with no need for feelings or sensations of any kind...

... until the next time......!

***

(15.09.99) I sent the above essay, 'The Mind of God', along with a letter to Barry Long, and asked if I was Enlightened now, as I have the feeling of having arrived and have nowhere else to go, and described how this has stayed with me for two or three months now. I honestly may be Enlightened?! I don't know whether I am or not. I feel I've got as far as I can and now I just continue with life, in this state.

My letter included the following description:

> About three or four months ago, shortly after starting a new job which required me to remain extremely conscious, something happened. The best way I can describe it is to say 'The bottom dropped out!'
>
> I found myself in a state of no effort, and no trying, as if I was floating – not physically, but everything else. (I'm sure you'll recognise all this.) I wondered straight away whether or not this was 'Enlightenment', and held the state of mind, not knowing what it was. I've had many realisations in

the past and you have been kind enough to confirm them for me, but this time was different. With the feeling of 'floating' (best I can come up with, a better may be 'global weightlessness') was the feeling or knowledge of having arrived! I felt I had arrived and had nowhere else to go.

***

(27.09.99) Today I received a reply from Barry:

Enlightenment is a constant state of Consciousness in which the knowledge is implicit. There is no knowing in it for it is nothing to speak of; it can't be known.

So you are not enlightened, or put more really you have not realised that state.

Nevertheless your description of being shows a profound realisation or realisations. But all the truth is in the actual living of it and shows itself eventually in the entire physical external circumstances of the life. And only you can know or see the extent of this manifestation in your life, or where it is not so yet.

Barry Long

***

I am twenty-six years old. I have left the IT recruitment as it didn't get any better, but out of the frying pan into the fire a little bit: I am selling advertising on the back of Safeway's till receipts. I have little savings and no money at all for the first two weeks, and am now self-employed. I am a little worried (though this is by now becoming a regular occurrence). And of course, I knew this is exactly why it had to happen. I fought hard to stay conscious, and felt I filled my body. I actually felt my whole body at once. And felt complete. Barry has

152

described over the years that one should make one's body conscious. This must be it!

***

(02.10.99) Sent another letter to Barry thanking him for his reply, with the confirmation that I am not Enlightened. I gave him a further update:

> *Three days ago, whilst driving home following another financially unproductive day, I was using every effort to remain conscious. I became aware of my body, all over. I was fully conscious of my whole body from head to toe (you have of course mentioned this before). This has happened to a lesser degree before, but this time it seemed more complete. I likened it to feeling my whole body was a piece of iron: solid, strong, dense, impenetrable, totally complete. This has actually stayed with me ever since, and now I am conscious a large amount of the time (at least at present while the 'reason' is behind it) and whilst conscious, my whole body is conscious. (You again no doubt will know where I am.)*
>
> *On the personal front, I have now spent over five years with an emotional and moody woman (she is now fifty-two years, and I'm twenty-six years). In the first year I moved out three times. Each time I felt it wasn't really time and there was more to do, and returned. I told myself after the last time that I wouldn't move out again until I knew it was over, and there was little or no chance of my returning. For the majority of the years, I've half hoped that the coming week(s) may be the last. However, I never really felt it was over and that I had more to learn...*

and boy have I learnt from it!

About a week ago, I realised that I felt I'd learnt all I could from her. I feel now it is over and again I just wait for things to work their way round to the solution. I moved straight into Elaine's house from my mum's, and have never had to really stand on my own two feet. Never really had my own space. Maybe that has been the attraction of older women over the years. Not necessarily being 'mothered' as is commonly thought, but possibly looking for the security of a house, etc. and an established routine. Five years living with a woman who on a regular basis tells me to 'fuck off out of her life!' soon destroys any feeling of security... and has built instead independence and strength.

I thank you again for your reply, and hope this letter demonstrates that things are moving in a positive direction.

I trust all is well with you. Of course it is, but I wish you well anyway.

Yours Sincerely,

Nick Roach

***

I was chatting again on AOL last night. Met a new person and the lady told me of a dream she had had of delivering a baby. The baby had died and she had the baby's blood all over her. However hard she tried, she could not wash it off. She said she was trying to look up what the dream meant.

I asked how she felt in the dream, and she said she was irritated. I asked whether she was in nursing, and she said yes. I explained that I too was looking after people with illness, and they die, and their families and friends say they should have been able to do something and feel it was their fault. They would always wonder whether they could do more, and blamed themselves.

I asked if that was why she felt irritated in the dream, and that perhaps she blamed herself for not saving the baby; and being unable to wash the blood off her clothes could symbolise her holding on and unable to let go of the situation emotionally.

She was amazed! Said I had interpreted her dream! She wanted to learn about detachment so I sent her the link to Barry Long's website.

I spent quite a lot of time chatting online with various people over several months, as it provided an outlet for me to share what I was learning and seeing.

***

(16.10.99) I was giving a friend a lift home from work today. She had another friend with her who reads palms. She looked at mine and said my left showed an extremely unhappy childhood, verging on suicide! My right, she said, amazed her, as it was the hand of a very together person! Not many little lines: a very long lifeline and no career line, which surprised her, on the hand of such a together person (which she said meant I am not my career – true!) She added that she saw a problem in the lifeline of my left hand but that it was sorted in my right.

***

In the office for the company selling the advertising on the back of Safeway's till receipts, there are a couple of colleagues who go to something called the Landmark Forum, and they invited me to go along to a meeting.

The principle has to do with self-awareness and spiritual growth, and is taken from various philosophies and teachings. I arrived and sat in the large room with perhaps two hundred other people. I was trying to be open-minded but it quickly felt like we were being given a high-pressure sales pitch. Various people stood up at the front and described how wonderful the programme was and how much it had changed their lives. Eventually members of the audience were asked to put their hands up to indicate that they were already prepared to sign up for the programme, in which case their 'Landmark' would start there and then. For those not planning to sign up at this time, they would be taken away for their questions to be answered.

So, I was directed into a little side room with four other people and four or five 'teachers'. It seemed the aim simply was to convince us to pay two hundred pounds or so for a three-day course! One man stood at the front, between us and the door. The other teachers stood at the back.

He started by asking whether anybody knew why they were there. No-one responded, so I put up my hand and offered what I could: I confessed I was sceptical as to how much it would help me, as I had spent a few years practising self-observation and my life was pretty sorted.

He accepted this and then he talked and talked; I tried to get involved, answering questions when I was able to from what I already knew. But I soon found I was getting really bored and frustrated. I sat there for another fifteen minutes or so, shuffling in my chair, picking up and putting down my cup of water, looking around the room for any distraction, before I could take it no more. I finally saw why I was there, what my lesson was. My lesson was to walk out, and it frightened me as it went against all I had been taught, i.e. to respect your elders and teachers, and the formality of the situation.

As I sat there, continuing to shuffle, rocking backwards and forwards, I seemed to be waiting for the right time, but I was getting very uncomfortable and the feelings were growing inside me. How was I going to do this?

The topic was raised of interpreting a situation, and how one bad experience can affect all others similar from then on. One of the new people said perhaps we should speak up when in a situation with someone. The example was given of a boss looking at his watch when we are talking, and how there are many possible reasons for this. The person said that perhaps we should ask why he's looking at his watch rather than assuming he's bored or fed up with the conversation, and the teacher agreed.

At that point I suddenly put up my hand and said I knew what I was there to learn. He asked what that was. I said I was there to learn to summon the power to get up and walk out. He said, 'OK.' I said I'd found it hard thinking about it, in a small room full of people, just to walk out; but to be honest, I was getting really bored! He said, 'OK' again. I got up, picked up my papers and water, walked up to the chap, shook his hand, and said, 'Thank you for your time.' I turned and smiled at the others in the room, and left.

When later describing the above to the colleagues who took me to the event, both said that my actions were very much in line with what I would have been taught.

***

I continued speaking with people at work and chatting online with others, sharing what I knew and experienced. Several expressed an interest in learning more, and one was particularly insistent that I begin to teach formally, as I had 'shown [her] stuff in a few minutes that others hadn't been able to in years'.

However, one person who I had been speaking with for a long time now said I could not be in the state as I described it. She said this was for ascended Masters only, as they vibrate at a higher rate, and that no-one can be in that

157

state whilst they are in a physical body (unless channelled through a psychic). I said, 'Barry Long is, and I nearly am!'

She didn't believe me, and it was clear that we may not talk again.

***

I was earning very little at work, and then I realised that is what I was being taught: my attachment to money. The day I saw this, I made three sales on the same day.

***

I wrote the following essay relating to reincarnation:

The Ocean Containing Bottles of Water

Reincarnation is like a shaped bottle containing water, floating in the ocean, but there are holes in the bottle allowing water to pass through in both directions: the shape of the bottle could be said to be the water's personality or character – that which makes it different from all the other water. Pour the water out and into a different shaped bottle, and it is still the same water but now a different shape – different personality or character. All that makes it different is the shape of the bottle, and of course the bottle itself which is left behind (discarded) when the water is emptied.

When the water is finally emptied out of the bottle into the ocean (in death), the water itself doesn't actually change. It is still individual because it is the same water. There actually only ever was one body of water. Just for a while it was in the bottle, and the water thought it was different.

Enlightenment is the process of the water in the bottle realising it's part of the ocean.

***

(16.10.00) I sent the following letter to Barry today:

158

Dear Barry,

I hope all is well with you.

I just wanted to write to thank you for allowing your videos of the Australia meetings to be shown in London. I was not organised – or awake enough (see below) – to get to the first two, but went to this Sunday's, and obviously intend to make it a regular appointment from now on.

Everything is right, but I feel I've been asleep for a while. I have been busy getting on with my new job and everything else that takes one's attention. When you were physically in the UK every few months, I had a wakeup call. The last couple of years it has been difficult to get over to see you, not least of all because my partner of six years decided a few years back that your teaching was/is not for her (she is now fifty-three and I'm twenty-seven).

That is not to make excuses, rather just looking at possible reasons why I have all the knowledge (as much as I do) and yet no longer have the drive to do anything about actually advancing, or living it (it seems). I take it at this time that this is a natural state/phase I am passing through, and perhaps it is just the trying and effort leaving me, but I didn't expect that to mean I would just let myself think rather than using effort to stop.

But as I said, everything is right, and I thank you for all your help and giving, and thank you for continuing through the videos.

It would be great to see you in person again sometime.

With thanks,

Nick Roach

***

(04.07.01) Several months later, I wrote the following letter to Barry:

Dear Barry,

I hope you are well.

This letter is regarding a dream I had two days ago. It is not urgent as all is well with me. It is just interesting (apologies if wrong word) at the very least as I see it perhaps indicates my progress with overcoming fear. A part of me would like to think there may be more of a landmark connected with it, which is why I am writing to you. I know you cannot and do not reply to the majority of letters (not to mention gifts) you receive. As I said, all is well, and I see the dream as positive and thank you for your time and knowledge and love.

The dream:

I was seated just inside a large old-style L-shaped room. Very high ceiling. Shelves with books all round the walls. I think there was an old grand piano in the corner. The room was very gloomy, dusty. The windows looked as though they had not been cleaned for years.

I was waiting for someone, I think. It felt like an interview of some sort. Quite formal.

After a little wait, I got up to walk around the room and I began to slowly walk towards the other end.

160

There was a large window there, too dirty to see through, with shelves under it. Again, the books were dusty and covered in cobwebs.

As I faced the end of the room, perhaps ten feet away from it, I felt a cold chill. It was as if there was a presence there. The chill quickly became a blast of cold air hitting me from the front, with this powerful presence around me. The presence and the cold chill were extremely intense, like putting the air conditioning on in the car full force, and it became stronger and stronger, almost pushing me back. I stood my ground, largely due to being paralysed on the spot, unable to move. There was nothing I could do. I don't recall if I was fighting to stay where I was, but the pressure pushing me back was extreme.

I looked down at the carpet in front of me to find I was being forced to the floor. This I did try to fight, but had no chance. The floor came closer as I was forced face-first towards the ground, unable to move.

Once down, I lay on my side, fixed in the same position.

The knowledge in me was to stay conscious. That everything was OK and I must stay in my body. This was what I was doing.

Then I felt myself being lifted up. I still could not move a muscle and could only watch as I was raised up and carried to the centre of the room, towards the door, the way I'd come in.

I was now in the middle of the room, 'suspended'

(though not from anything), paralysed in the position I had landed in, a semi-foetal position as I had fought against being pushed back, and then on to the ground.

Then I found myself being turned upside down, still in the air in the same position. The knowledge was still in me to stay conscious and everything would be OK.

Then I remembered that however much I surrender and may (or may not) have realised immortality, I am still in a body and as such it is right that I fight to live as long as I can, fear or no fear.

I was unable to move or fight in any way, so I did all I could do: I found myself saying the word 'Hello' (even this was a struggle). I don't know if this was to the presence, or to attract the attention of anyone outside, but suddenly I awoke with a start in my bed, to hear myself finish the word ('Hello').

(The end)

It was a strange feeling to wake from this dream, as I wanted to go back to find out what would have happened had I not woken myself up. It was very real and powerful. When reminded of it I feel it is not far away.

This could all be imagination; and as I said, it is interesting to see how I dealt with being attacked and hung upside down by a psychic entity, in a strange house, alone.

However, having listened to some of your tapes recently, I remembered 'The Keeper of the Threshold' that you talk about. This name means

162

little if anything to me. I have had insights and realisations, but have no experience of this 'Threshold' guy. Did I meet him, or would I have done had I not 'chickened out' (if that's what I did)? Or was the dream preparing me for the real experience in the 'waking world' later?

I do not know.

I do know all is well here. I know all is well with you, and would gladly help if it wasn't and I could make it so.

Thank you again Barry for all you do, and have done.

Thanking you in truth, honesty, and love,

Nick Roach

Master Session
2001
(4 – 17 November)

It's been over a year since I last made any notes. In that time I have left the selling of the advertising on the back of Safeway's till receipts (after only six months – not very productive). I then joined a carpet cleaning company, selling their services to residents. At first I seemed to do OK with this. A lady from telesales made my appointments and I would visit and make the sales. But I soon learnt that the manager was skimming commission from the sales team when he did our wages each month, and we didn't always receive wage slips at all; the company was not VAT-registered as it claimed, and they were not declaring our wages, National Insurance and tax deductions to the Inland Revenue.

As I had been self-employed and my parents were still doing my accounts (my mum and stepdad were bookkeepers), we had to take this seriously. I made sure I challenged all inaccuracies on my wage slips, and these were corrected; but I also had to report them to the Inland Revenue for my own protection and future legal security. (Their office was based in the next town. I took my wage slips and appointment sheets in, which they photocopied, assuring me it would be kept anonymous.)

One day I returned to the office to see some men in suits speaking with the manager. The company claimed at the time that the men were raising money for a police charity, but I was informed later they were from the Inland Revenue. (I had my suspicions anyway, but felt I had to ask so as not to imply I already knew.) What I did know was that I had to find another job quickly.

***

I did quickly secure another job. It was still using my sales background, but this time for a debt collection agency. Again, appointments would be made for us and we would go and do the visits. The company was based up north in Leeds, where

167

they had the majority of their work and agents. But they were now getting more in the south and, being based in Guildford in Surrey at the time, a little way outside South London, I was going to be the agent for the south. The job was visiting customers of Ford Credit and other car finance companies, who were in arrears, collecting from them the debt, any current charges plus our own costs (which were not small), or persuading them to hand the vehicle back voluntarily. If it was to be the latter, this involved the signing of an agreement to this effect as well as agreeing a monthly payment to clear any balance outstanding once the car had been collected and sold. Our costs, which were added to the amount owing, were to be cleared with the first few payments.

In principle this was not an awful idea. Usually the balance owed far exceeded the value of the car. And in such a situation the person would not only have to struggle to find the arrears and our costs, but would then continue as they were, paying a large balance for a vehicle worth little. But by handing the car back voluntarily, it was agreed that it would not affect their credit rating further; they would not have to find the large lump sum to get the account up to date, and instead could make other arrangements to get another vehicle to use as a run-around. So this could save them a small fortune, as well as a lot of stress. As the agent for the area, I would also collect the vehicle, using a little 4x4 van, towing a trailer, and deliver the vehicle to the auction or storage area, filling in the necessary paperwork and doing the required checks at the time.

The trouble for me was that, being the only person in the south, my area stretched from the far end of Kent, all through East Sussex, West Sussex, Surrey, South Hampshire, Dorset, Berkshire, Oxfordshire, AND much of London – even, if required, areas beyond these.

My first appointment would be at 9.00 in the morning, then with an hour being allowed for an appointment and an

168

hour for travelling, my next one would be at 11.00, then 1.00, 3.00, 5.00, and 7.00. I was expected to advise the office well in advance if I was unable to make any appointments. The appointment schedule would be sent to us the week before to check, but only the first two letters of the postcode for each address would be supplied. And in my area, some of the postcodes are huge and it can take an hour to get from one side to the other when traffic is good, and that's before one travels through the next area to the address. In busy times it could mean rushing and running late all the time. And with the first appointment being so early I would have to leave home at about 7.00, usually too tired to have breakfast; I quickly learnt that a cup of coffee in the first house would get me through to my first petrol fill-up where I'd grab a sandwich and another cup of coffee.

The days would be long and hectic, leaving the last house at about 8.00 at night, often having to drop a vehicle off at the auction and getting home at about 10.00. I would then have to write up my reports from the day (by hand), fax them over, and then try to grab something to eat. By this time I was exhausted and almost too tired to eat. So I might grab a bowl of cereal and go to bed, setting my alarm for early the next morning to do it all again.

As you can imagine, after several weeks (never mind months), I was finding it really tough. But the worst part was repeatedly describing to the office (on the telephone) what I was going through, and being told initially that they didn't believe me, and later that I was clearly doing something wrong! After a while I took to stating what time I left home on my report sheets, what time I arrived and left each appointment, what time I arrived home, and what time I finished writing my reports and sending them over. But this was never even acknowledged. (I was later told they even found them amusing!)

The feeling of helplessness that developed was overwhelming, and on several occasions I sat in the van on the side of the road crying, through a combination of tiredness, lack of food, frustration, feeling of isolation and stress in general.

What made it worse still was that we would get a monthly bonus depending on our success rate. The guys up north would complain that they were bored, often having an appointment early morning and then one late evening, with nothing to do all day! They would even visit the same person on two or three occasions to get the result, whilst I would have to dash through an appointment and try to do everything the first time because I barely had time to call anybody back, let alone visit them again. This meant the guys up north were actually being paid more than me down south. And it was this sense of unfairness and injustice that was perhaps another major factor in the way I was feeling.

***

I was still living with Elaine, but otherwise we were hardly together as a couple. It had been a long time since I last went to one of Barry's talks. In some ways I felt I had little to learn, but was beginning to appreciate the benefit of being in the energy of an Enlightened Master, at least theoretically. Barry had always talked about this, and often said that much of the teaching is done energetically and not by words; but I had always focussed on the words as I seemed able to understand them.

I booked the time off work to go back to Australia for the next Master Session. It had been eight years since I was last there, and it had been about six years since I last attended a talk of Barry's. It was now time to go back. I went alone.

***

170

The Barry Long Master Session
4 – 17 November 2001

(03.11.01) We arrived today at the Bond University where the seminar is being held. It's a very nice campus and I'm in one of the student accommodation rooms. The choice was between one of these which are actually on site, or sharing an apartment in a block of flats some walk away which was overlooking the beach on the Gold Coast. The apartment sounded lovely, but I felt I needed my own space and as little hassle as possible. I also wanted to save some money.

Sitting in the apartment, I wrote the following insight:

A child comes into the world with no sense of its 'being'. It cries instinctively, without perhaps being aware that it's crying, and certainly not why. There is no sense of self. There is only what is seen or felt, but no sense of separation.

Immediately it begins to see the separation; it sees objects 'over there' and begins to see that 'I' must be 'over here'. Everything happens to 'me'. I feel hungry, tired, hurt or happy. Me... Me... Me...

Soon the child learns that it has an imagination, and can use this to imagine its 'self' in another time and place. This is its own world where it is King, where its self gets everything it wants, and everything it doesn't, but still it can't help imagining. It spends more and more of its life in this imaginary world, the feeling of self growing stronger and stronger. It has its own likes and dislikes. It holds on to all its hurts and pains, and relives them time and time again in its own 'reality', defying anyone who would tell it it's not real or necessary, that it brings it all on itself for its 'self-gratification' and 'self-experience'.

The 'spiritual life' is simply to make an effort to spend less and less time in the imaginary world, and where possible and when seen, purposefully deny the self what it wants.

The pull to return to its own world where it can have all it wants immediately is extremely powerful. It takes years of (whenever it remembers) pulling itself out of its world and back to face what is.

Bit by bit, the pull of its world becomes less and it is easier to again just see and feel what is. If it perseveres and is earnest enough, with grace and love it may again return to its original state, where there is no 'self'.

'I' then begin see and feel what is, and from my gained implicit experience I act accordingly. But now without indulging by creating my world (and thus my own likes and dislikes), the sense of 'me' stops there.

The more I see only what is, and feel only what is, with no imaginings, the impression of being 'over here' lessens, as in reality there is no 'over here'.

My 'Being' is creating what is to give me a sense of being, but it is not the truth.

NB. I asked that this be given to Barry. He said when I met him later that it is all very good, except the last part.

(Note: I now know it's not the 'Being' that is doing it at all. It is the emotion, and the emotional attachment to being separate.)

172

***

(04.11.01) I asked for another letter to be handed to Barry.

Dear Barry,

Thank you for your time and love.

You have seen I'm doing well, or perhaps more accurately life is doing well through me.

This morning whilst seated for a while on the side of the bed, I had an experience of knowledge:

I 'knew' the 'Lord' was entering me.

The 'Lord' means nothing to me, except to say I have heard you mention it. I do not know what this means, or even if I need to know. The word 'Lord' was the knowledge of the state I was (am) in. There was no other experience or knowledge or insight. Just the knowledge that the word was/is the state.

Please note Barry that I did not wish to get 'above my post'. I just wished to let you know that I'm still doing well.

Continuing to thank and acknowledge you, in consciousness and Being.

Thank you, Barry

Nick (Roach)

***

Barry approached me. He asked how old I was, and when I told him I was twenty-eight years old he stated (and repeated) how wonderful it was that I had got so far!

In the morning session that day I was seated in the middle of the audience behind a lady wearing a yellow mackintosh-type coat who had long brown hair, and from behind looked exactly like Sophie from the first Master Session in '93. (Sophie had had an almost identical jacket, and amazingly the same long brown hair.) But it so happened I had just met this lady, Natasha, an hour or so ago elsewhere on the campus, so I knew it wasn't Sophie.

Natasha and I talked outside the meeting and began to spend a bit of time together, going for walks, travelling and spending the days together on any excursions that had been arranged. And it was as if everything was perfect, because we not only had a lot in common, with Barry Long's teaching, but we were of similar age, and she only lived about half an hour from me in the UK; I was actually driving through her village two or three times a week on my way to work! Whilst talking about our progress in the teaching, when I asked her whether she had realised 'there is only one "I" in the universe' (a term Barry used when describing the insight of there being only 'one' here, and on one occasion had added that he had heard of someone being institutionalised when they got this insight too early), she said, 'Yes, of course!' I did not press her on this point, but knew if this was the case, then she was the first person (besides Barry) I had met or knew of who had done this; who knew she was 'alone'.

But it was probably too perfect. It felt a bit like a setup, with everything falling into place so as to raise my hopes just to knock them all down again.

Even though Elaine and I were largely living separate lives, nevertheless I was still in her house. And when talking with Natasha one evening, and endeavouring to explain this (and my eagerness to leave my current situation), she expressed obvious and not inconsiderable concern and doubt as to how I could possibly be living Barry's teaching properly if I was in this situation. She felt strongly that I could not, and was not, living the teaching correctly. (A huge part of Barry's teaching was to 'live rightly'; to live consciously and be true to what feels 'right' intuitively. To do this one needs to be honest

174

(with one's self), and strong enough to face a situation and take action as required.) It was clear Natasha had decided I was not doing this, and the atmosphere changed.

***

The next day when considering the situation, I saw myself as a fish that had jumped out of its tank, and after perhaps flapping initially had actually calmed down and found it was not so bad on the soft carpet after all; it felt 'right', if not actually enjoyable. And it was as if someone had come along (Natasha) and pointed out to me that I was on the floor, dying. To which I shrugged my shoulders (as much as a fish can). She had said, 'I can put you back in the tank if you'd like, but I'm not going to if you're just going to jump out again!'

I shrugged again, and off she went.

Later, I (the fish) called her back, and asked to be put back in the tank and assured her I would not jump out again.

***

(13.11.01) Natasha had hired a car and took a few of us on a forest walk yesterday. It was very nice indeed, but we spent no time at all alone. In fact, I felt I was pursuing her, so backed off and went off alone, leaving her with one of her friends. I had a nice time, but had to face and accept the possibly that it was over between us, before it had even started.

She dropped me off last, but then drove straight off. I had a little time in the car to tell her my fish story, but when she asked what the moral was, I smiled and shrugged.

As I got out of the car I said that I might see her tomorrow (emphasising the word 'might'), to which she replied that I would.

In my room that evening I felt it was finished. That was, at least, unless she approached me.

**

(14.11.01) This morning I awoke and had a new insight relating to the fish story and 'the Lord'.

I was reminded that Barry, who had on occasion described himself as being the Lord, had often said that truth and love are realised separately. If you realise truth first, then a woman will come into the man's life and make him realise love, and vice versa. I saw that whereas before I had no knowledge at all of what the 'Lord' meant, I now know the Lord is 'Love'. My knowing the word only at the time was the very start of it. Now it has entered me a little to let me know it is love.

And this explains the fish story. In jumping out of the tank, through 'right' suffering, I have realised the 'Truth'. Now it is time to realise love. But I cannot do that alone (as Barry has also taught), just as the fish cannot get back into the tank alone.

To 'not jump out again', I see as perhaps knowing I do not need to suffer any longer. I have learnt the lessons and can now get on with enjoying life through realising love.

This also explains what Barry meant when he said Self-Realised men have asked him why he says life on earth is paradise, or The Garden of Eden, when it is not (to them). I too have questioned this. I knew that all was 'right', if not fun. I now see that I, and perhaps they, had realised the truth but not the love.

**

(14.11.01) I asked for the following letter to be passed to Barry:

Barry,

I apologise for the following question. I thought I was past questioning, with the knowledge that ultimately

176

there are no answers.

The following question has arisen a few times over recent years, when I hear the explanation regarding reincarnation. The question is regarding the explanation itself and not the fact (as I know the fact is OK), and it is for that I apologise.

We know there is one life, one Being. It is said the consciousness comes back into existence with a 'predisposition'. This consists of 'stuff' not faced or 'got rid of' in previous incarnations, as well as a portion of the world's 'stuff' (the essence behind the saying, e.g. the sins of the father).

This is my question:

The world being a projection of myself, surely that has no 'stuff' of its own, and there are and have been no other individuals to leave stuff behind for me to face, as it is all me. There is only 'me'. Therefore, whatever predisposition I bring with me into existence can only have been created by me. If this is correct, when explaining predisposition, why do we not say it is my own stuff not faced before?

I thank you for reading this Barry, and do not mean to be argumentative. Perhaps I have missed the point, or there may well be more beyond my current position that you are not able to go into.

I thank you Barry again for your love and consciousness.

Nick (Roach)

***

I really thought I had found a problem as I described the above. What I had seen, if only partly in logic, seemed to contradict what Barry said. And my letter was telling him so. I had even asked one of his staff members and she straight away said, 'That's a great question. You must ask him that during this session!' But I was concerned it could be embarrassing to him, if I really was pointing out a big contradiction. So I wrote the letter instead.

And this question seemed to send me into a mini crisis. I had trusted everything Barry had said for so long, but now seemed to see a hole in the teaching. What was I going to do?

The next morning there was a video instead of a talk (allowing Barry the morning off). Having gone through the crisis last night I actually didn't know how I could ever listen to him again. And then in the video I thought I saw another small inconsistency.

Having realised the truth for myself, I then saw that there are different ways of explaining it. It seemed totally clear to me that this was the problem, the cause of the contradiction, and that I am now far enough along to be my own teacher and do not need an external Master anymore.

I left the video with a beaming smile (and felt as if I had connected with something really powerful), and half expected to be asked to leave that afternoon after Barry had read my letter with the challenging question.

But there was no direct response to the letter during the afternoon session; though he did say to everyone that he reads them all, and thanked those concerned.

He also mentioned reincarnation again in another session, and repeated that 'The "legacy" continues with the intelligence taking responsibility for some of the world's stuff as well.'

***

178

It's been a couple of days since I last had contact with Natasha. I have actually been avoiding her. I have had a mild but constant attachment to get rid of. I saw that her reaction to my relationship was 'self' or emotion in her. And I'm seeing that if she sees this herself, and also sees that just because a situation may look wrong from the outside, that it may still be 'right' for the individual, that she may feel she has judged me Harshly; or she may not. In the meantime, it's served me by exposing some more attachment within myself to be got rid of.

***

(16.11.01) I still have had no contact with Natasha. I saw her when entering the seminar today. She smiled, and I returned the smile and then sat away from her. Barry came to me at the end, put his hand on my shoulder and said, 'Predisposition is a huge subject, and if I ever write anything about it, I will send it to you.'

I saw Natasha speaking with some people afterwards and again I walked past. I imagine she knows that she can approach me if she wants, but she seemed to make her feelings clear.

***

That evening, in my room on the university campus, sitting alone writing to Barry, I started with the following:

Thank you, Barry

I want to thank and honour you in the strongest way. I do not know where I am with regards to the levels of Self-Realisation or Enlightenment, but it has occurred to me that perhaps the greatest service I could do is to tell you before you die that I am Enlightened.

179

That is, as far as I can see, why I have been moved to write the letters describing where I am. So you can see your teaching is being lived successfully, truthfully, with love and acknowledgement.

I do not know if I will be able to tell you I am Enlightened, but please know I do not know a greater way to thank and acknowledge you, and will be doing my best, with life as my trainer and my coach as you are my Master.

Nick (Roach)

I went on to write on another bit of paper, still to Barry, what I was realising about 'legacy' and 'predisposition'. And towards the end of the page I wrote the following:

I am now questioning whether the last moment ever happened. And if it did, when was it?!

And then suddenly, it was as if some sort of round energy 'portal' opened up or appeared on the wall behind me. It was about eight feet across and high, filling the wall. For a minute or so I looked into it, into the doorway to heaven, as that is how it felt. I felt an extreme, almost bristling, blistering coldness (not unlike that of my dream where I was forced to the ground and then hung upside down), with an eternal fullness and incredible potential.

As I looked into it, the question I was psychically or intuitively being asked was whether I would like to be One with it. I didn't need to get up from the chair. I only needed to say yes internally and I would be 'One'. It was as if the doorway was genuinely open...

As I sat looking into it, I knew this was what I had struggled and strived for, for so long: to wake up from the dream, to end the pain, and to be One, and be gone...

But only in the last few days had I been shown I could now start to realise love (with the knowledge of the 'Lord' – love – entering me). Finally it had looked as though I would be able to start enjoying life. Was it really possible, if I was to stay, that this would be the case?

As I looked into the 'portal', facing the large expanse of intense energy, considering my options, I came to the conclusion that if I truly am allowed to stay here and realise love and enjoy life, that is what I would like to do.

With this thought, and with the decision apparently having been made, the portal evaporated.

The letter to Barry continued:

Barry, I'm sitting here, saying 'Jesus' and 'fuck' repeatedly. As I see it, you might never get this letter. I might not be here!

Bit of a shame perhaps. It may have been lovely to realise love with a beautiful woman.

I'm sitting at the desk, in only my boxer shorts and socks, wondering what now?

Have I just been asked if I'm ready to die? I guess so. And I wanted you, Barry, to get this letter, and I want to realise love.

My 'existence' has been about reducing pain. Facing emotions and dissolving the past. I would like to stick around and enjoy the Enlightened state, to be consciously in both places at once. Real or not, am I allowed to enjoy it? Or is the choice pain, or nothing?

Thank you, Barry

P.S. The clock says 9.24 p.m. I'm going to bed. I imagine I'll awake tomorrow. But if not, thank you for your love and your giving.

Once in bed, lying in the darkness reflecting on what I'd just seen or experienced, I felt a little distressed. I saw that I had been asked, invited, to be 'at One' with 'Being' and with 'Life'. And I had said, 'No thank you.' What have I done? I lay with this for a couple of minutes.

Then it occurred to me that maybe this was the point. I had been put through so much pain, so much unhappiness as to want to end it, for so many years, and maybe the whole point was to get me to a point where I would choose to stay? Maybe I was supposed to choose to stay. Maybe my journey, my life, was now complete.

And with that thought it then occurred to me, if my life is now complete, maybe there is no need for tomorrow. Maybe these few thoughts will be the last thoughts I ever have and I will not wake up in the morning. Will there even be a morning?

(Continued letter:)

Barry – 9.37 p.m. Just got up to say I feel like a fallen angel. I have been given the opportunity to unite again with God and have said 'No'. We'll see.

4.50 a.m. Still here and going for a walk.

***

On waking that next day, it was truly the first day of my life that I had chosen to be here. There were no excuses, no ifs and buts; I was here for one reason alone: I had chosen to be!

And it felt amazing. As I got dressed and left the building, walked across the campus towards the lakes, it felt as if everything was here for me. I turned right at the first lake and began to walk along the shore. It had an underground connection to the sea, which was not far away; this meant some sea creatures could find their way in. As I walked, to my right I noticed two very colourful birds sitting in the branches of a tree nearby (it's been a while, but I think they were lorikeets). They looked amazing, and I knew they were there for me.

Then to my left, in the shallows of the lake was a stingray, perhaps three feet across, swimming alongside me. It was also truly amazing, and I knew the stingray was here for me too.

I watched as it swam ahead, gliding, flying effortlessly through the water. I looked around. Everything was incredible. Everything was here for me.

And as I walked, I knew this included all the people as well: everything I had never experienced, anything that I knew. Even Barry Long was here for me. It was all me.

I returned to my room and wrote the following:

(17.11.01. The last day of the Master Session.)

5.35 a.m.

A New Beginning

My 'spiritual life' so far has been with the one aim: to realise the Truth and wake up from the dream of existence, as soon and as fast as I can.

It has been said that I am here to enjoy my life. In my conscious mind this has certainly not been the case.

Last night I was told I have realised the Truth, and was offered the opportunity to wake up... I chose to

183

stay...

The reality of it is really, there was no choice. I was never going to choose to end existence; although the doorway was indeed open, it was only to show me.

It is as if I died last night. Died to struggle and fighting. This is my life, and I have 'chosen' now to stay and enjoy it.

Thank you, Barry.

Nick (Roach)

(Note: Barry had described how he was asked if he was ready to die on three separate occasions: the first two times, he said there was a reason why he wanted to stay, something he still had to do. But on the third occasion, he was already gone. He had already passed through the psychological death.)

***

(That night) I did not see Natasha at all today. It is important to me that if we're not to be together, that we make sure it's not for the silly reason that she thinks I'm not earnest enough for her, as my life is not 'right'.

I took the liberty of putting copies of the letter to Barry on the windscreen of her car so she'd get them. I don't know what reaction there will be.

I had to rush to buy some cassette tapes. I placed the letters on her car window beneath the wiper and went inside the building, and the car had gone when I came out.

I took the bus to the Pacific Fair shopping centre and walked back slowly along the water and beach, trying not to think about her.

I got to Burleigh Heads (the beach area near the University) and began to see her in the seagulls. For a moment I didn't want to see the physical manifestation of Natasha, because it was nice to see her all around me.

Then I began to see her in the trees and plants also, and in all the sounds of nature.

I went along the nature trail and smiled at the noise she was making. The mantra 'Hello, my love' seemed to come up in me to each animal, each plant, each sound. My love was indeed all around me. I was standing in my love.

Back in Burleigh, I saw her car. I looked for her briefly, but saw it was best to leave it up to her now. Her friend had said she is taking him and another to Cabarita tomorrow, and invited me. I said she may have asked someone else, or it just may not be right. I said to call on me if it was 'right' in the morning, and gave him my room number.

I am more complete now!

They didn't knock for me the next morning. And I didn't see her again.

Back in the UK

(29.11.01) Back in the UK now, and things have been better since my trip to Australia. Elaine, perhaps due to my being away, stated that she is now open to growing in consciousness and love. After a couple of days she even said, 'Though we are two bodies, we are one,' but then immediately added that she didn't even know what it meant. Nevertheless, it was true for her.

She also said she feels the 'Nothing' a lot.

One night when together, she said (after hesitating) that she just felt 'space' inside and out; the same space! It would appear she's doing well.

I'm staying as conscious as I can, especially in the car all day between appointments (I'm still doing about a thousand miles a week) where I listen to Barry's talks on tape. I don't want to lose the state now that I'm back.

**

(25.12.01) I received a letter from Barry today, probably just getting round to reading and/or responding to letters from the Master Session.

This was quite a long letter, typed rather than handwritten as Barry would normally reply, and included the following:

> Human nature is at the base of everybody, ...and is the cause of the war in Afghanistan, the terrorist acts, and all the killing, fighting and conflict going on all over the world. Liberation is simply liberation, by grace and living, from my human nature and my self-made world.

**

(January 2002) Things are nearly back to how they were previously with Elaine. I'm spending more time with her cousins up the road who have become good friends.

The other day they asked me if Elaine knew where I was. I replied, 'No!' and smiled. They said she would go mad, to which I responded that she would be in a bad mood anyway, so it didn't really matter either way. (This was quite a big change for me.)

***

(End of January 2002) We were in the car, having the usual negatively charged discussion, and Elaine suddenly said, 'We can't go on like this! We've got to decide whether we stay together or not!'

That was it. That was the sign I was waiting for, and had been for so long. The very next day I found a room to rent in a shared house (just up the road), and paid the deposit.

I broke the news to Elaine in the form of a 'nice' card and wrote the words 'You said we've got to decide whether or not we stay together, and I agree with you. I am going to rent a room up the road!'

I had realised that things had not changed at all since my trip to Australia. And we could stay together for another ten years and nothing would change. I could not learn anymore with her. If I stayed, I might as well have died then, as it would have been a waste of my life.

It took three weeks to get a phone line installed in my room (which was imperative, as I still had to fax my reports to the office every night), and then I moved out. It was all very amicable.

It was ironic though, as I continued to drive fairly frequently through the village where Natasha lived, but of course that seemed to be a non-starter.

***

(27.02.02) New experience: I have been out of Elaine's house for a week or so now.

190

It feels strange, but I have the experience that I sort of feel genderless 'inside'; as if, were I to wake up tomorrow in the body of a woman, I could surrender to that, be that, and all that being female entails. It is understood that most people associate or relate to the gender of the physical body they're in. And for those that don't, they say they feel they're in the wrong body, and can have operations to correct this. But the state I feel now, it's as if my sense of 'being' is neither male nor female, but could be either, or at least act as either, as required by the physical body I happen to be in. It's as if I am no longer identified as being a man – male – anymore; or identified as being anything at all, come to that. Something has changed.

***

Insight: **'Me', 'Myself' and 'I'**
I have seen that the word or title 'me' is what I call 'myself' in existence.

'Me' is what I call my body. There is only one 'me' in existence, but it also has an opposite, 'you'; so it is not the ultimate truth. All opposites are in existence.

'Myself' is my identification with 'me', with what is best for 'me', but not for 'you'. That is why 'my-self' is <u>self-ish</u>. It is identification with being separate.

'I' am the intelligence behind it all – there is only one 'I', and everybody calls it 'I'; there is no opposite.

'I' am out of existence. 'me' and 'you' are both in existence.

***

Another insight: **Choicelessness**
'We' think we have choices, but as it is my intelligence creating my existence each and every moment, situations are 'tailored' to me and I really can only make one choice

191

according to my past and level of knowledge. I cannot make the 'wrong' choice as really whichever I choose was predetermined. It's not that I don't have free will, because I do. I just have no choice. I just do what I do and can only be what I am.

***

(03.03.02) What a turnaround: the next day after writing about being genderless (inside), I decided in the morning to go and pick up the little King Charles spaniel and have him with me for the day. (It had been agreed that I would look after him when Elaine was working nights; I still had a key and would collect him after work, by which time she had already left. But I now thought it may be good to have him when she was at work during the day too.) Elaine called me in the morning to remind me to feed him and collect him that evening; she would normally text me, so this was unusual. I said I was going to call in for him anyway.

For the next forty-five minutes my mind was racing with the possibilities of what could happen when I went round there. I had not seen her since I moved out.

Well, I won't say it was inevitable (as I can be a bit unpredictable in situations like this), but we did 'spend a little time together'. I was confused and a little disturbed. What was happening? I had no intention of getting back together, but for some reason this felt right.

***

(07.03.02) It is now four days later and it's been on my mind a lot. I don't know what is happening or why. But after much looking and searching, for whatever reason, I have to go along with this.

I sent her a text this evening asking if I could pop by tomorrow and she replied 'yes'. I intend to make it clear that we cannot live together (as I would become a part of the furniture to her after only a day or two). I'm going to suggest we still 'see' each other but do not live together.

It feels like this new 'relationship' would be on my terms (instead of my feeling like a spare part). I will be able to stay away (or leave) in times of negativity, and spend more time when things are good. This way no-one feels trapped or compelled to do anything that they don't want to do. We each have our own space.

***

(15.03.02) I received an NIP (Notice of Intended Prosecution) today for speeding. I would receive a further three points on my licence, bringing it up to nine! (At twelve points, a person has to go to court, and may lose their licence). When driving over a thousand miles each and every week, passing literally dozens of speed cameras every day, and all the time rushing to get to the next appointment, it is quite tough to stick to the speed limit. But I will have to try to do so!

The ticket has slowed me right down, unsurprisingly. I feel grateful for this.

***

Insight: **Why no <u>man</u> is God!**
If 'I' was God, I would find my body constantly changing, from one animal to another, one colour to another, then even a mountain, then a flower, then into a lake. I may become a star, the solar system, then the smallest microbe – or a combination of new or existing forms.

But whilst restricted by a body and its needs, having to eat, sleep, wee, have sex, etc., how can 'I' be God? God <u>is the</u> body and the environment; 'I' am *in* the body, and am therefore not God!

This takes me back to my LSD experience of realising 'I am God', but then not understanding if I am God, why could I not create a beach, or some equally attractive

193

environment for myself – why was I still stuck in a dark bedroom?!

No, no man is God! But he can realise God within himself!

***

I have been seeing Elaine quite a lot, and the current arrangement seems to be working for us both.

***

(19.03.02) I wrote to Barry and shared with him my insights regarding 'Me, Myself and I', 'Choiceless-ness', and 'Why no man is God'.

***

I read Barry's book *Only Fear Dies* several years ago and I nearly cried when reading the very last section where Barry ended with the words 'Until next time', when the dream of life and existence had dissolved all separation, and was due to start all over again! At the time I was stunned. I was still struggling to deal with this life, and was now reading that *I* will be stupid enough to go through it all again later. That shocked me, and I felt sadness and despair.

However, I recently saw that it doesn't really matter if *I* do this again, as nothing ever really happens here anyway.

***

I am much stiller it seems now. And I'm looking for a new job.

***

I see the meaning behind the saying 'Healer, heal thyself!' I must be Enlightened before I can teach properly. (A point Barry has repeated, in his warnings about 'phoney Masters'!)

***

Am I nearly Enlightened now? I do see it as a beginning, another phase. I used to find the idea intimidating, mainly due to it taking so long to get 'there'. And yet I feel I'm getting close.

***

(29.04.02) I fell asleep last night with the TV on, and woke two or three times in a catatonic state.

The first time, I heard men's voices in my room but found I couldn't move. I pushed and pushed and eventually managed to open my eyes to see it was the TV, and went back to sleep.

Later, I woke again and couldn't move. Forced myself to sit up in bed, and woke, still lying down. Turned off the TV and went back to sleep.

Then later woke again to find myself in the same space. I could hear the 'clicking' of the water pump in the fish tank, and was again fixed in my position. I had no feeling of any sort and couldn't move.

I knew what the noise was and what was going on, and just went back to sleep.

I explained it to myself by saying that my mind was awake but my body had not had the signal to wake up; but later I saw my body was not still 'asleep' – I didn't have a body! It had not been created yet. I was in the original state of just 'being', and I had only the sense of hearing (no other senses). If it happens again, I will know this and just enjoy being 'nothing', with no body.

***

I have been told it is currently a time during which the five planets are in a line, and this is supposed to mean a time of union (?) I am however finding it easier to be totally conscious and still.

195

(22.05.02) It's been a few months since I moved out of Elaine's and have been seeing her once or twice a week. This seemed strange, but it also seemed 'right', so I went with it. On the occasions it may become negative, I stay away for a week or two before she'll call me for something. And all is well again for little while.

I have asked to be shown (internally) what is going on and why this is so powerful for me.

She's gone away to visit her family for a couple weeks; due back in a few days. I keep being reminded of us together, and it's not even a feeling of wanting anything. It's just an image in my mind of 'us'. I have not been able to understand why this has been happening until this evening.

Whilst walking, and acknowledging the images in my mind of us together, I noticed I am in the same state of mind or experience, whether they are there or they are not there. And furthermore, I feel I am in the same state all the time as I am when we are 'together' for real.

This suggests I really am becoming 'one' with my love for Woman (as Barry taught). To 'be with a woman' is the highest 'good' and I feel I'm in that state all the time.

(Note: Barry explained on a number of occasions that the saints and Enlightened Masters who taught that one should be celibate were only partially Enlightened. 'They have realised God out of existence, but they have not realised God as love in existence', he would often say. He explained that once they have realised Truth 'within' and freed themselves, they should turn their attention out into the world and love rightly, realising love and loving enough, so as to free their love in form, which is woman.)

(June 2002) I had a dream:

I was kneeling on a square piece of wood, paddling around a small 'harbour' with manmade islands and brick flowerbeds, and it looked familiar but I wasn't sure where from.

I noticed the water disappearing, and soon I was left on the brick bottom, kneeling on the wood with no water at all. I began to try to shuffle back to reach the water, but had trouble getting between the brick structures.

As I struggled between two, the board banged down loudly on the other side, and this woke me up. Once awake I noticed the bang had coincided perfectly with the post arriving and the letterbox banging. (This was probably what had woken me up.)

Once awake, it was only then that it occurred to me that I should have got up off the wood and walked, once the water had gone.

What amazed me was that it had not even occurred to me to do this. Why not? It was obvious now I was awake.

And then I saw that the thought was not 'given' to me. And if thoughts are 'given' or not 'given', then I really do not have the free will I had thought. If I don't even create 'my' own thoughts, then I really am nothing.

This has opened up a new area for me...

I used to 'watch' my actions and be aware, but now I see that to watch implies duality (the watcher and the watched). I see that as I become the action, I cannot 'watch' anymore, as I am already there. I am the action. This seems constant as an experience here and not as a past insight.

I see that this also creates its own questions (as much as I have any questions at all).

If I am the space in which all occurrences happen, that itself implies duality (the space and the happening). And yet in the experience of it, I am the happening, so there is little or no duality.

197

And If I am the space, I am not even 'responsible' for my own thoughts, and therefore 'I' am not really responsible for doing anything.

A few days later it occurred to me that I am actually the 'parasite': the 'knower' and 'doer' contaminating the perfect 'space' that sustains my existence.

And then I saw that ultimately, I am both! (Possibly best to stop questioning.)

***

(13.08.02) All is going very well. Elaine has been away for a week. I feel I am already 'One' with her (but more so, the experience is that I am 'One' with all women: 'One' with the energy within).

***

At work yesterday I saw something that I don't want to lose: my manager gave some of my paperwork to a colleague to read as part of his training. I felt bad as he had to read my bad handwriting. I saw then that when I write, all that matters is that the information is put on to paper with no regard or thought for the person who has to read it. That is to say, my bad handwriting is a lack of respect and acknowledgement for the person who has to read it. This has changed since, and it seems my speech has also improved as I seem calmer.

Let's hope it lasts.

***

(23.08.02) On the radio today they were debating a march or rally about to take place in support of Osama Bin Laden by some Muslims.

For a moment it occurred to me that I wished Jesus and Mohammed were alive today, to see what was going on. So they could try to sort out this fighting and killing that is going on in their names. I believe they would object strongly.

198

Suddenly I said out loud from deep personal knowledge, 'I am Jesus, and I am Mohammed, and I AM OBJECTING!!!'

And this reminded me that Barry has asked in his talks before, 'Why follow Jesus? Why not *be* Jesus?' I know what this means now.

Jesus was the Master consciousness; he had realised the One Being. I have the knowledge that I am realising, becoming, the One Being as well.

***

(07.09.02) The challenging situation at work continues. I have been with the company a couple of years and have not had a pay increase. I have done a huge amount of work during this time, each and every week, but not received even a cost-of-living increase; so in effect am being paid less this year than I was last.

When I spoke to the manager, his response was that the bonus scheme is in place to reward good progress, and the better one gets, the more one earns. But I reminded him that when I had previously questioned them about moving the goalposts and making it harder and harder for us to attain the bonus, he had replied saying the bonus is there to reward outstanding performance and that people are not expected to get it! These two seemed to contradict each other.

However, finally, back in May, the message was passed to me that I would indeed be given a pay increase of five thousand pounds per year *if* I achieve the targets for the next three months: May, June and July.

I didn't trust them, and I sort of felt life was setting me up (again). However, I also knew I had to throw everything I had into this, so I did.

I put in a huge amount of emotional energy as well as time over those months, starting earlier, finishing later, and even driving into London for follow-up visits on a Sunday when I wasn't working, just to try to increase my success rate.

And it worked. I was on ninety-seven per cent each month, putting me in the top two of the advisors. I literally lived the job for twelve weeks. But, as feared, they are not going to honour it. They are now saying that my performance dropped in August, which was outside of the term set by them, and as a result they may not pay!

They also said that they never actually promised to pay. They only said they would consider it, and having considered they have decided not to pay!

I've had to work extremely hard to deal with the emotion connected to this.

Today I saw that having a problem is like holding a ball, mentally, and once holding this particular ball, it is nearly impossible to stand still. And the bigger the ball, the stronger the urge to play and run with it; so, one runs with the ball. But if you can stand still with it, the ball begins to shrink and as it does so, so does the urge to play. The trick is to stand still, mentally, both with the ball and even when you're not holding a ball (when faced with a problem). The more you play with a ball (think about the problem) the bigger it gets.

I must stand still and not play, not 'run', at all. I must stand firm and hold on to this!

***

(15.09.02) Sent a letter to Barry describing my recent progress.

***

(17.09.02) I feel much stiller now. I sat at Newlands Corner tonight on a bench (Newlands Corner is a 'beauty spot' with great views, not far from where I live), and I saw (it occurred to me) that I'm ready to die. That is to say, I am so still 'inside' (and this feeling has stayed with me) that I could stay there forever; or indeed the images of the physical world could evaporate totally, and it wouldn't matter.

It is only six weeks until the next Master Session (with Barry in Australia), and I thought I would have wanted to see Barry. But I seem to be so much in the stillness that I have little need to do anything. Good; at last!

(It had occurred to me to ask again, 'Am I Enlightened now?' We'll see.)

I have also just seen that I must not be 'together' with Elaine again. It has been a couple weeks since I last saw her. It not only may give her false hope that there is a future for us, but (and possibly remembering what happened at the last Master Session with Natasha) it could also interfere with my moving on.

***

(18.09.02) Again, I seem very still now. I see no point in imagining other bodies, as they are no more real than mine. I am alone!

I ordered three more tapes of Barry's talks: two mentioned his approaching death (due to prostate cancer); the last was called 'Seeing through death'.

Whilst listening to the tapes, I saw very clearly that the purpose of life is to dissolve as much emotion and self as possible, so one can be as conscious as possible when one dies – so God can know himself!

But I also see now any emotion left does mean another body must be created to act out and satisfy and dissolve old wants, hurts and emotion, so that ultimately there is no emotional 'need' left to return.

***

(19.09.02) Wow...

Today has been easier to remain conscious, but has also been more like those experiences on LSD when I felt separate from the actions of the physical. I am the space surrounding and supporting all existence, but I am not it.

I remembered the phrase 'to realise I am not the doer', and that is what has been happening. I have just been watching my body act and feel that I am not actually doing anything myself. My body acts but I do nothing.

***

(21.09.02) I am staying in Somerset with family at the moment. I go in and out of consciousness (in the sense that I lose my self-reflection, not that I am passing out). It is easy to feel and be aware of my body, but then I lose it and come back shortly after. Earlier, I saw I have thoughts that pass through my mind, but I am not actually thinking anymore, or at least it seems that way.

Insight: **How heavy is your backpack?**
A person carries an emotional rucksack on his (or her) back. Each time he (or she) is hurt he throws the rock of emotional past and memories into his sack. It gets heavier and heavier and weighs him down.

As with karma, which is the past repeating itself, when a situation similar to the one that caused the rock of emotion earlier comes up, he tosses this into his rucksack also, becoming bitter and twisted and even hateful with the effort.

If he's fortunate, eventually, he may begin to face each situation as a new one (thinking less). Now when a situation comes up similar to an earlier one, he faces it consciously, does not get emotional, and does not add this rock to his baggage. He drops it and moves on (to the next).

202

This 'facing and letting go' automatically releases the older rock from the bag, the one that was related, so both he and the bag become a little lighter.

This is repeated time and time again until all the rocks in the bag are gone.

Soon there is no need for the bag, and it too is gone!

Then, if he meets a situation which stirs emotion, it is also faced in the moment with no holding on. And he soon has little memory of it, and no pain associated with the situation; and should he come across the situation again, or even the same person (if it was related to a person), there is little or no emotion connected to the past situation. Everything is new.

***

(22.09.02) Insight: **The difference between believing and knowing**

The people *believed* the earth was flat. Captain Cook set out to discover and prove otherwise, and returned and told the people it was round, not flat.

Perhaps some people believed him and some did not (still believing the earth to be flat). The point is that none of them actually knew, except those that were part of the voyage. They could only 'believe' one way or the other.

Believing and disbelieving are both futile. The point is, you either know something, or you don't!

***

Am I Enlightened?

Since around the seventeenth, when I sat at Newlands Corner on the bench, I have felt very still.

***

(04.10.02) I have not seen Elaine for over a month now. I see that continuing to see her kept it going, even though I wasn't seeing her very often. Though I confess that knowing the option is there may help as the situation is not imposed upon me.

***

Yesterday, the stillness or feeling of 'nothing' did not seem to be enough; it seemed a bit abstract. I wanted more. But it has been much easier to stay conscious.

I woke early this morning and put on one of Barry's video talks before leaving for work. And on my way to work, something changed.

We were having a team meeting and I had about an hour's drive to get there. On the way, it felt as if I had found a 'centre' within the 'nothing', within my body. At the time, it seemed like it was the 'idea' of me.

This tiny point expanded gradually through the day. By midday it took up perhaps half of the space within me and now, as I write this at 5.00 in the evening, I cannot even say there is a 'nothing' at all. The point has expanded to fill me and then kept going. All I can say now is, 'I just am.' Maybe there is not even 'I'. There is just this that is writing this, and what is being written. There is no 'I'!

It feels as if I 'have all the time' (whatever that means). Is this Enlightenment? It seems so!

***

(05.10.02) I'm still in the same state.

This evening I visited some close friends and told them I may be Enlightened, and had a good chat with them about it.

Later in bed, when I had finished saying, 'Thank you' (something I've said every evening for a week or two now at the end of each day), I said out loud, 'I will never think again!' and meant it.

***

204

(07.10.02) Insight: **Woman and Man**
Life wants (or moves) to be whole and complete.

As Man, 'I' have separated myself from life with my selfish wanting. I see the reflection of my life, my love, in 'form' all around me, in nature.

Nature is life, love, God, in form, and I can wonder and be amazed at its beauty.

Wouldn't it be lovely if God was in a body similar to mine as he/it is in nature, and this body would fit together with mine and we could interlock, and be as One again in form? (e.g. 'Eve' – the original Woman.)

Love, God, or life also wants to be complete, and the female form will have this driving force to be One with me in form (with Man), as I wish to be One with her.

But she will be affected by my sexual aggression if I am not ready for her. So I must first make myself 'as One' inside, so I'm complete within, and will find a female partner who is receptive, and together we will make her 'One' inside also. We would be united both within and without.

Phrase for the day: '**Don't make anything of it!**' (i.e. don't interpret or imagine.)

***

(10.10.02) I'm still in the same state within: no feeling. Though I do remember my friend last week saying he thought I was on drugs due to the large, fixed smile across my face all evening; such is this experience.

***

(11.10.02) It seems quite easy to stay conscious now, but thoughts or images do go through the mind.

Today I had emotion rise (due to a potentially unsuccessful visit at work). So even though I am in this state, emotion still rises. It was not enough to really make me think though; I absorbed it. But even this took some effort.

***

(12.10.02) Observation, written in car this evening:
Enlightenment seems to be a little like the expression: 'Now that you've passed your driving test, you can learn to drive!'

Enlightenment means not reliving or thinking about your problems (so not creating new emotion), so now you live your life in the moment, facing and dealing with any new emotion arising in any situation, thus increasing in stillness and consciousness.

Enlightenment is indeed a beginning, not the end!

***

(17.10.02) Despite being 'Enlightened' (I'm taking this to be the case), I find I allow myself to imagine speaking to an audience, answering the questions: teaching. It is usually Barry's audience, and he is sometimes in the audience, sometimes not.

I know this is 'thinking', but the truth that is revealed is very fine and seems to serve: it may be that I need some sort of reflective teaching experience. Barry began teaching prior to being Enlightened (as I understand it), and I have no experience at all so this may be a 'loose' way of getting some sort of sense of experience before jumping in at the deep end (if that is to happen).

***

(18.10.02) Essay:

'The Dream of Life' and 'The Dream of Living'
They are one and the same, 'The Dream of Life' and 'The Dream of Living', from different sides. Life is dreaming this

206

and we are living it. Many of the attributes of a dream whilst asleep in bed can be given to 'The Dream of Life' as well.

Life is a mind, empty and open like your mind before you imagine anything (like in dreamless sleep).

It develops a need for experience (I don't know how this need arose). The need in this mind makes objects and forms, and it dreams (i.e. creates) a form for it to interact with the forms it is creating (its body). The purpose is to satisfy the need for experience to return again to just 'Being'.

It enjoys the forms for a while each time, and then lets go of The Dream, passing through a state between The Dream and its pure mind. This is our dreaming state where it is not physical but has some forms and is still emotional with need and wants. Then, on to deep dreamless sleep where Life has actually 'woken up', or is at least in its pure state. The need for experience still needs to be satisfied so Life after a while (we cannot say 'a time' because there are no objects so no time) returns back through the emotional world to its Dream where it is 'awake' (aware of itself).

The need keeps it driving for more experience, and when in its Dream something goes 'wrong', it uses its imagination to get even more emotional experience – soon doing more and more imagining about its Dream world and getting more experience through the emotional ups and downs it creates.

Perhaps after driving out (into the world) with a body, it begins to get tired of the form and its Life is withdrawn (old age), eventually to 'die' in The Dream. Life is then awake again (from The Dream), but the need for experience is still there and may be stronger than when it started due to all the emotional wanting and striving from the last Dream. So it returns through the need to a new Dream with a new form. (This is the truth behind the theory of Reincarnation.)

After many lifetimes it looks for a greater reality, and as it always gets what it wants it creates a teacher to teach it to go within, to the stillness before The Dream existed.

A few lifetimes later it may be in a state of constantly knowing it's dreaming, so does not add to the need for experience through emotional wanting, and is instead dissolving the past need through facing each moment with no holding on to the last. Eventually there is no need for The Dream and it ends.

However, just as when dreaming whilst asleep in bed, even if you have the knowledge that you are dreaming you have no knowledge of your body in bed. Likewise, even though the Enlightened person knows s/he is dreaming, they cannot know what is beyond 'death', beyond the mind that is creating The Dream.

Other similarities...

Just as in a dream you cannot study the objects to find the truth because they are just forms in the dream, scientists will never find the Truth. Every atom, insect, blade of grass, animal, building, mountain, planet, star, etc. is within the Mind of Life.

When in bed and dreaming that you are in a room, what's on the other side of the wall? Answer: There is no other side to the wall, though you can certainly create one. Walk round and take a look. It will be there.

There is an old philosophical question: 'If a tree falls and there is no-one there to hear it, does it make any sound?' This was a question raised, and answered – with a 'No' – at that talk at the College of Psychic Studies some years ago. But now I understood why:

As above, if you dream you are in a park under a tree and in the same dream return later to find it lying down, the truth is that not only was there *no noise when it fell*, but in reality *it never fell*. You dreamt it standing up, and you dreamt it lying down.

Space (between objects) is the mind where it has not dreamt a form, so space is the truth (as much as we can get it in The Dream). Space could also be said to be Love in form, as without the 'no-thing' between the objects there could be no objects, almost as if the space has had to sacrifice 'being' to allow the objects to be. Or you could see it from the other side, in that the forms have had to sacrifice their state of not being, to allow the space to be seen.

Being within a mind, you will also see that if it was 'right', anything could happen. In your mind (The Mind), 'your' Dream is creating the space and the trees. All are one and the same. Some Enlightened men have therefore apparently had the ability to change these forms – e.g. walk on water, levitate, walk through walls – just like in your dream in bed.

Nature is Life (the 'Being' or 'Mind' behind The 'Dream') expressing itself in the many forms, from each tiny flower and insect to the largest animal. Each form has no knowledge that it is (we describe this as the inability to reflect) and acts according to the nature given to it by Life. The person may have occasional feelings of being somehow connected, or even have 'insights' of being 'One' with nature. Eventually in Enlightenment there really is only One, as the one dreaming recognises nature as their 'Being in form' around them every moment, and expresses this feeling of completeness and peace as 'Love'. Not a love for an individual, but as their state of Being.

Once Woman is in the constant knowledge that she is dreaming (that is, in touch with her inner 'Being' behind The Dream, felt initially as the stillness within), she has no need of experience in the same way that Man does. In fact, it could be said that her Enlightenment is closer to the true Being: it is more pure. And she still lives The Dream, enjoying each moment without fear of death as she knows there is no death, and without fear of losing as she knows she cannot lose.

Man's Enlightenment is the same, but the need for experience that started The Dream in the first place still is. He therefore must live in this state, and continue to dissolve the need through living out The Dream. This need in Man is expressed in The Dream as his sexual wanting; and even once Enlightened, although the wanting is no longer the same as it was, the attraction remains with the knowledge that Woman is his Love and his Being in form, as he is hers.

The Dream ends....
Once all need is dissolved and The Dream ends, there is only Mind. As I said at the start, I do not know how the original need arose so I can't say whether or how it may arise again. And as all knowledge is within the Mind within The Dream, one cannot know if anything is beyond it.

***

(18.10.02 continued) I have found it more difficult to stay conscious today. Then noticed the thinking was always about teaching (others); so was doing this coming from an attachment? If so, that's a little worrying as I had been feeding it, indulging it for the last two days!

Though, it is not really surprising it has come up, as it has been a major driving force behind my spiritual growth for the last eleven years (along with wishing to be free of unhappiness). And now it has got me here, it must go as well! Otherwise, if I'm not careful, this will also stop me getting any further. It is an attachment like any other!

***

(25.10.02) I sent Barry a letter yesterday with my piece above entitled 'The Dream of Life', and described my recent experience of the 'centre point' expanding and filling me.

210

I have been finding it very hard to stay conscious of the physical; it feels as if I keep drifting off into imagination even though the Being in me is so strong. The 'Being' is totally solid. I cannot say it is nothing, as I used to be able to look into that nothing. I can only be this.

It has been easier to be still today though since listening to one of Barry's cassettes yesterday which had mentioned again that I (the listener) am projecting this.

***

Insight: A wanting person wishes to satisfy and fulfil their wanting, and being in the physical, s/he looks for forms to fill the void, to fill the sense of wanting within them. This may be food, which we feed into our bodies and which fills the need for a while, only to hunger for experience again soon after.

Or it could be sex; again, in an attempt to fill the void, which will only hunger again later.

In fact, only 'Being' can fill, and indeed fulfil the void of wanting. And in this sense, I see cigarette smoking (which admittedly I've never done) also as an attempt to satisfy the wanting emotions, filling the void with a form: first the end of a cigarette is put into the mouth, thus satisfying the first void. Then smoke is inhaled and fills the lungs – the second void. This then makes the person conscious of their lungs when they otherwise would not be (making them more conscious), thus the third void; and finally the nicotine enters the system as a drug, calming the nerves and filling yet another need, another void.

However, all these voids would be filled by 'Being', where the person is conscious and knows they are creating all the forms as well as voids, and therefore there is no emotional void. There is nothing to fill.

NB. Another void I have seen is the space between the fingers, which the cigarette also satisfies by being held for a while.

211

Question: If in deep dreamless sleep I lose all knowledge of this 'reality', is it not unreasonable to wonder whether I actually wake up in another place on the other side of dreamless sleep, and then fall asleep here and wake up again in this dream?

(PS. When dreaming at night in bed, the forms there are based on the nature of reality here. Taking the dream analogy further, perhaps the images, the forms in this 'dream' are based on a reality elsewhere?)

***

I keep getting 'flashes' that this 'dream of life and living' could end for me before I get to Australia for the next Master Session with Barry (it's only about three weeks away), as there will be no need for existence and the dream, as I am 'still' or conscious enough.

But I still would love to be with a woman, in love, and live the dream in Enlightenment with a woman who is also Enlightened. This may be enough to keep me here, but I will let go of this too if I must.

And I may be approaching the state of the LSD experience that night, when I knew I could stop breathing and end the dream, but didn't have to...

Barry told me I didn't have to do anything I didn't want to, so he has had this too, and chose to stay and live out the dream.

It seems daunting to have the choice, to just let go of the dream and be in the state of Being; but not because I want to do anything – except, that is, to love, here in form, as there is no love outside the dream, just Being.

I don't seem to have the choice yet, but the suggestion seems to occur.

But then again, as there seem to be no consequences for staying (except to pay for everything in one

212

way or another), good or bad (it is after all a world of opposites), I think I will soon have the choice whether I stay here or go.

I was asked this last year and chose to stay. Then a couple of months ago it seemed I was already 'there' – or I just 'am' – and ready to let go any moment if required.

Still, I love to love, and love is only here, so it would be nice to stay.

Master Session
2002

(3 – 16 November)

The seminar this year was again held at the Bond University on the Gold Coast. The talks were in the same hall as last year, as were the meals. And again we had the same choice of accommodation: either staying on campus in the students' accommodation, with each having his or her own room, or sharing an apartment overlooking the beach a short walk away.

I had saved some money so was not so concerned about the cheapest option. And having only attended last year it seemed good to have a new experience. There would be three people to each apartment: one in a double room, and two sharing a twin room. I decided, as much as I didn't mind sharing the whole apartment, I preferred to have my own room, so paid accordingly.

The apartment was quite a few floors up in a very smart block, on the road that ran along the beach. It was amazing, as was the view. We were told that the whales (I forget which type) had their annual migration at this time of year, and we could indeed watch them in the distance as their backs broke the surface of the water.

Though as nice as it was, the university was a bit of a walk away and therefore I knew I would not be spending much time there. (It was really too far to pop back during the day in a spare few minutes, so it would only be to sleep and for a short period either side.)

***

A couple of days into the event, as I was leaving one of the talks in the afternoon, shuffling through the double doors of the hall with everybody else, my exit coincided with another chap's. We noticed each other, and I smiled and acknowledged him, and he looked shocked. Once outside of the room he turned to me and asked if we could have a chat.

We stood on the landing watching everybody going past, and he explained to me that he was about to go home.

217

He had not heard of Barry Long prior to a few weeks ago. He lived fairly local and had seen an advertisement for an Australian Spiritual Master who was holding a residential seminar and decided to give it a go.

But since arriving he had been stunned by how unfriendly everybody was. Everybody he spoke with, everybody he *tried* to speak with, immediately jumped in and pointed out where he was being emotional with what he was saying. He said he had never met a more unfriendly bunch of people, and couldn't understand how they were supposed to be spiritual and following the teachings of a Spiritual Master!

I was able to explain that I too had been like that for many years. And in a sense, it is an inevitable result of being strict with oneself and one's emotions. One ends up seeing emotion everywhere; and in one's eagerness to identify it, when with other people who are doing the same thing, it is not uncommon that the emotion starts pointing out the emotion in other people. (There could also be an element of the emotion trying to deflect the focus from itself by pointing out emotion in others.)

David and I spent a lot of time together during the rest of the event.

(Note: Despite saying above how much I'd calmed down, as you read the following you may notice it is still quite (very, even) harsh, quite severe. And I have to say, as I'm typing this now, nearly fourteen years later, that I am pleased everything has settled down. But anyway, on with the story.)

***

(07.11.02) I spoke with Barry the other day on the university campus. (He actually approached the person standing next to me, to talk to them rather than me, and before he walked away I asked him if he had seen my letter.)

He said he had received my letter. But when I referred to my description of the centre point expanding to fill me and how it now felt solid, he hesitated, did not seem very happy or pleased at my progress. And as he turned to walk away he said abruptly that I have had insights, and must live them! I thought I was! I felt like I had just been told off.

Today I think I saw what he meant, having been thinking about what he said (and knowing he can be fierce at times, a little unpredictable. And I felt a little like I was challenging him as I now knew this stuff too), I suddenly felt I was the one 'I', and knew it didn't matter what he said as he cannot hurt me (emotionally) in any way whilst I am in that space. I saw this is the realisation of the one 'I', and whilst I previously had the knowledge of it, now I had (and have) the experience of it.

I have spoken with people this evening and tried to hold on to this. It seems to be vital that I do not think or imagine anybody, as thinking about them gives them a separate 'I' which is not the truth (and lets go of the 'I' within me). I am indeed the only 'I' and must live this as a constant state, and not just the constant knowledge.

To be the only 'I', I must be here and now, as this is all there is. To imagine anything else is to create other 'I's. I am the only one and must live this as a constant knowledge... BY NOT THINKING.

***

Later in one of the talks, Barry said something I've never heard him say before. Having always warned people to only accept the teachings of an Enlightened person, as only an Enlightened person can talk as he does (of love, God and truth), Barry stated emphatically, 'Not all Enlightened people are the same!'

219

He didn't elaborate further. It was a simple and direct statement, almost out of the blue. But I was sure this was aimed at me.

***

(08.11.02) I went on a bus trip on my own to Byron Bay. I spent the day doing my best to live the one 'I'. That is, to be conscious of the surroundings, and when talking to anyone, be aware that 'I' am the only one here. It has been good.

I found I do not need to look at the face of every person I pass. (I now perceive this as being a search for them to reflect my 'I', to acknowledge me and my existence. This is no longer necessary.)

One of the ladies I met on the bus (who had also come to listen to Barry Long) shared that she has had some psychic experiences, and added that she sees me as being a great teacher one day (I had barely said anything to her. We were just sitting, chatting). She then turned to the person with her and laughingly said, 'We could be sitting with our new Master!'

But if I am *now*, and am the only 'I', then there need be no effort to do anything, let alone teach.

***

(09.11.02) **Living the one 'I'**
I have been working hard to keep the experience of the one 'I'. It has been good, and two things have happened:

1) I found myself sitting with people to teach, but with the experience of my being the one 'I', I knew, as has been said in a tape of Barry's when reporting of another Realised man, 'there is no-one to teach'. So I could teach if required, but with no attachment to the teaching, as I am alone.

220

2) I saw that eye contact is also 'I' contact. I used to seek eye contact from passers-by, to reflect to me my 'I', and thus affirm the illusion of theirs also.

I do not need to reflect mine from them now, and can look down or ahead with no problems, but I feel that they may be looking for a reflection of their 'I' from me, and for me to feed their self, to acknowledge and like them, by a smile and a 'Hello'.

It is easy to keep away from them when surrounded by strangers, but harder when on campus surrounded by people I know and who may not understand the change. (I have noticed Barry does the same: not looking at anyone specific, he walks past, and yet sees everything.)

So, for me to acknowledge this feeling in them is to credit the person with an 'I' they don't have, and ultimately consider their feelings which are not true.

I need to practise actually looking at what I look at, but not seeking eye (I) contact with another to feed their feelings or mine.

Insight: I have seen there is a connection between my work and my relationships, and my work situation will probably change around the same time that I get a new partner. (Besides any other reason, my hours are still long and pretty antisocial.)

***

(10.11.02) For the last couple of days I have been reminded more of love, and of being with a woman in love. The strange thing is, when I looked inside for any deeper knowledge or

221

understanding, the knowledge there was of Elaine. But we have not been together for two months, due to her moods and the emotional ups and downs, and I wish to make myself available to loving another woman should the opportunity arise (having scared Natasha off last year).

The image of Elaine and me together keeps coming back despite my efforts to push it away. It always returns.

This morning I decided to give up and would try a new approach: it seemed trying to get rid of the desire for her the 'old fashioned way' (involving avoiding any images) was not working, so I thought that perhaps I could 'go through it'; face and dissolve it as I always have every other feeling, but would instead work with the images.

So I allowed myself to hold the image of us together: first just her, then once this had stopped generating any feelings I imagined us together, but freeze-framed (so as to be a still image, so not actually 'thinking'). It was actually difficult not to allow any feelings or sensations to arise, but I felt in control.

I did this all day, holding the knowledge of us together in my mind, and it felt good.

Then, during the last session of the day, this afternoon I felt Elaine and I were together in my body, as if we were sharing it! I was aware of her presence throughout my whole body: toes, feet, legs, hands, torso; and particularly in my face, looking out of my eyes. It was lovely and overpowering. She and I in the same body!

I went to the toilet immediately after the session and sat down in the cubicle. It was amazing, but strange (of course). As I sat there, looking down at my body and my hands and looking around the cubicle in the gents' toilet, the thought occurred to me, *I wonder if Elaine has ever been in a gents' toilet before?* And though my eyes were looking, exploring (it was quite a clean, well-maintained toilet), I knew

222

it was she who was doing the seeing. Not me! It was very real.

This evening this has progressed to only Elaine sharing my body; it is as if I have stepped aside and allowed her to take over. She is my body and my consciousness, and although 'I' am aware of everything (as I always have been), she is here and doing it, not me.

This feels wonderful and I must not drift off into thinking. Here we are indeed 'one'!

***

I spent this evening walking and talking with David. I'm still in the state of oneness. The knowledge of my being 'one' Elaine in my body is becoming integrated with me, and it is not as easy to put her name to it anymore. But it's certainly the same state nevertheless. It is as if this is love. I am united with the love.

Intellectually, it could be explained as my love for Elaine. But this is bigger than that. I have known and experienced love as a knowledge (rather than an emotional feeling which comes and goes), but it has now become real in my body; and as 'love' (consciousness) is my true 'being' anyway, it is more powerful than any person or personality.

Of all the experiences I've had and can remember, this is the first in which I feel I have stepped aside and allowed another to take over in love and being. It is as if Nick Roach is no more. Only his love (currently, for Elaine; but there is really no person in this) remains. And that is what is acting now.

***

(11.11.02) The idea of being with someone in love is back, but it is still with the knowledge of Elaine. This is different from a sexual feeling; it is far deeper than that. It still feels like we are together in this space. And I don't know where this is going. (I thought that was finished).

***

A few days later, one evening after that day's session had ended, I was sitting on a bench in front of the hotel overlooking the beach, speaking with a lady. And as I talked to her, something amazing happened:

Quite suddenly, I felt a shift in my awareness or sense of being. And then I was no longer sitting on a bench speaking with someone else. As I looked at the lady and talked to her, the experience was that of speaking with my own reflection. Her appearance had not changed; she was still very much 'her' as far as one could see. But I knew she was actually a(nother) projection of 'me'. She was 'me'! I really was speaking with myself in another place! Then as I looked around, it was as if it was ALL my reflection; the bench, the sand, the trees, the sea. It was all me! I was in my own reflection.

I continued the conversation as if nothing had happened. The experience lasted the duration of the conversation and then came and went several times over the next few days. But it was gone by the time the seminar ended a few days later.

(Note: I was later to refer to this experience as a major step in my becoming 'Enlightened'.)

***

(13.11.02) It seems I am no longer attached to the idea of teaching. With experience now of being the one 'I' and being alone, there really is no-one to teach. So, although I still do teach, if it occurs (I talk with people at the seminar and answer their questions if they ask), there is no need to be attached to it.

224

One particular lady has approached me a few times with questions, and today was quite concerned as she had not been able to go into the sensation of the body as Barry had instructed. I was able to direct her in the moment, and later she expressed how wonderful the chat and experience had been and how grateful to me she was. Again, I was not attached to the gratitude as I was not attached to the teaching; I was not trying to get anything for myself.

The knowledge or idea of being with Elaine keeps occurring when I am alone, but evaporates as soon as I am in the company of another woman.

And yet I am not out for sex at all, but to be with a woman in love (in the sense of conscious acknowledgment), and this knowledge is given to me via the image of Elaine.

(Even though this does not feel overtly sexual, it may nevertheless be partly my going through or facing my sexuality. We'll see.)

***

(14.11.02) All is still well. People have been coming up to me and asking questions, or just making a comment, and in the moment I am moved to reply, to teach, but without attachment to the response.

This evening I began to see that if life – having got me to this stage, through my love of Elaine and hers for me, despite the emotions (as she has been open to it at times), and as I have had experience of being one with her, and as we've been apart for three months – has any integrity, then it may be right (as she has made me 'pure', i.e. God-Realised) that I now go back and do the same for her. I feel I owe her that. And then if we do part, I have lost nothing, owe nothing, and have given what I can. We'll see.

(NB. In the talk yesterday Barry shared that he is now on morphine. He may not be around much longer.)

(15.11.02) Still people approach me and ask questions, or I find myself chatting and a question comes up from them, and the person is amazed at what I know. The words just come. As I am the one 'I' now, I am not attached to teaching them and so it flows easily.

Barry did not come out after tea break for the second one-hour session, as he was not strong enough. His voice had got noticeably weaker at the end of the last hour and it was announced that they cannot make long-term plans for more sessions in the future.

The knowledge feels very strong that if possible I should return to Elaine to make her pure (at one with love), as a service to her for making me this way. I also see that most likely her past emotionality was only to teach me, as it was what I needed at the time. And I feel strongly – if our psyches are indeed joined, united, and one with love and being – she may be able to live it now as I am already one with the love in me, and am ready to love. We'll see.

(That night): I have been trying to sleep for an hour now, and the knowledge is really strong that I must love, and it is still to be with Elaine.

The last session is tomorrow morning, but I am booked to stay in Australia for a few more days. I will send a postcard (in an envelope) tomorrow asking to spend time with her when I get back. Again, we'll see.

***

(16.11.02) I did send a nice postcard to Elaine asking if we could spend time together if she would like and is available. The knowledge still feels very strong that my job is to return to her with the sole purpose of making her 'at one' with love (God-Realised).

The seminar has now ended and I am in a new apartment, some distance further up the Gold Coast. All's well. There is a slight sensation or emotion in me regarding the seminar (and it ending), but mostly about returning to my new 'job', with Elaine. It is good I have these few days to get things straight in my mind.

As Barry left the building after the last talk, he saw me and said, 'Goodbye Nick. Keep up the good work!'

I replied, 'Thank you, Barry, I certainly will!'

**

(17.11.02) The apartment is over the road from Underwater World and I'm visiting it today.

The knowledge and images related to my making Elaine pure (God- or Self-Realised, and at one with love) are very strong.

I see one thing I must address is her seeming to have an ingrained resistance to enjoying being together (possibly this could extend to really enjoying anything; at least, that's how it seems). This could be from her mum, but it's as if she's always looking to criticise things, to see the negative. This is contrary to my own way of life and perspective. I need to get her to open up and express the positivity more, to enjoy and appreciate more.

**

(18.11.02) I have been reading a couple of books on love and relationships and have picked up the following important message:

> *The more loved, cherished, and appreciated a woman feels when not making love, the more open and loving she will be when making love!*

From the above, I see now how I probably contributed to the problems between myself and Elaine. Due to her reluctance to show positivity, love and enjoyment (and enjoyment in love), I too had been less than positive with her generally, and had focused instead on facing and dissolving emotions within me. And, as David had experienced, this can seem cold and unfriendly to people around.

This must change now. I cannot expect her to be open and positive and enjoying love if I am not open and positive and enjoying love all the time either.

***

(19.11.02) I visited Australia Zoo today. I saw Terry Irwin, but not Steve. (He was away filming the movie, apparently.)

At first I had feelings and thoughts about what he has and is achieving. His zoo is currently 40 km^2 and he is to spend the money from the movie on enlarging the zoo to 240 km^2, with elephants and other large animals. He is famous!

Then I had an insight that being famous means nothing compared with loving rightly, and helping a woman to realise love and union within herself, as Barry has taught. Freeing her from emotional unhappiness through conscious love is the most important task. But to do this, first the man must free himself of attachment to the past, and then the highest achievement is to free her. My job is to love as much as possible. Her job (the task of the lady I am with) is to be open to the love, and to point out any way I can love her more. To not point out how I could love her more is to not help me do my job, which is to love and help her.

(Note: This was with regard to being famous specifically and in no way a slight on Steve Irwin. In fact, not only did we love watching his programmes (and we watched them a lot), but his love of nature and animals – and indeed his love of life generally – and the way he lived his life spoke to me in a way I didn't fully appreciate until he died. It was several days after his death, during which I had been struggling hard to face and dissolve the resulting emotion, that I finally saw why I was so affected: I saw that he was the embodiment of what I longed

228

for, of what I felt was lacking in my own life: sheer love and passion for life and everyday living. To me, watching his programmes, it was like watching a real-life superhero. He had been a valuable reflection to me, filling a need. (I would have loved to have been him and living his life as it seemed perfect in every way.) And when he was gone it was like my own love and enjoyment of life had been ripped away. It was tough for a few days.

But as we know, if one consciously faces and dissolves the emotion from a difficult situation, one replaces that emotion, that unconsciousness, with love and being. Thus, one grows as a result, but not in emotion and unhappiness like normally happens, but in consciousness and love.)

***

Free will

I also saw today that whilst there is free will, in the sense of an energetic movement to be separate or free, independent from the whole, there is no free action, choice or thought. The free will can of its own self do nothing. It merely provides the impetus for everything else.

***

(Later that same night, after visiting the zoo): I have decided to get Elaine a very nice card to stand by the bed (so not accessible to anyone else visiting), as a written reminder of what we must do. I could not sleep until I had made some notes as to what it will say:

There were to be five points, relating to us loving each other, acknowledging and appreciating each other correctly and positively.

On the reverse I wrote a reminder of the purpose of this:

The purpose for loving like this is for you to realise and become the state of love in you that is already there. So that you will never again be separate from love, as you will know we are one in your body as we are already in mine. I am the love and the space within you. Be in that space and you will know we are truly together in love, immortal and eternal. Love is all there is. To be love, is to be all there is.

Tomorrow is my last day in Australia.

The feelings have settled in me about needing to love (as opposed to needing to *be* loved).

I see that love must surpass all personal likes and dislikes, opinions and wants, about what we may think find attractive, e.g. hair colour, height, age, looks.

At this moment as the feelings have gone, I doubt whether I should even return to Elaine. However, I know from experience not to trust feelings, whether present or absent. The knowledge is in me about what I should do. I must not look for feelings. I am looking for the stillness behind feelings (within), and to bring them out in another. And who better to do this with than the woman who unknowingly brought me to this level of knowledge and being?

Anyway, I am not with her at this moment as I am alone in an apartment in Australia, so why should there be any feelings?

We'll see.

Becoming the Master

(29.11.02) I have been back in the UK for over a week now.

The first day back was extremely busy, as I had not allowed for the time difference to the UK and thought I had a day off. Once home, I barely had time to get changed and print out my paperwork before I had to dash off to my first appointment of the day!

On the very next day I saw a job advertised in the paper for a rent accounts officer for the local authority, and applied for it.

I have spent a lot of time with Elaine since I got back.

I've continued to have glimpses of being the one 'I' rather than just knowing it, and since yesterday afternoon this seems to be almost constant (but not quite).

As I was going along the A3 today (a large dual carriageway near home), I passed a white van parked at the side and saw it was a traffic/speed control vehicle. I was speeding but maybe by only three miles per hour (allowing for discrepancies in my speedometer), so may or may not be OK; but this has been enough to bother me all day, and I had to work very hard to stay conscious. This has probably served me.

***

(02.01.03) Thankfully the speeding ticket never came. But it did continue to make me more conscious through the emotional fear of facing the possibility of it.

I have spent most of the time when not at work with Elaine. At the moment all seems to be going well.

The experience of being the one 'I' is growing more constant. 'Real' Enlightenment may not be far off. (Since returning from Australia and carrying on with day-to-day living, doubts have surfaced as to whether this is actually Enlightenment.)

***

(21.01.03) I received a letter the other day saying that Barry Long will no longer be holding meetings. I am grateful I was able to go to the final one.

I read the book *In Heaven as on Earth* a few weeks ago, by M. Scott Peck. I sent him a letter offering an alternative ending to the book, as the man in the story did not find the answers he sought, i.e. God as himself. *(Note: Perhaps not surprisingly, I did not receive a reply.)*

***

(March 2003) The pattern seems to be that I see or understand an aspect and after a few months I'll have the experience of *being* it, if only for a moment, and a few months later it becomes a constant state.

Recently, whilst sitting watching a band perform on stage at the holiday caravan park where we were staying (and as usual practising as much as possible being conscious), I experienced something new (to me). Some months back I saw that I was 'nothing' besides what I see around me. But it was only intellectual or informational in nature. This is what I then experienced:

I was in the audience listening to the music and watching the band. The room was quite dark. Suddenly I had a shift of perception, which can be summed up by the famous state or experience 'The perceiver and the perceived became One!'

Everything external remained the same: the stage, the room, all the people, the table in front of me, and the people sitting round it. But 'I' was not there! There was everything that was seen, but there was no-one here to see it. I was gone! There was no me! There was nothing, literally nothing. And I saw then that I am nothing. The objects and the external world 'over there' give me a sense that 'I' am over 'here'. But I'm not. There is no-one 'over here'. There are only the objects: the images of the physical world as if projected on to a screen, creating a sense of personal being and identity which is not the truth. There is no person. There is no identity. In reality there is no perceiver.

I then saw that the reality behind the idea of the perceiver and the perceived becoming One is when the perceiver has dissolved himself or herself to such an extent that there is nothing left. Leaving only what is perceived.

As is usual, this only lasted long enough for me to enjoy and marvel at it before it left me; or perhaps more accurately, I left it (?) It could be a few months before it returns and becomes a constant state. We'll see.

***

(28.04.03) Letter to Barry:

Dear Barry,

I trust the quality is with you. I wished to write to you to thank you again for your teaching, and to tell you of my progress. All is well here. I am very grateful to have been able to be present for the last Master Session at the end of 2002 and have meant to write to you since the session.

During the previous Master Session in 2001 you expressed how wonderful you felt it was I had got so far; yet in the recent meeting you seemed to express concern at my rate and level of progress, perhaps seeing that it is potentially possible for a person to claim to be the 'new Master', even at twenty-nine yrs. (I am thirty in June).

I wish to thank you for the words of caution. They were made clearer by the experience of being the one 'I' becoming very apparent after only a couple of days into the Master Session (due to being in your presence) rather than just the knowledge of it, and clearer still when reading one of the pages at the back of the hall answering the question of whether or not there is Free Will. The point for me was that these supposed Masters could not agree on this. This was big in showing me not all Masters have the same level of knowledge, and perhaps more importantly not all Masters are really 'The' Master. I have yet to confirm in my own being the experience of what The Master is, but I can explain perhaps some of the theory behind it.

My present view on the subject of Free Will is at the end of the letter.

It has been an aim of mine to teach from when I first sat in front of the psychic eleven years ago, stammering very badly, and he told me my stammer was due to strong energy I could not control. He said if I chose to follow the Spiritual Path I would reach a very high level very quickly and have many followers. The latter point has been repeated recently by a lady I met who turned out to be psychic. However, as the experience of being the only 'I' has become more constant, so the wish/need to teach has diminished.

I certainly would not claim it is a constant experience, though the knowledge and experience are certainly available should I be reminded to look. However, it is present enough that I feel no need to teach. As a result my life has now changed giving me both the time and the opportunity to teach if I wish to, but at present there is no movement in that direction.

236

I don't know if it makes any difference to you at all, but you, Barry, are the only Master and yours the only teaching I have ever followed. As a result, should it ever be for me to teach (if only to give back some of what I have received), 'my teaching' cannot help but 'fit' with your words which have and still do teach me. I don't wish to say my teaching will be your teaching because as you have said, your teaching will be complete. And I don't want to say it will be different, as that may sound contradictory. I am just trying to say I feel you have taught me well and set a great example. I can see though a little of what you mean when you say it would be nice to just live away from all the hustle and bustle and let the world just get on with doing its stuff. I see also this would not be of service.

Thank you again Barry for all you have given. You have made the state of Enlightenment a reality rather than an Eastern myth we Westerners read about, discuss and debate.

Should the movement arise I would like to write to you again if possible.

Keep well & thank you

In Love and Truth,

Nick (Roach)

I didn't expect a reply to my letter, but it was good still to be able to write to Barry.

***

(May 2003) I started the new job with the council (chasing tenants for the rent) about four weeks ago now, and it's going well so far.

I am still spending time with Elaine (though I have not given up my own room in the shared house and still spend time there as well).

The moods are generally much less, but the issue now is with her making plans which include me but not asking me first. I see that she expects me to do something and denies me the choice either way, and then gets moody when I choose not to do it, blaming me for messing up her plans.

So this new issue seems to require that I stand up for myself, for my ability to do – or not do – as I wish, and standing up to face her moods which emerge as a result. This teaches Elaine she should not expect or demand, should not take for granted (which has been part of the problem all along). It requires that I be stronger. (I tend to go along with other people's wants and demands so as to avoid stress and conflict.)

***

(16.05.03) I have been enjoying working on the pond in the garden of the house where I rent the room. There are newts in it, which are lovely to see.

The pond (fibreglass, perhaps ten feet across) had been neglected for many years. (There had even been a fallen tree lying over it for some of those.) I wanted to clean it, and carefully sieved all the mud so as to safely remove (save) all the newts. There were quite a few and I was very pleased. (I later saw that I was excited to see them, so I was emotionally attached.)

I came home the other day to find five of the newts trapped in the new water pump, four of whom were dead. This did concern me. But then I felt better when I saw three swimming in the pond.

238

This evening I came home to find two more dead in the pump, despite thinking I had blocked up the hole they got through. I think I have now blocked them all.

Life will take everything I love from me! Everything I am attached to! I am truly alone. I am not allowed duality within.

I am still having to be strong with Elaine, not allowing her to make plans for me as if I'm an object to be moved around. It is hard but I must not give in to the expectations.

I sent an email this afternoon to a lady at work who seems to arrange or advertise yoga courses for staff. I asked her how I would go about arranging to teach Self-Awareness classes at work.

***

(02.06.03) Once I had accepted I had probably killed all the newts in the pond, I then found there were actually at least eight or nine still alive, as I could see several at once. Life is amazing!

I have written 'Introduction to Self-Awareness' as an introduction to my classes at work, and posted it on the various notice boards around the building.

Everyone who has read it says it's really good. One lady said I need to sell it more, but actually I do not want lots of people. I couldn't cope, and they would be wasting my time. It seems strange, but now I have written it, I don't mind if no-one comes. It was my job to offer it.

Even since sending the letter to Barry, explaining how the experience of being the one 'I' is continuing to grow, I noticed I still did not know what 'The Master' was.

Then, when out for a walk the other evening, I saw that if a name has to be given to the state or experience that I am in now, of being the one 'I' in the universe, the 'One Being', then 'The Master' would seem to be as good a name as any. So I am becoming 'The Master'! I will turn thirty in nearly two weeks.

I would like to write to Barry again very soon, telling him I am seeing that I am becoming The Master, and send him a copy of my advertisement, 'Introduction to Self-Awareness'.

My poster:

Introduction to Self-Awareness

By way of introduction, first we need to establish what is meant by 'Self'.

In the first instance, we are referring to the person's individual likes and dislikes, opinions and beliefs, hopes and fears; in fact, all the emotional attachments which make up the personality. In some teachings this has been called the 'Lower-self' (note the small 's').

Behind all the above, before we want anything, is the space of openness. This space is what people try to tap into with practices such as meditation and yoga. In this space is the 'feeling' that all I need is right here now. Here is still the definite experience of 'Me being Me', but if asked what 'I' am, the immediate response would be 'I' am nothing, since there is no wanting or trying.

This space has been called the 'Higher-Self' (capital 'S'), since it is the original state of each person before the personality is created.

So Self-Awareness is both being aware of my personal wants and dislikes, whilst being aware of the space behind the wanting. As the person's awareness of the

---

240

'Higher-Self' grows, so the focus on the 'Lower-self' diminishes. Eventually the person is in constant contact with the space where all is well and they have everything they need at any moment.

This state has been given the name 'Enlightenment'. This is because the individual is enlightened of their problems, and enlightened in that they see life more clearly.

By Nick Roach

I am looking to begin holding meetings, perhaps weekly. It will need to be only a very small number of people at first as it is likely to be very new to most people, and no doubt will result in a lot of questions.

It has not been decided when or where to hold the meetings, and I would welcome any suggestions.

At this time I am not looking to charge anything unless money is required to pay for the venue. This is because I feel it is as much for me as for those who may wish to learn, as I wished to give back some of what I have received over the years.

For more information, or suggestions on possible venues and times, please contact Nick Roach, Housing.

***

(07.06.03) I saw some family this week. I showed my dad my advertisement, and he was not happy at my failing to include physical considerations in the descriptions as to what is meant by the word 'self'.

I have not talked to them, or indeed anyone really (besides Elaine and the people in Australia who are following the teaching), for a long time about Barry's teaching, nor my progress, as they had made it clear they did not agree (or like) the principle. And one aspect some of my family had not agreed with was my withdrawing emotionally, as well as physically, to some extent. But it had been necessary at the time (imperative, even) and has resulted in my making so much progress in a subject that the world's greatest philosophers, spiritual teachers and indeed scientific minds are exploring.

Of course, as usual, I made a light attempt to explain my reasons for leaving the word 'physical' out of the article, and then left it. There is no point in arguing.

***

(12.06.03) I turn thirty years old today.

At work I have asked for my article/advertisement to be posted on the intranet. I'm told it might be online today.

***

(23.06.03) Finally the advertisement for the meetings went online. One person phoned after only two hours (they have an interest in Buddhism).

Today I also received a reply from Barry:

14.06.03

Thank you for writing Nick, (28 April) & you come from a good & right place. Sure, you may write to me any time, but you may have to be quick to catch me.

It seems to me, your qualifications to serve by teaching the people are solid or well-founded. It is

*true that at 30 there is still much living to do, as J.
Krishnamurti found. But that did not stop him. At
that age – and I suppose at any age – one must
face the testing circumstances of the realisations of
truth and/or love. At 30 however, with profound
knowledge already realised, there's a lot of living to
do.*

Yes, your piece on Free Will is correct to me.

*So there you go in Nick – or on you go. Time will tell
but you do have the right stuff as long as you keep
any arrogance at bay. This you have done well
since we first started to speak.*

Barry

***

(26.06.03) Two more people have shown an interest in my
class at work. One has an interest in spirits and mediums (it's
sort of relevant, I suppose); the other said she knows about
the higher and lower 'self'.

I sent another letter to Barry:

Dear Barry,

*Thank you very much indeed for your letter. For
both your time in writing, and for the words.*

*...I am writing so soon after the last letter as you
mentioned I may need to be quick. I wished to tell
you that the one question in my last letter seems to
have answered itself (as is the way when people
write to you).*

*I said I still didn't know what 'The Master' is. A few
days after writing it was suggested to me internally
that if a name is to be given to this experience of*

being the only 'I', 'The Master' would seem to be as good a name as any. This suggestion has stayed with me ever since.

So, as long as I am not deluding myself, this is it. No flashing lights, no levitating or appearing and disappearing. Not even any real answers. I had major expectations as to what 'The Master' means, but there is really not much else it can mean. To be The Master, is to be the only one here (and not just to know it).

It would still be lovely, Barry, to have you here, to lead me deeper into it.

Thank you so much for your love and your Being, as well as your Truth.

I wish you well on your continued journey into the depths of Being.

With love and eternal gratitude, Barry.

Nick

The teaching

(10.07.03) Last week I sent an email to the three people at work who said they wished to come to the Self-Awareness class. I then booked the room in the council building for the next two Wednesdays: 16 July and 23 July 2003.

I told the three people of the dates and one replied saying she is away for the next three weeks, and another said she can't make next week either. Then the last person came to me and said she has family problems so she also may not be able to make it!

So I am left with possibly one person, but probably not, and a room booked for the next two weeks!

I looked at the situation and saw that it was make or break. As it was already arranged, I created a new, updated advert and posted it throughout the council offices, giving the time and date and the room details for the meetings, and would just see whether anybody would turn up.

***

(16.07.03) **The first teaching session**
It was the first meeting this evening. Of the three people who had originally said yes, I knew two would not be here tonight; the third had said yes this afternoon, but later cancelled anyway.

But there was a new person, one who had asked me about it briefly over the counter (when I had been downstairs speaking with the customer services officers) a little while ago, but had not confirmed she would be attending. Her name is Sally.

We sat in the meeting room facing each other, perhaps six feet apart. (There was no point in making it out to be more than it was, with some sort of formal layout. So I kept it light.) I just talked, being 'still' within and directing Sally to connect with the same space within her.

The meeting went very well. Sally described how, having begun with her mind being very confused and hectic, she soon felt very calm. She described feeling a tingling sensation throughout her body. Later she said she felt like she was in two halves: the front being her body, and the back being the space that was expanding.

She very much enjoyed it, but said she would not know how she would ever explain the experience to her friends.

Later she said the two halves became entwined, but somehow still felt like two definite halves.

She added that she was very pleased there was only the two of us! We'll see what happens next week.

***

(17.07.03) The next day I received an email from Sally saying she had suffered with sciatica for some years, and last night she walked to her car free of pain for the first time in a long time, and still today there is no pain.

She said she felt we were destined to meet, as if she knew me, my name, before she'd even seen or heard of me. She said that she had not even been sure she was going to come to the meeting and had completely forgotten about it, but had been getting ready to leave work that evening and a colleague had said to her, 'Sally, aren't you going to that thing tonight?' and she said, 'Oh yes,' and found herself walking up the stairs to the room.

She also said she had tried to speak to some of her colleagues about the experience: some understood some of it; others claimed they did but didn't at all. But she knew this didn't really matter.

***

(21.07.03) Today I received an answerphone message from a lady working for the magazine *What is Enlightenment?* Apparently they were inviting me to join a discussion in London tomorrow regarding one of the articles in the recent

248

magazine entitled 'Can God handle the 21st century?' It is to be the day after tomorrow. But that is the evening of my next teaching class and I can't change that now.

I sent an email saying I would not be able to attend, but did offer my perspective on the subjects up for discussion:

> *I have followed Barry Long's teaching as earnestly as I have been able for twelve years now, and as my own state deepens I find it increasingly difficult to ask any questions, but here goes:*
>
> ### Can God Handle the 21st Century?
>
> *The question seems absurd to me (sorry for any offence caused) as the word 'God' I see as being given to the one Being and intelligence behind all existence, holding it all together and creating the image each moment. Whether God, the intelligence, is creating a sunny day or nuclear holocaust, a blade of grass or nuclear bomb, I don't see where the question is 'Can God handle it?'*
>
> *From the perspective of the God-Realised man or woman in constant contact with the stillness of Being behind all forms, in this space of truth that is (to the experience) eternal and timeless, the question of whether or not this truth can handle the oncoming circumstances of the formal, yet temporary, world is also absurd. Especially in light of the knowledge that it is his/her own world anyway.*
>
> *With regard to the question 'What is Enlightenment?', in my own experience, Enlightenment is the process of shedding attachments to the forms, in favour of uniting with the truth and 'Being' behind all forms. There is*

another term, 'The Master', which marks the point in the process where the individual has reached a level of awareness where s/he is the only one here. Hence the name 'The Master'. There really is only one.

I don't know whether these views would be of any benefit to the discussion. As you know, Barry Long's teaching is about 'Being', not questioning. I am grateful to have recently entered the state which they call 'The Master', and as such see whatever is here and now as existence in its perfect entirety. It will continue to unfold, and I will continue to be, and interact with existence as it progresses.

***

(23.07.03) The second teaching session
Only Sally attended again this evening, despite two of the others saying yes. The third emailed me to say she was too busy. There was one other who had shown interest in the beginning, but didn't attend either.

Sally described how she had had a wonderful week. Said she felt 'Enlightened', and had then asked herself who she thought she was to say that? She had got a book from the library by the Dalai Lama, and understood it! But she did not like the word 'emptiness'; she instead prefers 'stillness'.

She had borrowed Barry's tape 'The way to Enlightenment'. She said she liked some parts; the others she was not sure about.

Having had such a great experience last time at the class, and having had a great week since, and with her being my only student, I was determined for this one to be just as positive for Sally.

So, when we were sitting together talking and going into the space or stillness, I intentionally went as still as I

250

possibly could, knowing that energy would help her go stiller too.

The meeting seemed to go well. She said her heart was pounding and she felt energy was surging all over her body. She said it was so strong she felt she was going to burst.

During the meeting she said that at times in the week she felt she may get lost in the feeling of 'Being' and asked whether this could actually happen. I told her only the mind would get lost, and it was this that was afraid. She, her Being, the one watching the mind, can never get lost. It is the source of all things.

At the end I asked if she would be here next week as well, and she replied that she didn't know!

This blew my mind. I didn't mind the other two not showing, whilst I still had one student. But now this one student, who had been having great experiences beyond her (my?) dreams, was saying she may not come again!

I saw I was becoming, or had become, attached to teaching again. It then occurred to me that perhaps Sally was doing as I had been teaching: when unsure of what to do, do nothing.

***

(24.07.03) I attended a sitting with a psychic at the College of Psychic Studies today. I was curious as this was where it all started thirteen years ago.

I wasn't interested in being told my past or future. I was looking to see if there was anything new from the perspective of spiritual growth.

She told me that I will teach whether I like it or not. And she said I will be a healer. I said I wasn't really interested in healing, more in spiritual teaching. She said that nevertheless, at some point I will be able to heal people by touch alone. She also said I need to teach in order to use the

251

energy and earth myself. ('Earthing' or 'grounding' myself, my energies, has always been an issue for me – as I was originally told at this college thirteen years earlier.)

She said that holding one-to-one meetings will be good, but that I must also write. At times the energy will be too much for the people (as with Sally when she felt like she was bursting). She added that I could work with her if I wanted, or have my own course at the college, and to send my letter and CV if I felt I was ready.

***

(25.07.03) I arrived at work this morning to find an email from Sally, sent yesterday afternoon.

> *Hi Nick,*
>
> *I know that you are not in today but just feel that I have to put this down. It may take me all day to write it and sorry if it's long.*
>
> *The experience this week was very different from last, but I know and understand why you can only learn something new for the first time once. When you felt that we had been talking a lot and not actually sharing feelings or energies, you changed. Staring at me and drawing the energy inside me to the surface was a very powerful thing to do. It felt quite aggressive and wasn't a pleasant experience. I'm not being negative about it. I just want you to know as this is also a learning experience for you (as you have said). It's a powerful thing that you can do but not everyone would be able to go with it or handle it. I feel that it was a little too much for me to take at this time.*
>
> *When I was walking through the car park after the*

meeting, I suddenly became totally aware of my existence. The clouds got darker and the wind was very strong. I felt a deep sense of fear that I could not control. When I got home I just felt I needed to protect myself. I felt physical nausea. The realisation that I am a part of all this was difficult to comprehend.

Today I feel elated and scared at the same time. My energy is flowing quite strongly, though not as much as yesterday. This is not something I feel I want to run away from; I want to go further but need to do it at my own pace and not yours. This is not criticism and I don't want to upset or offend you, but I know that I can tell you without me feeling bad for saying it.

I don't know if I will come next week, I feel I want to talk to you and it's already been decided whether I do or not anyway!!

Hope your meeting with the people you hadn't seen for such a long time went well today and you had a good time. Keep well and I look forward to seeing you on Friday.

Sally

(Sally later described how, when she got home that evening, it felt as though the whole world was closing in on her. She drew the curtains, turned out the lights, disconnected the telephone, didn't even bother to put the television on, and just lay on the sofa in the dark trying to cope with the extreme feelings.)

***

I replied:

Dear Sally,

Thank you for your email. You are absolutely right, as you know.

I apologise for it being too much for you. I wasn't aware that it was possible to give someone more than they can handle. I didn't know I could give anyone anything at all, except their own reflection.

When I met the lady yesterday (she is a psychic at The College of Psychic Studies), she said I will teach whether I like it or not, but she also said it will be too powerful for people at times.

I am truly sorry. It was not my intention to do harm. The intention was to do the very best I could and not to let anyone down. I suppose there was a need in me to recreate some sort of experience for you, so you would not think it had been a waste of time. But I see that there was no need, and I should have let life take its own course and not try to make anything happen. After all, that is the essence of the teaching.

I understand if you do not wish to come again.

The fear will pass. It is the mind seeing you are going to a greater truth than it can give you, and it sees its independent existence is threatened. I am happy to see you before Wednesday if you feel you need a more light-hearted reflection. I know you can't really tell anyone to ask for help, so it may be quite lonely.

I hope things are calmer now.

254

Thank you for your input and honesty.

Love, Nick

***

So it looked like the teaching might be over for now.

Then a short while later one of the other ladies came up to me in the office and said she wished to start attending, in two weeks when she was back from her holiday.

Sally told me she had spoken with the lady (which is why she came to see me, though I don't know what Sally said to her, especially considering the state she was in herself).

In my email reply to Sally I suggested (offered) to let her teach me – to teach. She liked the sound of this. And I told her again that I understood the fear.

***

(26.07.03) I have been shown the next phase:

Whilst sitting in an armchair (in Somerset, visiting family), and seeing that not only was I the 'Being' here, looking at the image (of existence), but I had the experience of my 'Being' being above, and even behind the image. That is to say, the image (of the formal world) was <u>within</u> my Being – not as a knowledge or insight but as a real experience.

Then, as usual for first experiences, it was gone!

It did however minimise the experience of being the only one here. (Being 'everything', and the 'nothing' beyond that, is very different from just being the only one.)

I may call them phases one and two of Enlightenment.

When sitting with my dad in the living room one evening, he stated that he felt I had an air or an atmosphere about me, as if I had done something great – achieved something. He said it did not feel good as it gave the impression I had done something valuable, something important, and was better than others.

I replied that I may indeed have done something great, and he perhaps just didn't know about it; but I took the point, and immediately was able to drop the arrogance, as far as I could see it.

***

(30.07.03) As suggested by the lady at the College of Psychic Studies last week, I sent them a letter offering to hold the talk or meeting looking at Enlightenment/Self-Realisation. When I was there for the spiritual awareness course all those years ago, this was the ultimate aim of the course (perhaps of all the courses), so I hope they will be interested. After all, it was where it all started for me so it would be a nice place to return to.

Sally is working late this evening and then going away on holiday for a week, so there won't be a meeting today.

***

(01.08.03) I received an email from Sally saying everything is AMAZING, and about how calm she felt recently at work, despite being very short-staffed and working very hard. She said it was almost spooky.

Insight: Existence is like being born and brought up in a house. No-one ever leaves this house; instead, they spend all their time eating, sleeping, playing and worrying about the house and where to put things. And arguing with others in the house, fighting with them, etc. No-one ever asks whether there is more than this.

When a person does finally begin to wonder whether there is more than this, they begin by looking in all the cupboards, under the bed, behind the wardrobe, in the attic, etc.

256

Eventually they begin to notice the windows, which are covered in paint. And one at a time they begin to peep through the paint on the glass which is obscuring their vision, seeing a little more each time.

Seeing the outside world through different windows, different views, the person has insights into the 'real world' the others don't have. However, they are still only glimpses.

They may describe what they're seeing to the others in the house, but they will either not be interested or won't believe them. The person begins to peer through more and more gaps in the paint-covered windows, moving from one window to another, fascinated by what they see outside. But still no-one else wants to know.

Over time they develop quite a substantial knowledge of what is outside the house, and are able to describe it in some detail; but nevertheless they are still inside the house.

Eventually, 'Enlightenment' is when the person not only has a clear view through the many windows, but walks out of the front door and away from the house. They then find they no longer have just a view of three hundred sixty degrees, but are also met with all the smells and sounds, etc. that go with it. They are immersed in the experience. Previously, when just glimpsing through the windows, they had a little information which they could relay to the others. Now it is their living truth – their living experience.

However, whilst the person can call back into the house to tell the others, most would not want to know, and most would not believe him (or her) anyway. Only those ready to look out the window for themselves are ready to start the journey.

***

(07.08.03) All is going well. This evening the meeting with Sally was good. Very easy and light. I feel I have nothing to prove, after her experiencing too much too fast. And she stated emphatically that I had nothing to prove to her, and this meant something to me.

Her main question was how to get back the stillness when she loses it. She said her friend did not 'get' it and this affected her, and she had been disturbed ever since.

I lent Sally one of the tapes of Barry's talks at the Gold Coast. We'll see.

***

(13.08.03) I left Elaine this evening, for the last time.

I had had another meeting session with Sally, and one other lady did turn up but left before the end (though she had stayed from 5.30 p.m. to 7.00 p.m. The meetings tended to last two hours). She said it was good but that she needed time to think about it.

Sally and I talked after she left, and I shared that I felt it was strange I was to go on holiday (camping, in a few days) with a lady not at all interested in Self-Awareness, and that she (Sally) would be perfect! (Admittedly I was fishing a little, to see how she felt about things.)

She agreed, and it was said that we both liked each other and would get together if I was not with Elaine.

I did not know in that moment how or when I would end it, but driving home after the meeting I knew putting it off would not make it any easier, and would not be honest or fair on Elaine (as I would be with her but wishing to leave to be with Sally). And it would not be fair on Sally, knowing I was with Elaine, and this may put doubts in her mind about my integrity (I'd been down that road before). And it also would not be fair on me, to spend any more time in a habitual going-nowhere relationship. Especially when Sally had said she wished to be with me, and had been thinking about the possibility, as I had!

258

So I went straight to Elaine's this evening and told her I had a problem: that it looked like Sally and I were going to get together, but added that we hadn't yet, and that it would not be right to go on holiday in two days to Cornwall for two weeks as we had arranged.

It was strange, sitting in Elaine's living room telling her this. I knew it was going to be hard, but I also knew I had absolutely no choice. I just had to get on with it.

So as I sat on one two-seater sofa, with her on the other, talking to her, the experience was literally as if I was observing somebody else saying the words. It did not feel like I was saying it. I wasn't involved at all. The body was just doing the talking.

She immediately packed my things, requested my keys back and gave me mine... It's over!

***

(14.08.03) I emailed Sally this morning, telling her I was no longer with Elaine and that I was now available if she still wanted us to get together.

As I was sending it I knew, from my experience with life, that there was always a chance she might have changed her mind and the situation had just occurred to force me to end it with Elaine and to make a fresh start.

Thankfully this was not the case. Sally did indeed reply saying she hadn't changed her mind and would like us to get together.

***

(18.08.03) I spent the weekend with Sally. It was wonderful! She repeatedly expressed how she had never experienced anything like this before. She even said she now knew she had never 'made love' before, and said I am her first love!

I also introduced her to a few friends in Guildford at the weekend. All went well.

But, as wonderful as it was, it was not all easy! When the emotions have been allowed to play havoc for so many years, doing their own thing, it can take a little while to get them back in check. It is one thing to be open and conscious for two hours once a week, but quite another to do so all day for several days.

By way of example, on the Saturday night when getting ready for bed, I was second in the bathroom. I came out to find Sally in bed, tucked up in the blankets, facing the wall with her back to me. Elaine had done exactly the same thing nine years earlier! I was horrified! Was this it? Was it over by the second night? Our whirlwind passion and my visions of future love extending into the depths of God-Realisation, was it just another of life's teachings for me, showing me I had got attached to the dream, and now it's been taken away...?

It was a tricky conversation. I did my best to explain and describe as much as I could and in the best way that I could, what I had learnt from Barry as well as from my own experience, the difference between conscious love and acknowledgment, and the emotions of sex and excitement. (We had not talked about this before, and she had heard very little of Barry's teaching. So this was all on me):

I explained that in this world of sexual and emotional excitement and unhappiness, love (in the sense of conscious acknowledgement and openness) has been smothered by emotions, and instead of conscious love there is sexual excitement (or the lack of, in the form of indifference, or even rejection, for example).

With the normal situation where the man is unconscious and sexually excited, he has not been able to love the woman consciously. And with the woman being unconscious, largely through not being loved consciously, she too is governed by the emotions. So when the two come together with the possibility of 'making love' (i.e. having sex),

260

there can be the situation where a woman who is emotional (not united within, with her love) is faced with a man who is unconscious (emotional and sexually excited), and her emotions have to decide whether they feel like playing with his emotions. So a person either feels like it, or they do not. (And as we know, even when the two do indeed both feel like it, it is not uncommon for one to receive the physical and emotional fix they desired, and the other not. So one can be left unsatisfied and even more unhappy.)

As we were talking, Sally saw and shared that the whole situation (of us being together, and my being in the bathroom) had reminded her of the times with her (now ex-) husband. And she had indeed closed down and behaved as she always had done with him. She saw that this was not necessary, that this was fresh and new, and we were together in love.

***

(19.08.03) I have noticed Sally's eyes are quickly becoming very still when we look at each other (they would previously be flitting around). She said, when her eyes are still and we're looking at each other, it's almost as if it clicks into place and it feels like (she has the knowledge of) the one 'Being' looking at itself. She even said this morning, when looking in the mirror, she could see the stillness in her own eyes.

We did have to have a discussion though, because I was learning here too about my trying too hard to teach her and help her to remain conscious. It was through a fear that we could fall into a routine and habitual life like everyone else (and as we had, in the past), and we would never get it back. I said I would watch this as well.

We had a funeral this afternoon. It was for Sally's favourite aunt. Sally said she was amazed that she did not feel sad, and when I asked, she agreed that it is as if her auntie is with her, her love within. She knows she has not gone anywhere. (This was something I had seen Barry demonstrate to people a number of times in talks and meetings: uniting them with their love of the person they had lost.)

Sally also said at breakfast today that it feels as if time has stood still. I asked if she knew why she felt like this, and she said no. I explained the space – the love within – is the same space and love that existed a thousand years ago, and will exist in a thousand years to come. It is the intelligence creating all the images, and although out here we have time, and clocks, and work to do, when in touch with the love we know really there is no time.

***

(21.08.03) Sally said each day it gets better and better.

When we wake each morning, I tell her I am so pleased she is here and give her a kiss. She said today it feels like we are melting into each other. I agreed. It feels like we are becoming one and the same. We were shown that we do have to be careful though. The other day I woke to see Sally putting on her dressing gown to go downstairs. I said to her, 'Where are you going?', and she replied, 'I am going down to iron your shirt for work.' I said, 'But we haven't even said good morning to each other yet.'

Sally then pointed out that I hadn't said good morning, or given her a kiss on any of the previous two mornings, so she didn't think it mattered!

I was shocked. I had not noticed that I had let this slip. I don't know how it happened because it had been very important to me. But already, in only a few days, we had begun to take each other for granted; everyday living and the chores of the world had taken over and we had forgotten each other (or I had forgotten Sally, and she had accepted it). We would never let this happen again!

262

I am off work this week: I was due to be with Elaine in Cornwall. Sally is at work so I'm at home (her house; I have not been back to the flat since we got together).

Whatever I am doing, I have the knowledge of her, of her love for me and mine for her. And in that knowledge we are complete and whole. Sally feels the same, and when she described a little to one of her friends at work, they replied, 'Young love, I remember that!' But we are determined to keep the love new, fresh and alive, and not to lose it over time.

Sally met with the other lady (who came to the last meeting) recently and they talked about the classes with me. She said she would like to meet on an ad hoc basis, not the Wednesday evenings. This was what Sally and I wanted too, as we are together and don't need to go there anymore to meet. So that is the end of the classes at work.

***

(22.08.03) Things are still going very well indeed. Sally feels she's getting stronger and stronger – expanding. She is becoming more conscious and less controlled by emotional likes and dislikes. It is as if we're going beyond feelings.

She said yesterday whilst at work, she had the sensation that I was putting my arm around her. Then her thumbs touched each other and it was as if I was touching her. It was very tangible. The constant experience of us being together within her is growing stronger.

This morning just prior to getting up, we were lying against each other and I intentionally went stiller and stiller inside (as I did at that second meeting), and each time I did so she felt the energy increase inside her. It was quite amazing for us both.

I feel I am able to 'read' her eyes more and more. The stillness is there, but when a thought passes through her mind I can see it; though of course I can't read the thought. And whilst I may acknowledge that I've seen it, I do not ask

263

what it is. I have seen that it may have no relevance beyond its passing through, and for me to ask what it is/was can inadvertently give it some validation. (This can also cause problems, if it was not a nice or good thought; so it's better dissolved and got rid of rather than shared and aired.)

I have also noticed Sally's eyes becoming fuller, energetic, and there is an amazing softness in them. Not emotion, just softness – love.

***

(23.08.03) Sally got home yesterday evening and asked whether I enjoyed the cup of coffee at 10.30 a.m. I was puzzled and tried to remember a cup of tea or coffee anytime, and what I was doing at 10.30 a.m.

She smiled: she had been in the staff canteen drinking a cup of coffee and suddenly I was in her too, drinking the coffee; both of us were in her body! This is of course the same experience I had in Australia last year when Elaine was in my body with me, sharing the same space.

I feel it is wonderful and amazing Sally has progressed so far so fast, through our love for each other, and our loving together. Sally has referred to me as her 'tiger'. It's a lovely name. She came home the other evening with a china mug for me with a picture of a tiger on the side, so I would have my own mug at her place.

The mug is white with a colourful drawing of an orange tiger jumping for joy as a beautiful yellow female tiger approaches him, smiling. There are butterflies and flowers all around them. The grass is lovely and green, and there is a beautiful sky. Around the scene is a border: at the sides, top and bottom are triangles in the colours of the tiger, and the four corners of the scene are either the yellow or the female tiger with a black swirl in the centre.

To me, the scene shows what is happening in my life right now and reflects the knowledge that we are one.

264

Sally returned home this evening from her hair appointment to say she feels like we are 'together' physically (making love) even when we are apart, and that she needs to stop doing this when she's driving or she's going to crash! (Though she did say it felt lovely.)

***

(25.08.03) Last night, when I was in bed with nothing on, I had a strange sensation and knowledge that I was wearing a suit: a really smart suit, 'James Bond' style, with a crisp white shirt and a bow tie. It felt wonderful.

Looking at the sensation I saw it may be representative of the power and authority entering me from loving and being loved 'rightly'. And looking at it further still, it was almost like the original idea behind the word 'suit', in its perfect glory and power, and all other suits in existence are an attempt to recreate the power and glory and authority of this original and pristine idea in 'God's mind' of a suit.

When talking about it to Sally, she said she feels what it means to be a 'complete woman'. She feels she is, and must give me everything, and more, as the more she gives, the more she grows.

Later that night when in bed together she had tears in her eyes, and said it was so loving and beautiful. Later I mentioned the words 'making love' in a sentence and immediately tears came to her eyes, as the sensation came over her again.

And later that night she said, *'Sexual man takes what he wants. Loving man gets what he wants because the woman freely gives it!'*

***

(26.08.03) Sally says repeatedly she feels she needs to give me more and more, and just keep giving, opening up, surrendering to love. (And only to love. Not emotional demands.)

However, we noticed that I was finding it hard to relax when we made love, as if after all these years of watching carefully to make sure there was no sexual excitement, no emotional wanting, now it was time to stop watching and trying. To just relax and enjoy it as the work has been done.

Then at breakfast I was reminded that Barry has said at some point the man has to detach from detachment, from his emotional wanting or needing to be more detached than he is already. After so long of focussing on detaching, it is difficult to let go and stop trying, but I feel this is the phase I am entering.

This evening I am still practising relaxing and enjoying not trying (if that's not a contradiction; it does take some effort to break old habits, even when the habits are themselves the dissolving of old habits).

Whilst sitting with Sally on the sofa yesterday, looking at each other (she's getting really good at reading me through my eyes), I felt myself let go of all trying. At that moment Sally expressed amazement! She said I suddenly grew and filled the room. I was the room, and she could see that the room was in me!

I see, as I am writing this, that this is not just her seeing me grow. Whilst I am indeed doing so, her own Being is opening up and she is beginning to see everything as being One. Having already experienced my 'Being' in her body (when we are not together), and now saying I am the room, it looks as if she's nearly there, Enlightened (or at least making huge leaps towards it).

All evening I held the space, doing my best not to hold back, or to want, but to act naturally and easily in the moment. For the rest of the night I felt I could just watch what was there to be watched, feel what was there to be felt, hear

266

what was there to be heard, but I was not actually doing it. The body was just doing what it does.

***

(28.08.03) This evening we watched the film *The Others*, in which Nicole Kidman and her two kids realise at the end of the film that they have been ghosts the whole time. I understood the fear of having one's beliefs shattered with regards to what you are. Then I was given something; the knowledge came to me clearly: *I am walking around in my mind!!!*

I repeated this to myself a few times as the fear grew. I have distanced myself from it so far, by referring to it as God's mind for many years, but as I have already realised there is only one mind, this has to be my mind!

The knowledge was so clear and blunt that it did scare me. I thought I had got past the fear years ago, of being alone, but I now had tears in my eyes.

Then Sally appeared and gave me a big kiss. When I told her what was happening she smiled and said, 'But it's a lovely mind!'

(Note: This can happen a lot on the spiritual path: one has insights followed by realisations, each going deeper and deeper into the truth. And knowledge one already had can take on a new strength, a new dimension with each new insight.)

***

(29.08.03) Sitting with Sally after tea, looking at each other, the stillness was strong and she said she felt her body was about to disappear, and the fear was strong in her to fight to hold on to it.

In my own body the understanding of 'having no personal consideration' (for oneself) has been growing, and I

267

find by looking at what is (here and around me at any moment) and feeling with no words, it's often as if I have no being beyond what is seen and felt.

***

(30.08.03) This morning when lying together in bed, we both experienced the same thing at the same time. It was as if we both lost sight of the other's body; all we could see was the other's eyes. Everything else was like a soft grey mist of energy between us. It felt as if the detachment to the physical was so strong that even the forms were disappearing, but in both of us at the same time.

***

(01.09.03) Elaine met Sally.

Elaine called me this morning and asked that I collect the rest my things. She had heard (from friends) that I was giving up my rented room and was moving in with Sally. We agreed I would pop by this evening.

I actually wanted them to meet, to help Elaine put a face to the situation and for Sally to see my past, so as not to feel threatened by it. Also, if I was ever to be able to see our little King Charles spaniel again, it would help if they had met.

First I met Elaine on my own. She is OK now but has had a tough time since we separated. She agreed she would like to meet Sally, so I collected Sally from our friends' house up the road.

They got on OK, and at the end Elaine said to Sally, 'Take him home!', and we left.

In the car, Sally said she didn't wish to talk for a while. I knew she was upset. Once home she got out of the car and I asked her whether she still wanted me to stay (I could go to my rented room as it was still available to me). She said she did, and began to really cry.

268

We stood in the car park for a few minutes holding each other, with Sally crying. Once inside I asked her if she could tell me exactly what was upsetting her.

She explained that when she heard Elaine describing how she felt and what she went through not knowing exactly where I was for two weeks (though she knew I was with Sally), it was exactly what Sally went through when her husband left her for someone else. And she swore she would never do that to anyone else! She knew Elaine's pain and knew she had caused it, and she could feel the pain she went through five years ago.

***

(02.09.03) Last night, looking at Sally as she faced the situation within, with conscious presence and all the strength she could find, she looked very, very still. She said it felt like she was set in concrete inside.

I also had to spend the day facing the emotional disturbance within me, partly due to the end of the nine-year ordeal, as well as the knowledge of what Elaine had gone through, but also due to the idea of not seeing the dog and cat (with whom I was very close) ever again. (Elaine said it would be harder for her if she saw me, so it would be better if we drew a line under everything and made a clean break.)

I did talk to Sally about the situation. I explained it had all happened in the best way. We/I had done all we could to be as honest as possible to Elaine and to the situation. And meeting Sally would actually make it easier for Elaine (this is something Elaine said herself). We were doing everything for the right reasons and in the best, most loving way possible.

Soon the pain was gone (in me) and by this evening there was nothing left of it at all.

However, there has been the constant knowledge of all that has happened since that Wednesday evening on the way to tell Elaine, prior to Sally and I getting together. As I dissolve it by holding on to it in knowledge but not thinking about it, I seem to grow even more in stillness within.

***

(03.09.03) I likened the situation with Elaine to having an old car and working on it for nine years, lovingly, painstakingly, struggling to make it as good as one can and it is still not right. And then someone comes along and offers a better one, one that is nearly there, and with a little effort will become perfect. The catch is you have to give up the old one.

I have to accept the new one as I can see I have done all I can with the old one, but it is still hard to let it go after all the work and effort I've put in; and it was still a good car!

Sally said there are so many similarities between her house and Elaine's. Even the woodchip wallpaper with fern green paint in the living room; it's uncanny. Then she added that it's almost as if it was nearly right the first time, but not quite.

I agreed that is how it feels to me too. Though I still have the knowledge, the connection, with the one love, the love I made through being with her, within me.

***

(04.09.03) Sally has said more than once that when we are together making love, she feels the energy in me growing and the release of energy is extremely strong. And she continues to feel the energy surging round her body for quite a while afterwards.

Elaine had expressed this only as far as saying it woke her up and she couldn't sleep afterwards. This is the difference between somebody who wants to grow in love consciously and one who does not.

And I now see very clearly, however advanced a person is, s/he cannot do this for another, no matter how

270

much s/he loves them. It is not enough. It must have both devoted to the same cause.

***

(08.09.03) looking at each other this evening, I went very still (intentionally) and my focus on (or ability to see) my surroundings became vague. And at this point Sally announced my eyes had turned from brown to yellow and my pupils were also faint. She said it was as if I had withdrawn and was not there at all. This is of course exactly what had happened.

***

(09.09.03) After making love, Sally asked whether I saw the lights. I asked what lights? She said there were bright lights behind me, like car lights, but one big glow, like in the films when they portray angels!

Then later that night she had a vision of herself approaching the Pearly Gates of Heaven and them opening to accept her.

***

(10.09.03) As well as seeing the glowing lights behind me, Sally explained this morning that during making love it was as if she had no body, as if she was just a space. I also had no physical body to her; I was just energy.

When walking together this morning, she said, 'It's still there!' She explained it was as if she had no body, and yet was aware she was moving. She is becoming pure energy. Love.

***

When sitting on the side of the bed last night, before getting in, I felt a feeling like a spider sliding or crawling across my leg. I looked but there was nothing there.

I looked around the room to see if I could see anything – I had seen programmes with psychics recently, and wanted to see whether I could see any forms. Sally was sitting on the other side of the bed, and asked me what I was looking for. I didn't tell her as I didn't want to spoil (or scare away) whatever it was.

As I sat there, it happened again. Sally was looking at me, puzzled, seeing the expression and question in me. And then I felt the whisper or light touch slide over my thigh again and she suddenly jumped and clutched her side. She felt it too!

She was shocked and amazed, and looked around on the bed to make sure there was nothing there. She said it was as if this hand had moved across my leg, across the bit of bed between us and over her side. She found this more disturbing than almost any other experience, as it was so definitely real and unexplained.

(Note: I have no explanation (even as I write this in 2016). It occurred to me that it was definitely a psychic experience rather than a spiritual one. 'Truth' is the 'Being', the love, and this was not that. This was more physical, more definite, as if something was touching us from without. I thought that had there been a psychic in the room with us (physically, a real-life person), perhaps s/he would have seen an entity connecting us both. There was no malice in the touch, and no emotional feeling in us – just amazement.)

***

(20.10.03) I received a reply from the College of Psychic Studies regarding my offer to teach Self-Awareness and Enlightenment at the college. They advised me that they had carefully considered my proposal at a recent meeting, and whilst they can see that I am highly skilled and trained in this area, and that it is valuable work, they do not feel it is quite right for the programme as they are now focussing more on psychic development.

I feel this is a shame. I thought this would be a perfect environment for me to share with others who are seriously on the path, earnestly searching. At the same time it seemed an opportunity for me to give something back to the college. Oh well.

***

Sally is developing quickly in all areas, but it was not an easy process at first. It involves – requires even – that one be as conscious and aware as possible at all times, not only of the physical body and what is going on around it, but of any emotional movement within. And when an emotional disturbance does arise, rather than permitting it to do whatever it wants, to have whatever it wants, one treats it like one would treat a spoilt child that needs to be put in its place.

The trouble is this child is now in the body of an adult and has had its own way for a very long time, and is very strong. Inevitably it objects angrily to being questioned, or even for its existence to be pointed out at all, come to that. Its strength has been in its ability to act as a sort of puppet master, controlling the person from behind the scenes. But point out to the person that they are being emotional, that they are being controlled by the emotions, and they cannot help (being under the control of the puppet master) defending themselves and their position. This can be from the smallest thing to the biggest thing. It doesn't matter what it is relating to. It is amazing how we have given total control of our lives to the emotional puppet master. And regaining control is inevitably a painful process.

It takes a great deal of inner strength because, just as the emotional puppet master has taken control, it has entwined itself with the person's personality and sense of identity. Most people would not know where the division lies.

And if they're not feeling unhappy about something, most would deny that they were emotional at all. They do not know that this emotional puppet master is controlling everything they think, say and do, each and every moment!

The process of disentanglement, or separation, can literally feel like a death. And it's not just a one-off experience. It can happen several times a day, all day or night, for weeks, months or years. But with each situation in which the person is able to remain conscious and regain that bit of their true nature, they regain that bit of energy, that bit of love. And in that way they grow in love and consciousness with each and every experience. But it isn't easy!

***

Sally has been making huge progress at work as well. She has noticed how she used to approach members of staff (in her capacity as an officer and manager) to ask them to do something, with emotion in her, expecting a fight before she even got one. And of course, inevitably, she did get one. And so the cycle would continue.

This new knowledge, regarding facing and dissolving emotions, and not giving in to them within herself, has also made her stronger with other people, and she went through a period of several weeks at work which unsettled quite a few of the staff. She was no longer approaching them expecting an emotional battle. She was approaching them with strength and confidence and with the knowledge that she was not going to give in to their emotions any more than she did her own. But this strength was a cold, hard strength – an unmovable energy. Some people became distressed at this, but that wasn't her problem. They were their emotions; they were their problem! (I of course recognised this, as I had been through this very thing. For me it lasted about ten years!)

Thankfully it did not last very long for Sally. After only a few weeks she was finding it easier to face and dissolve the emotions within herself, which meant she began to soften in her approach and attitude. She was still able to have the same detachment from an emotional perspective when speaking with the staff, but she developed an empathy and an acknowledgement of what they felt and went through. This meant not only was she not affected personally, emotionally, by their feelings, but she was able to express an understanding of them nevertheless. Suddenly everything became easy. Relationships at work became easy. Managing the staff became easy. And it wasn't long before the old Sally was little but a distant memory for those who had known her for years. Now Sally was the go-to person for anything and everything. She even found she didn't have to ask anybody anymore to do anything. People knew what needed to be done and would come to her and offer.

***

(28.10.03) I wrote the following essay today:

Mud-tinted Spectacles

People talk of rose-tinted spectacles, saying this applies to anyone who sees life in a positive, joyous way. But I see the truth as being the opposite.

The Being inside the person is free from problems and troubles. It is not attached to the issues of the world, the goings-on, with all the pain and struggle. The 'Being' is the original state of the individual before s/he becomes attached to their physical life.

The person then sees his/her life through these attachments, their hopes and fears, beliefs, opinions, likes and dislikes, and all his/her past hurts and pains, and suddenly the physical world becomes a hard, cruel, painful place, in which we each do our best but no-one really enjoys anything for long.

These attachments I am calling 'mud-tinted spectacles'. Take them off (that is, let go of your beliefs, opinions, likes and dislikes; in fact, all of your attachments, and just be where you are and what you are feeling now), and you are in touch with the 'Being', your Being, behind all the problems. Here you are free; that is, until you allow your mind to take you away and focus on something separate from the Truth. Anything imagined cannot be the Truth, and holding on to any belief, judgment or past fear is not the Truth.

What is true is whatever you can see in front of you now, and the Truth is the space inside you, the space you feel when you are aware that you exist now. Take off your mud-tinted spectacles and be where you are, and you will be free, wherever you are.

***

(21.11.03) I took Sally up to London to listen to a talk by an established spiritual teacher (the same one I had been to previously). I wanted her to see the 'competition', and it was very similar to the last one that I had attended; I wasn't impressed and neither was Sally.

This teacher did announce that whilst being around Enlightened people can put you into a deep state of Being, his enlightenment is the modern enlightenment, which looks to the future of mankind in the world.

I could see this idea would be more acceptable to the majority of people, but it was not the 'Truth'. To the Enlightened person, the world is within their own Being. The world is a projection, a manifestation, of their own emotional self, presented in form so they may interact with it and learn. Focussing one's attention on improving the world outside may be very noble but it is not Spiritual Enlightenment.

276

I was sitting at the computer one evening, conscious and aware as always, when I suddenly noticed something was missing! There was no feeling in it! All this time, when 'aware' (of being aware), there would be something to hold on to, some sensation; but now, whatever that something was, I couldn't find it.

For a few moments I wondered whether something had gone wrong; was I not doing it right? What had happened?

But then I noticed that I was still aware, so I clearly was still doing it right. As long as I could say (and *mean*) 'I am', that's all I could do. Then I remembered Barry always said that 'Being' has no feeling. This was it!

***

(29.11.03) Sally and I have had many experiences together over these months.

We recently visited her parents in France and we slept in their old room upstairs. They had moved their bedroom downstairs into the dining room as Ivy had had a back operation and couldn't manage the stairs.

Both Sally and I had a tough time with nasty dreams of being attacked. Sally even dreamt she died and was standing over her dead body!

Barry has described how unhappiness can get into the walls of a building, and psychics say this too: that the psychic imprint is left behind. I asked Sally whether her mum had had a tough life. She replied that she didn't know. She said her mum had lived for a couple of years as a child with a man who was later found to have been sexually abusing his own daughters. I asked whether it was likely that Sally's mum was also abused whilst she was there. She said she had never considered it, but added that it would explain a lot about her mum: the fear of the dark, the fear of being alone and the fear of sex.

The room had an awful feeling to it and made us both feel very uncomfortable for the two or three nights we were there.

***

(06.12.03) Barry Long died. It is said that the Master will appear outside when the person is ready. And Barry also taught that the Master – he, Barry – is only outside until the person has realised the Master within themselves. I would have liked Barry to stick around longer, so I could have shared with him what I was doing, what I was learning, how I was growing. But he was no longer needed. The Master outside was no longer needed. It is within.

Going public

Sally and I wanted to begin teaching again, outside of the work environment. The first thing to do was to set up a website. Everyone seemed to have a website.

So we bought the domain name, chose a package, and set out learning how to use a basic WYSIWYG software ('What You See Is What You Get', which looks and behaves like an MS Word document, enabling one to write on the page, change fonts, colours, add pictures, insert tables, etc., and the programme writes the html code). The first few attempts were very basic and clunky, and we made all the common mistakes of first-timers, such as inserting pictures full-size and then dragging a corner in to make them smaller. (We soon learnt that this meant the original information was still stored on the page, and in the days before broadband this made the page very slow to load.) We also did not standardise the font on the website, thus it would change from page to page, sometimes even on the same page.

Then we learnt that what we see on a computer at home is not necessarily what other people see on their computer; we had set our default font on our PC to a certain type and this meant we would see it as this on our home PC regardless of what it was set to on the website. We also learnt that pictures would be invisible to anyone else if we linked to a folder on our PC and not on the server. And at times, even when all was perfect, the browser could take a little while to refresh the page, and we thought it was not working when in fact it was fine. (At times it was a bit of a mess.)

But we persevered and it got better and better. (Every couple of years or so we started again with an entirely fresh layout, enabling us to remove many inherent issues with each attempt.) The content on it grew and grew. I was writing a lot of my insights under various headings on different pages, and it was not long before we had quite a sizeable website.

***

281

I then went on to the Internet forums to let people know about us and the website. This was an interesting experience. I had, rather naively, assumed everyone would want to hear what I had to say! After all, my only experience of spiritual people was at the Barry Long seminars and we were all like-minded. But on the forums it was very different. Everybody wanted to give their opinion. Everybody wanted to be the one to tell others the truth. It was all about one-upmanship, and it was quite uncomfortable. A few memorable examples include:

I started on spiritual forums, which I thought were a safe bet. But the fashion at that time was for an Indian teaching or philosophy called Advaita, and the way the people seemed to understand or learn this was to repeat, almost hypnotically, 'There is nobody here' and 'This is nothing happening to no-one!' (The latter being designed to sound clever rather than just exhibiting poor English). And these comments would be the reply regardless of what I said or asked. So even if I asked them whether they had any experiences relating to what they were saying, the reply would always be that there was no-one here to have experiences. This led to a lot of frustration. How could I teach these people?

My next stop was to join a Buddhist forum, in the assumption that everybody would be delighted to speak with an Enlightened person, with the word 'Buddha' meaning 'Enlightened one', and all of the members of the forum supposedly looking for Enlightenment. I started a thread and announced that I was Enlightened. People began to post challenges to me, asking me questions they thought I wouldn't understand, and I was able to answer all of them in my own direct experience. The trouble was of course, none of my experience related directly to Buddhist teachings, and it was Buddhist teachings they were following. It was not long before the moderators closed the thread, posting a note saying that whilst I may indeed have something, I did not follow Buddhist teachings and the forum was for Buddhist teachings.

As a final attempt I joined a forum on philosophy, again assuming people posing philosophical questions would want to know the answers. I was of course very wrong! Every post of mine was removed by the next day. At first I thought there was an error and so would re-post my message, and again it was quickly removed. After a few days of this, when I finally realised it was not a glitch, I emailed the moderators asking what was going on, asking was it really the case that people could ask questions but no-one was allowed to answer them? I didn't receive a reply but suddenly my membership was removed.

***

So we gave up with the forums and began to look for something more formal. I approached the organiser of a psychic/holistic show and offered to give talks at his events free of charge, giving me the experience, and he would have something else to offer visitors. It was agreed and we did this for a few events in the south.

These talks enabled me to record a couple of CDs, based on what I had been asked at the shows. We bought ourselves an inkjet printer which printed directly on to CDs, and made them ourselves. Then we noticed the ink on the CDs could smudge (as it was water-based) and worked out that if we sprayed them with art and craft varnish it would seal them. We then sold these at later talks. We also created a PayPal account and were able to sell them online through our website.

Working for the local authority, we knew about the adult education scheme. Sally had also attended a couple of classes herself in the past. So we filled in the forms, attended the interview and began teaching through the county council. We ran a couple of weekly meetings running for perhaps ten weeks, and perhaps three one-day events on a Saturday. The longer courses seemed quite successful, but the Saturday classes seemed to be attended mostly by people who were looking for something interesting to do on a Saturday afternoon, rather than those really wanting to know about the purpose of life and how to grow in consciousness.

We were then invited to go to Leeds and talk to an Eckhart Tolle discussion group. We accepted. It was quite a long way to go and would mean staying overnight, but it was nice to get started. The first meeting had about forty people, and was apparently very well-received. We went twice more after that with numbers dwindling each time, so much so that it wasn't worth doing again. It seemed that some people really 'got it' – but to such an extent that they didn't feel the need to come back. Then there were those that didn't get it and/or didn't want it, and therefore didn't come back. So we were pretty much left with a few who wanted an argument and/or would turn up to any spiritual talk to give their opinion.

Whilst we were giving the talks, we were recording them digitally. This enabled me to tidy them up later and put the talks on to CD. By this time we had found a company to make and print them for us.

We also made a friend online who was a graphic designer who created the CD artwork for us, with photographs he had taken himself in Canada.

***

We saw there was a community centre in the village near where we lived where various courses and events were regularly held, so we wondered whether we should offer a regular weekly meeting for anybody local who was interested. We would keep it more 'light', more focused on meditation (which was popular). I didn't actually do a lot of meditation personally, but as 'mindfulness' is an extremely popular form

284

of meditation, and was what I was doing all the time, it was a pretty easy thing for me to teach.

We booked an inexpensive room for a couple of months ahead and reserved it for a few successive weeks (so we could see how it went). We created posters and fixed these to the various notice boards in the area, and waited.

We held three sessions in total, with only about three or four people coming each time, but they seemed to be mostly people who just wanted to get out of the house for the evening. This was not for us.

***

Sally and I had been together a few months when we took our second trip down to stay with my family in Somerset for a couple of days. We went out for a meal to the local pub with my dad and stepmum, in celebration of their anniversary, along with my sister who was also staying with them for the weekend.

It was a meal like any other. And we were keeping the conversation light when suddenly my dad asked, 'So what is this Enlightenment stuff about anyway?' It had been many years since I last spoke with them about it; there had really been no point. The conversations always took a turn for the worse. I had sent them our first CD several months earlier, which I didn't think they would necessarily listen to, but at least it was there if they were interested. But now I was being asked directly what it was all about. So here I went:

I started by saying simply that it is realising that 'I' am 'at One' with everything.

My dad immediately replied, 'I don't think I'm at one with everything!', to which I said, 'Maybe you don't claim to be spiritually Enlightened,' and then followed it quickly with, 'but in the end they are only words; the words mean different things to different people!' But it was too late! The damage had been done!

I forget who said what, because they were all talking over each other at us, but each was trying to make their point and show us where we were going wrong in our lives.

This was by no means new to me. My family telling me (telling anyone, come to that) that I am wrong was a regular experience. And as usual, I just sat quietly, watched and listened. I knew that after a few minutes (when the emotion in each had said what it wanted to say), things would calm down again and it would all be forgotten. But for Sally, such behaviour was not a common experience. She was not used to other people telling her (or me) that we were wrong and that we should change the way we think and the way we live our lives (and with such negative emotion). And she let them know it.

She told them she was appalled and disgusted at the way they were behaving; that we had done nothing wrong but come down to see them, and had been friendly and helpful to them, and we had done nothing to justify an attack like this! It shocked them so much that my sister even remarked to Sally, 'I can't believe how angry you are!'

We finished the visit, going home the next day as planned, but the matter was dropped there and then and not mentioned again that weekend.

Once home, I certainly felt no need to make contact. Sally had been absolutely correct. I had been brought up 'to do as I am told' and 'not answer back', and actually this had kept the relationship relatively civil all these years. We were so different, that if I was to speak up and 'be myself' with them, we'd probably never speak again. As it happened, it took Sally – a new person, an outsider – to see and expose what was going on.

We had no contact with my dad and stepmum for about twelve months after that. At which point my dad did actually phone, and said, 'Let's make a pact to never talk about your Enlightenment stuff ever again!' To this day we still haven't.

***

We saw an advertisement for a week-long New-Age event which would take place in Surrey not far from us, near the end of 2004. Those attending would be staying on campus, with activities, talks and entertainment going on all day. The people giving talks and teaching classes would not be paid but would receive free entry to the whole event.

We, not living far away and having fulltime jobs, and not being what would be regarded as typical 'New Age' types, did not wish to attend any of the other events. So we agreed for our talks to be at 5.30 p.m. every evening (after work), finishing at 7.00 p.m.

It was mildly interesting, but also clear that we were in the wrong place. For example, we were challenged over why we were not telling people to go and save the whales! I explained that I was not telling them *not* to go and save the whales; I was only suggesting, whatever one does, that one is conscious whilst doing it.

We gave the talk every evening, but did not book for the following year.

***

In 2004 we decided it was time to write a book. It would be a how-to guide, describing in simple terms (as simple as I could make it) the process of reaching Enlightenment. And we called it *Enlightenment, The Simple Path*.

The writing process itself was quite simple: Sally would give me a list of suggested subject titles or questions, and I would run upstairs to the office and pick and choose which one to answer next, and type out the page. It took four weeks to write the book; the information was just flowing.

287

I then met online with Nitin Trasi, author of the book *The Science of Enlightenment*. Nitin was a doctor living in India who was also Enlightened. We became good friends and he agreed to do the foreword for our book.

However, getting it published was not so easy. After being rejected several times by publishers, we had to go for the self-publishing route. This was simpler but meant we had to pay. Thankfully there is the relatively new technology, print on demand (POD), which means that when a book is ordered, one copy is printed, thus avoiding the previously common problem of authors (or publishers) having boxes of unsold books in storage. Another good friend whom I had known for many years created the artwork for the original cover from a basic design I scribbled down, and the book was available in 2005.

***

We heard via the Internet forums about a teacher who gave talks in North London. We would be in the area that day, so thought we'd pop by for a listen. I had heard about him from the people on the forums who were practising Advaita, and I wanted to hear for myself what this teacher was saying.

And true enough the chap did indeed start off by stating, 'There's nobody here, and "This" is nothing happening to nobody!'

He then looked over to a lady in the audience who was crying. He said to her, 'Do you know why you're crying?' When she shook her head, he replied simply, 'You are crying because you are identified with being here, and there is nobody here! When you see this, there will be no crying because you will know there is no-one here to cry, and nothing to cry about!'

I was amazed. I had spent so many years facing and dissolving emotion, learning in my own experience how the mind and emotions work, and how one's emotional self is

288

what determines the circumstances of one's life. And here was this teacher simply telling people they're not here. That seemed to be the sum of his teaching.

Then another member of the audience said he had booked to go on the chap's retreat in a few weeks, and asked whether there was any point in him going. 'None at all!' was the reply. (Which admittedly was quite amusing, but I didn't feel it was very helpful.)

He went on to say, 'These so-called "teachers of Enlightenment" don't know that there is no-one to be Enlightened and no-one to teach!'

Now, I knew the point he was trying to make with the last statement. It was indeed true to me to that ultimately this is all 'One Being' – one's own Being (to me). But surely one still has to play the game, whilst one is here? And surely he was doing just that, by booking a hall, advertising his event and then talking to this audience. Here he was criticising teachers for teaching 'as there is nobody here to teach' to an audience who had paid to listen to him teach them about not being here. This seemed to us to be at the very least a little hypocritical, if not contradictory.

***

A couple of people approached us online and asked if I would help them with their new spiritual websites by writing articles for them on Enlightenment. This I did, sometimes submitting quite a number of pieces. But after an initial splash when each website was launched, all would seem to go quiet and I would not hear anymore; on occasion noticing I had been apparently demoted, dropping off the list of main topics as they found new and 'more interesting' or 'more prominent' people to work with.

***

By the end of 2005 we had noticed our own website was now extremely large – more than enough to make another book. Many of the essays and articles were taken down, and with the addition of a few more esoteric pieces they were put into a second book entitled *Essays in Truth, Glimpses into Reality* and was made available in 2006. I had recently read a book called *The Jesus Mysteries* by Timothy Freke. I very much enjoyed the book and it was in line with my own understandings. I contacted Tim and he was extremely kind to do a few words for the back of the book for me.

By now the self-publishing company we had used for the first book had gone out of business, so we took this opportunity to set up our own publishing company, registered the name 'NR Publishing' and completed the agreements with the printers. We did it all ourselves. We also re-released the first book which was now out of print due to the demise of the other company.

***

Having seen advertisements for teachers who had spoken at The Theosophical Society, we approached the society in June 2006 and gave a talk at their venue in London, under the heading 'The Journey of Self-Discovery'. This seemed to go well and the room was full, but they could only allow me a little under ninety minutes (if only so it fitted on the cassette), and this was never enough for me. Therefore, everything was cut a little short, a little rushed, and less than satisfactory to me.

At the end, the organiser thanked me and said to the audience that it was 'interesting'; but I felt that it was not their 'thing'.

***

We also submitted an article to the magazine *Healing Today* which was published in the August-October 2007 edition. A

290

number of people contacted us for advice and help after reading that.

We continued to look for avenues through which to teach. But generally, teaching and getting the message out seemed to be falling a little flat – not at all what I had expected.

***

At some point during this period, I became intrigued with the idea of personally speaking with 'dead people'. It was perhaps around the time when the series *Most Haunted* was beginning to make a major impression. So Sally and I spent one evening a week for a few weeks visiting a spiritualist church. (It was just a class run in a village hall.) I wanted to know whether we could do it ourselves.

We were only there for a few weeks and the experiences we had were limited. But there were a couple worth noting:

Sally was sitting opposite a lady, looking to 'read' her (the teachers would say we were waiting for a message from the other side, but we didn't see it this way), when she described to the lady that she felt she wanted to wrap her in a pink baby's blanket. The lady confirmed that she had only recently had a miscarriage! It had been a girl!

Mine was less dramatic: I was sitting opposite another lady and was supposed to describe her house. In my mind's eye, I saw a picturesque image of a white cottage with the traditional windows and a white picket fence. Again, she said this was exactly right.

However, as interesting as this was, it was not for us and we stopped attending.

***

(18.09.09) It was my sister's wedding. I was sitting in the garden area with my stepfamily (on my mum's side), when my dad walked up and sat down with us and introduced himself:

'Hi, I'm David, Nick's dad!' And immediately followed it with, 'Nick has never achieved anything, you know!'

'Oh come on, David, that's not true!' one of them replied, shocked and amazed at the statement.

'Oh yes it is! He's never achieved anything!'

They didn't know what to say to this, and that was the end of the conversation.

***

Relationship-wise my life was now perfect: I was with a wonderful woman who was growing in love and consciousness, becoming the 'One Love' as I had been taught and was now living; I had become the 'One Being', inside; we had set up a website; had four CDs; published two books; written articles; and had given various one-to-one meetings and held various talks and courses. Looking at this list, one would have thought the spiritual journey, my spiritual story, was complete. But this was far from being the case.

Between 2003 and 2013, the period during which the above list of 'achievements' happened, I was to come to understand what Barry referred to in his last letter to me:

'...one must face the testing circumstances of the realisations of truth and/or love... there's a lot of living to do.'

Facing the testing circumstances

I started work at the council in March 2003. It was as a rent officer for council properties. So far I had not had an easy time work-wise and was hoping things were going to change. I had been back from the last Master Session in Australia a few months and was hoping this was a fresh start, the start of an enjoyable period in my life.

I picked it up quite quickly, both the computer systems and the chasing of people for money, but I didn't like it. It's not what one would call a positive job; the constant threats to families that they may lose their home if they do not bring the account up to date (something many had heard many times before) was not pleasant. This was made more frustrating by the fact that for the vast majority of people their rent arrears were due to their lack of ability or motivation to fill in a form to apply for benefits, or their failure to supply the documents required in support of their claim; or they simply failed to respond to the housing benefit department when they tried to contact them for clarification of a point. The result of this was families with no money, no means to raise the money, entitled to full housing benefit, in rent arrears due to their inability to work within the system.

I would have to take them to court for rent arrears, fully aware of the situation; and the courts, not wishing to make a family homeless, would agree for them to pay less than two pounds per week to clear the arrears, which by this stage would regularly exceed a thousand pounds. Often the same people would be in the same situation time and time again, each time being given the same court order (Suspended Possession Order), and each time giving the same promises that it wouldn't happen again. No judge wanted to make a family homeless. And so it went on.

I was managing OK for quite a while. There were three rent officers managing the four thousand rent accounts. We were giving evidence in court every other week and due to our efforts the total arrears figure was reducing every two-week cycle.

But then one of my colleagues applied for and got the housing officer position (I applied for it as well, but he had a lot more experience than I had at the council), and instead of replacing him, his work was shared between me and the other remaining rent officer. And that's when the problems started for me.

Within a few weeks I knew I was struggling. I told my managers I was falling behind: I was not able to get through the entire list of those in arrears before it was reissued two weeks later. I was developing quite a pile of cases needing to be applied to court, but court applications took me some time, and in the same length of time that it took me to do one court application I could send a lot of letters or make a lot of phone calls. So as a result, people were not going to court and the accounts with big arrears kept piling up. But my managers weren't concerned. They just told me to keep going, as I was doing fine – but I knew I wasn't. I began blind-copying the manager of the human resources department into my emails to my manager asking for help. I didn't want HR to step in until I knew I could not take any more, but I wanted them to know the history for when I did finally approach them.

Months went by and I felt like I was becoming ill. The symptoms were difficult to describe but I knew I wasn't coping. And yet all my emails to my managers (I'd send one every couple of months saying I was struggling) would be met with the same answer: 'You're doing fine. Keep going!'

Eventually, perhaps a year later, after having been in the position for nearly three years in total, I started having spontaneous and fast-flowing nosebleeds. These occurred several days in a row on getting up in the morning. This was now getting serious! Finally, I approached HR and said I had had enough. The next day my line manager took me to one side, said she was to have a meeting with HR that day and

296

made it clear that she was not happy that I'd been to them to ask for help.

I sat at my desk all morning wondering what was going to happen. But I was confident that finally I would get the help that I needed.

A couple of hours later my manager came to my desk, stood over me, and told me that she had met with the HR person and had told them that nothing would change; I would carry on as I was. As far as she was concerned that was the end of the matter.

I was in shock. If HR could not help me then it seemed no-one could.

The next day I went to the doctor and was signed off with 'high blood pressure due to stress at work'. I was off for three months.

***

Whilst I was off I realised how ill I really was. The symptoms were so varied and each individual symptom may have meant little, but when put together as a package it was quite extreme. And with high blood pressure having the label 'the silent killer' (and I had a lot of time to investigate it while I was off), I had to accept certain possibilities.

One day during the first few weeks I watched the movie *Dragon*, the true story of the life of Bruce Lee. And at the end I sat there stunned. The similarities to my own life were too numerous, too blatant to ignore.

His perspective was a spiritual one: unique, non-traditional and philosophical. He struggled with not fitting in (first due to being Chinese, and then with the Chinese for teaching Westerners their secrets). He tried to improve himself by going to college and began teaching whilst he was there. One of his first students was his wife-to-be, Linda. He had been badly injured aged twenty-four, and Linda helped him write and publish his first book. Then in 1970, aged thirty, he made the film *Big Boss*. He died in 1973, aged thirty-two, three weeks prior to the release of his first big movie *Enter the Dragon*.

So here I was, also aged thirty-two, also a new spiritual teacher who had struggled with not fitting in throughout my life. I too had struggled during my twenties; I had tried to improve myself by getting a traditional job, aged thirty, and had also started a teaching class; my first student was to become my partner, and she too had helped me write and publish my first book (which was complete in all but the copy for the back cover), and now I was seemingly, potentially extremely ill, and was sat watching the story of this person who died the year that I was born. Was I to go the same way?

The hardest bit to cope with as I considered this (more so than my own, apparently imminent demise) was imagining Sally having to complete the book. She would have to write the words for the cover and I was imagining her having to do so, and what she might say. This was difficult. I did not want to put Sally through that.

***

Perhaps the amazing thing throughout the entire experience was that I still knew that 'I', the 'One Being' that is here and that I had realised as myself, was responsible for it. I did not know why 'I' was doing this, but I knew it was all 'me'. There was no-one else to blame.

And during those months I continued to answer emails enquiring about Enlightenment and taught as if nothing was happening.

***

I spent a lot of my free time whilst off work at a local gym. The doctor had said exercise was good, so I spent a few hours a day working out. This seemed gradually to help.

Perhaps midway through the three months, when I was still a little delicate, I was sent my annual competency review paperwork by the council. It showed that when I had taken on the extra work a year before, and we had been told we would be put on a higher pay scale to reflect the extra work, the manager had actually lowered my competency so I got no benefit from the higher pay scale as had been implied; and now that I was off sick and had not coped with the additional work it had been lowered further still. So now I was on a protected salary as a result of being given half the work again and not having coped. I had asked for help for an entire year and was ignored, and was now so ill that I didn't know what the future held (or whether there would be a future at all), and I was being penalised for this financially as well!

Shortly after this, the lady from HR visited us at home. She said it looked like it was not appropriate for me to return to the position of rent officer, but as the only other vacant position in the council was as a kitchen porter, on a far lower salary, I would have to take this job or I wouldn't have a job at all! This was also tough to hear. I had done absolutely nothing wrong besides work hard and put everything I had into doing so!

However, a couple of months later another position did come up. It was as a neighbourhood officer. This position was dealing with the public in a more positive capacity: helping them with their waste and recycling, managing the grounds maintenance contract in my specific area of the borough, and working closely with the councillors and public alike. It held a similar pay scale to my current/past position, and my experience and transferable skills seemed to make it a good fit. I could step straight into it.

I was still quite fragile even after three months off, but it was time to get back to work. The agreement for me to have this role, which had only just been created, was made between the HR person and the team leader. The manager of the department had been on leave and his first day back at work was my first day in the department, and he made it very clear that he was not happy I had been given the post. My first meeting with him was across a table and he said, 'Other people would have liked this position! Can you handle that kind of pressure?!'

Despite the managers creating the post – presumably because they wanted someone to fill it – it seemed they did whatever they could to make me feel as unwelcome as possible. I was on a three-month probation period, and I could tell early on that the plan was for me to fail the probation so they could get rid of me. So instead of trying to help me learn the role, I was told to sit at a desk in the corner on the other side of the office away from the team, and look at the folders and files in the shared drive on the PC and read the documents there. That was to be my training!

Knowing what they were up to, but also knowing that I needed the job, I could not let that happen. So I would often ask to tag along with other members of the team when they went on visits so I could learn the role. This worked for a few days before the manager noticed and told me to stop asking to go out with other members, because they were too busy to train me!

But I kept asking and kept going out, and bit by bit I did learn the role.

Nevertheless, in each of the monthly progress meetings they would pull me up on the most ridiculous of things (because they had nothing else): being too quick to answer the phone, or helping other people when I should be sitting at my computer reading the (mostly outdated) documents. But I knew I had to put up with this if I was to get through it.

After three months they had to agree that I had actually done very well (despite their efforts to the contrary), but they still weren't quite sure. So my probation was extended for a further three months, and after this I was given the position permanently.

It was far from easy though. Even once I'd passed the probation, the management style was extremely strict: micromanaging, hypercritical, judgmental, with very little praise of any sort. Whilst I no longer had the stress of the workload, and the work itself was positive, the restrictive management style produced its own stress. But I persevered.

***

I had been in the department for a few months when I noticed how slowly everybody seemed to be talking. It was like they were in slow motion and it seemed really strange to me. (I realised later this was an indication of how I was still 'racing' inside. The stress was still there.) Shortly after this we had a two-week holiday in Majorca. Sitting on the plane on the way there, totally conscious and aware and feeling my body, I felt energy surging through me. My mind was not racing. My mind was still. But the energy was very strong and very fast all through me. It took a few days of doing almost nothing on holiday before I was able to slow down. By the second week, I could feel the energy no more. By the time I got back to work I was speaking the same speed as everyone else (though the environment would inevitably take its toll again, as time passed).

***

Months went by and I continued to face and deal with the situation at work. It was still difficult, and yet I knew it was still me doing it, and I still had to go through it, for whatever reason.

Every so often I would have to tell people that I was struggling again, be it my managers or HR. Having already got stress on my work history and knowing that no-one would help me until they really were forced to, I was not afraid to tell them when I was finding it difficult. This happened a few times over the next few years. (Though I don't think I got much help. It's more difficult to ask for help when the problem is the manager's style of management.)

Eventually Sally and I decided it might be good for me to go down to working four days a week. It was getting too much again. By now we had bought a weekend retreat at a holiday park by a lake, but only being there each weekend was not proving enough time for me to de-stress. We would arrive Friday night, grab some tea, watch a little TV and go to bed. On Saturday we would do a few odd jobs and perhaps a bit of shopping, and then settle down for the evening before going to bed again, knowing the next day was Sunday. And Sunday would be spent preparing mentally for Monday.

The council was trying to save money by inviting staff to reduce their hours, and many people in other departments had done exactly that. But I knew my manager may not look favourably upon it. Nevertheless, I submitted a request and, as expected, it was rejected. The reason given for the rejection was that we would soon be going through a staffing restructure. I would try again later.

***

Despite the difficulties, outside of work I continued to teach. The second book was published and I gave a number of public talks, wrote articles, and met people for one-to-ones. To anyone looking in, all seemed perfect. And, intuitively at least, I would say it was perfect. I would acknowledge that I was struggling emotionally, finding it difficult to slow down and enjoy 'being'. But I also knew that, for whatever reason, it was necessary and that 'I' was doing it. I just didn't know why, and hoped it wouldn't go on too long.

***

I had now been with the council for about seven years and had always had my own desk. Several years earlier, when I was still a rent officer, it had been agreed that I could have the light turned out over my desk. After all, there were a hundred fluorescent strip lights in each open-plan office, so it didn't really affect anybody else if one bulb was disconnected. But with hot-desking this changed. With my sitting at a different desk each day, in a different part of the office, and with my not being allowed to stand on the desk each day to turn a bulb on and off, the managers became frustrated at several bulbs being off around the office and told me they all had to stay on. When I objected, saying it affected my eyes, they said in that case I would have to go and see occupational health.

As I waited to see occupational health I wanted to prepare for the meeting. So I did a search online looking for possible reasons for my sensitivity to the fluorescent lights. One thing that came up a couple of times was dyslexia. The first time I saw this I ignored it immediately. That would be ridiculous. But on the second occasion, I opened the page and began reading about dyslexia and the symptoms. I was stunned. It was as if I was reading about myself! It explained all my characteristics, all my difficulties that had been present throughout my life: the poor memory, terrible handwriting, poor sense of direction, dislike of routine and structure, reluctance to blindly follow rules, and even my stammer, my (emotional) hypersensitivity and increased awareness, my intuition, as well as an ability to solve problems (as expressed by the psychic in my first meeting many years earlier, where he was amazed at my clarity and ability to see above problems), to list a few examples. Suddenly everything made sense. (Note: Not all those with dyslexia will have the same symptoms, nor to the same degree.)

By the time I had the meeting with occupational health I had printed out a lot of supporting evidence related to dyslexia, also showing that sensitivity to bright lights can be one of the (many) symptoms. I also shared with the man from occupational health that I had a history of high blood pressure and stress, and that this could possibly be partly due to being dyslexic and the type of work I was doing, and that I needed to reduce my hours. He agreed and recommended in his report that I be allowed to reduce my hours and have the bulb turned off at my desk.

But my managers were less than pleased at this. They were also horrified at the idea that I could be dyslexic. Especially as not only was I obviously intelligent, but my letter-writing was pretty good, so much so that my colleagues would come to me to ask for help with their letters.

So the managers and HR arranged for me to have a formal assessment with a psychologist to confirm once and for all whether or not I was dyslexic. The assessment cost five hundred pounds and was to be three hours long. This was because dyslexia (as I learnt) is to do with how the mind and brain process information. It is said that the left-hand side of the brain is where speech happens, as well as reading and writing, structure, routine and memory to list a few. And the right-hand side of the brain is the creative area: intuitive, sensitive, artistic. Apparently in dyslexia the left-hand side of the brain does not do what it should, thus one can have trouble with reading and writing and with some or all of the left side-related thinking. But often, the right-hand side of the brain can compensate. The result of this can be a highly intelligent, creative, intuitive, sensitive individual, who can't read and write (for example), and can't remember anything. So a formal psychological test for dyslexia has to determine whether or not a person's difficulties in certain areas are indeed due to dyslexia, or whether they are due to any number of other factors, such as lack of education, lack of intelligence or even simply due to the person coming from a different culture.

The outcome of this assessment was to determine what would happen next.

***

(March 2011) The assessment came and went. The psychologist said at the end that she didn't really need the three hours, nor even to do the test. She knew almost immediately that I was dyslexic, and more so that I was a classic dyslexic. She said she was sure, had she met me at seven years old, she would have seen me struggling. And of course I had been! I remembered well my teachers screaming and shouting at me, and my mum trying to help me with my homework and becoming equally stressed, everyone asking (or often shouting), 'Why can't you get this?!' The psychologist stated that it was clear to her how hard I must have worked to have got to where I am, with my abilities of reading and writing. And of course I had. In a way it had possibly helped me that no-one knew I was dyslexic. Had people known, whilst I would not have had such a hard time growing up, there would have been no expectations of me either. So in hindsight, the two choices were probably: 1) be diagnosed as dyslexic at an early age and have a relatively easy time, having been labelled as having learning difficulties and in effect written off as a result, and achieve little. Or, 2) not be diagnosed, have a (seemingly, at the time) horrendous time at school, constantly have to find work-a-rounds in order to keep up and fit in, and constantly be labelled as lazy by all those around me (especially by those trying to teach me), often weighted with emotional frustration and even anger (an attitude which continued through to present day).

So back at work, armed with the large and extremely comprehensive document prepared by a qualified psychologist, which also recommended that I be allowed to reduce my hours and have the light bulb turned off over my desk, I expected this to be the end of the matter.

But alas, my managers still did not accept it, still did not accept that I was dyslexic, nor that I suffered with stress, and demanded that I be sent back to occupational health for another assessment.

It so happened that my appointment was with the same person I saw originally. I am told their response was less than favourable to the council, saying that not only had they made their original assessment and given their recommendations, and not only had the council chosen to ignore this and sent me in to see a formal psychologist who had given the exact same recommendations (and whose recommendations they were also ignoring), they were now sending me back to occupational health. The same recommendations were given: that I be allowed to reduce my hours and turn off the bulb over my desk!

My managers were still not happy (as one can imagine). They conceded that perhaps I was dyslexic, but said that it must be very mild, but did accept that I was perhaps stressed, so decided that one day extra off each week would not be enough. They insisted that I reduce my hours to three days per week!

I'd known these managers for quite a while by now and I was familiar with their mindset. I was pretty sure the intention was to claim later that they did not need a part-time post, they needed a full-time post, and they could therefore make me redundant in the near future if I went down to three days, and get rid of me once and for all. But by only reducing my weekly hours to thirty (from thirty-seven) as I had requested, this would still make me officially full-time, and the plan would not work.

306

So I rejected their offer, and they dug in their heels and rejected recommendations from the three doctors' reports. The manager said, 'I've made my decision!', and that was the end of that meeting, and it was expected (probably, by them at least) to be the last meeting on the subject.

That could indeed have been the end of the matter, but I could not leave it there. My requests had been genuine, and I felt I had no choice but to pursue the matter further. I submitted a formal grievance against the two managers involved. As you can imagine, this was quite a daunting prospect and process.

I submitted the grievance, and suggested that it should not be heard by the senior manager of the two involved, as that person had been aware of what was going on. My wishes were honoured, and instead it was heard by another senior manager, who apparently was appalled and horrified at what had happened, and it was upheld. I was given a desk with the light off overhead and permitted to reduce my hours. Every weekend would include Monday off.

As dyslexia is regarded as a learning disability, I was also given a PC with software to help me read and write (which I never used; I had managed so long without anything like this), and I would also be receiving a series of one-to-one meetings with a person from outside who would help me 'cope' with my dyslexia. This all seemed a little silly to me, at thirty-seven years old, but I had to accept it.

Now that the reduction of my hours had been formally approved and was going ahead, Sally submitted her request for a reduction in her hours so we could have the time off together. She submitted it mid-morning, and by the time she came back from lunch it had been approved; such is the difference between the managers of different departments.

***

307

It was around this time that I turned to Sally one morning whilst getting ready to leave home for work and said, 'I feel like I've had enough; I've just had enough!' I did not know what this meant, but it marked the beginning of a new phase for me, and this is described in detail in the last chapter of this book.

***

I continued doing all the same work I had been previously, but now within only four days a week. The stress in this department had been caused not by the workload but by the working environment. So by being out of the office for three days every week, I felt I had more energy and could therefore achieve more in less time. This worked for a while, and it was not long before I was not only doing my own work within those four days, but I was covering for other people as well. I was working very hard, very efficiently and effectively, but without the stress. At least, not the stress that I had had previously: the new stress which was growing slowly below the surface was due to simply rushing around all the time, putting myself under pressure to get everything done to a high standard in the time permitted. It was happening again!

***

During one of the early meetings at work with the lady from outside who was helping me with my dyslexia, I described to her my schooling, and specifically how the maths teacher had told my mum that I was creating my own ways to solve maths questions, the main example being long division. She was intrigued by this and asked me to show her what I was doing. I said that of course I couldn't remember now, it was over twenty years ago! But nevertheless she wrote an equation on the paper and put it in front of me, and said, 'Show me!' So I looked at it, explained that I had no idea what I used to do but logic dictates... and I just started doing 'something'.

308

She looked stunned and said, 'That's called "double division" and is what they're teaching in schools now!'

***

Near the end of 2012 I had my annual competency review. I had not had a pay increase since 2007, despite still being on the bottom of the pay scale for the role, and despite working very hard and achieving a lot.

On my own section of the form I listed what I had done, achieved and learnt: the new skills I had acquired and the courses I'd been on during that period. I knew the relationship with my managers was less than perfect (and this had been the case prior to my putting in the grievance), but I still wanted them to have to respond formally to my pointing out that I was being held back intentionally. I would have to wait for the outcome of this.

Some weeks later I approached my immediate line manager and asked whether we should have had our copies of our assessment yet. He apologised, saying he thought he had given it to me already. He said he'd send it over.

A few weeks later I asked him again, and again he apologised, saying he thought he'd sent it and assured me he would do so.

A few weeks later still, I approached HR and asked them if I could see a copy. They agreed to supply me with one, but expressed confusion because, as far as they were concerned, my manager had given me a copy.

When I got it, not only had everything I had written in support of my request for a pay increase been removed, my signature had been forged on the bottom!

This time I felt differently. My perspective had changed with this new phase and I didn't feel inclined to make a big deal of it, but I did have a quiet word with the relevant senior managers and they were grateful that I allowed them to deal with the situation themselves. Possibly as a result of the influence from above, the following year I did indeed receive a pay increase. But then changes were put in place by my managers and it was made clear, indirectly, that it would not happen again.

***

Staff started moving on, additional work was taken on by the department, and I had to do more and more in the four days each week. Again, I was physically doing the work, but it was beginning to take its toll. When I approached my managers saying it was becoming too much, they replied saying that I should tell them about anything I could not cope with, but of course there was nothing to show; the work was getting done. The problem was what it was doing to me, and I did not seem to be able to go on a 'go slow' (which is how it felt) intentionally so as to be able to point at work I couldn't do. So I continued.

Another colleague left, and in 2015 another retired. Suddenly I was given more than half my workload again (a repeat of what happened the last time, when I was a rent officer). It was described to me originally as being only a temporary arrangement. But having struggled for several months, knowing again it was becoming too much, I spoke to my manager and was told it was never temporary at all; this was how it would be and there was nothing that could be done. Again, I would have to carry on.

However, with the change in my attitude coupled with what I had learnt about myself and the reasons for this happening (again, this is described in the next chapter), this time it would be different.

By early 2016 Sally had agreed to take early retirement/voluntary redundancy, and having had this extended several times was now working on the final date of sometime in December 2016. I approached the senior managers in the council and requested that I also be allowed to take voluntary redundancy. This was agreed (seemingly without question), probably supported in no small way by my experiences over the years which were well known to them. We agreed a leaving date at the end of June 2016.

As I write this it is the end of August 2016. At forty-three years of age, the redundancy has enabled me to take the time out to write this book. And more so, circumstances elsewhere have made it possible for us to have a long-term (possibly permanent) change of pace and lifestyle. I now know what has happened since 2003 when I joined the council, and why it had to happen. And I am now free internally (as a state of mind), and externally in my physical life (at least, to an extent; I still have to operate as a human being like anybody else).

***

The cause of my stammer

I had also by now realised the three contributing factors responsible for my life-long stammer (albeit, it was far less obvious now):

The first, as mentioned above, is that I am dyslexic. For many dyslexics the difficulties associated with it (whilst actually numerous) may only be apparent to others in their reading and writing. But it's the same part of the brain which is responsible for speech. It is therefore not uncommon for dyslexics to have some difficulty thinking of and/or speaking a specific word. (It is just not so common for it to become an actual and established stammer.)

The second factor is emotional stress, or even just feeling hurried and under pressure. Stress is well known to affect a person's ability to think clearly, and even a person without dyslexia can stammer when unsure of what to say, or struggling to be heard, particularly when there is a sense of urgency.

311

It is the third factor which is perhaps the most interesting. I said near the beginning of the book that sometimes my stammer would be there and sometimes it wouldn't; and a little later on I discovered I was sensitive to the feelings of others. (Thankfully this has long since subsided into an intuition rather than an emotional disturbance in me, when around people.) And it became clear that their emotional state would directly affect me (and therefore my stammer). However, what I had not anticipated is how sensitive I actually am. When I'm speaking with someone and their mind wanders off or they are distracted by something, I have noticed that it is as if my energy and ability to speak is instantly affected. As a result, I have since learnt to not struggle on, trying 'valiantly' to speak when I know they're not really listening and the words therefore won't come. Though when I do this, the most frequent (and sometimes indignant) response is the statement 'I am listening!' (when it is clear to me they are not).

So the cause of my stammer, it turns out, is a combination (or accumulation) of my being dyslexic, experiencing emotional stress (whether in myself, or picking up on the other person's) and/or my trying to speak when I know the person isn't really listening. Quite a concoction!

312

Liberation

***

(March 2011) There have been two questions which have occasionally occurred to me during the last seven years since the experience known as God-Realisation (or Self-Realisation) happened here:

1) Why do people keep claiming 'There is nobody here' – when, to me, there clearly is, even in God-Realisation?

2) Why have I continued to experience (apparently) emotional stress, long into God-Realisation (Enlightenment)?

These two questions have recently been answered, and I would like to share with you what I have learnt...

I had assumed that the teaching that there is nobody here (in its truest sense – once the Truth of this existence has been fully realised) was simply a misinterpretation of one of the insights; for there has been no doubt that whatever 'I' am, 'I' am still 'here'. Sure, I have realised there is one Being here, and that this one Being is my own Being, but realising this did not make 'me' disappear. I simply became 'bigger' than I thought I was (the energy behind everything). But life went on.

I had also assumed that the teachings that describe everything as continuous peace in this state must be due to the environment in which the teachers in question live(d): invariably this would be some Eastern country, in the sunshine, where the spiritual life is highly regarded, and with very little else to do but enjoy 'being'. I have had no doubt that

I too could teach about the peace, if I lived there, instead of having a 'real' job working for a busy local authority in the UK. In addition, life has seemingly thrown situation after situation at me, and daily living has been far from easy – ever. I have just hoped there was some reason or benefit to it, and more so for an end.

***

As I write this (near the end of March 2011), it has been about two weeks since I turned to Sally, whilst getting ready to leave our home to go to work, and out of the blue said, 'I feel like I have had enough. I have just had enough!' I did not know that that was my turning point...

At around the same time, and it could have been the same day, I received an email from a visitor to our website who I had been corresponding with for a few weeks. We had exchanged a lot of information during the time, and this latest email included the words 'I think that Bernadette Roberts may be at a more "advanced" state than yourself currently' and sent me a link to a website with an interview with this lady.

I don't tend to read works by other teachers. Their teachings are either the same as what I say, in which case there is nothing to learn, or they say something different, in which case their teachings are contrary and often over-complicated (or just coming from a different place).

Anyway, I wanted to be open, to be able to explain away the apparent superior position of this lady, or better still, learn something new. But I could not see what could be more 'advanced' than God-Realisation. So, I read the interview on the page. At the time I was amazed. It struck a chord with me, so perfectly timed and executed that suddenly I knew this was it. There was something here that I had not heard of, or at least had not appreciated before. I had to find out more.

Bernadette's path is quite different from my own. She describes coming from a Catholic background spent as a nun, and her spiritual journey being one of contemplation, prayer and reading the works of the saints. However, Bernadette describes entering a new state some twenty years after (what she terms) God-Union – It was as if her 'centre' had gone...

She says at the time she looked everywhere for some reference to explain what this was. Surely someone else must have been here before? Eventually she found one line in the Buddhist teaching:

> Initially, I gave up looking for this experience in the Buddhist literature. Four years later, however, I came across two lines attributed to Buddha describing his enlightenment experience. Referring to self as a house, he said, 'All thy rafters are broken now, the ridgepole is destroyed.'
>
> And there it was – the disappearance of the center, the ridgepole; without it, there can be no house, no self. When I read these lines, it was as if an arrow launched at the beginning of time had suddenly hit a bulls-eye. It was a remarkable find.
>
> *(The above is an excerpt of an interview by Stephan Bodian and was published in the Nov/Dec 1986 issue of YOGA JOURNAL.)*

She goes on to say that the confusion occurs because teachings (both traditional and current) merge the two states together, God-Union and No-self, when they are very different... as I was soon to learn.

I knew this was my next step. I felt I was so close. But how does one make their self, their centre, disappear?

That night in bed, I was given a glimpse of the experience whereby the centre did seem to evaporate, right 'in front of my eyes' (as the saying goes), and was gone. Then, a moment later it was back, but now at least I knew what I was looking for...

I spent a couple of days doing what I have always done in these situations: holding on to a sensation within (in this case, the sense of a centre within) so as to dissolve it, but it was not working. As I held on to it, there it remained. I felt I needed a new way of dealing with this.

I then wondered, if I let go of the centre and instead focused outside of myself, on the world around me, what would happen? I was already Self-/God-Realised so I could not lose that. So, I tried it, and the moment I did so the centre was gone. There was only this space looking 'out' at the objects of the world – no centre, no 'self'!

That was a few days ago now as I write this, and it has continued to be my experience. It's a little strange and still new, but I will try to explain it more in my own words below:

The Experience of No-self

First, I am still 'Me'. By that I mean, to everyone who knows me, nothing has changed – I don't have a halo, or wear sandals. And, although internally something has indeed changed, it requires a little looking to confirm what exactly.

The slightly ambiguous aspect is the lack of a centre. I say 'ambiguous' because, even though it has only been a matter of days, I cannot, even now, remember what the centre was like. I only remember thinking that I had one, and one evening noticing it had gone. (In hindsight I can just about recall that the centre had been my solid foundation since Self- or God-Realisation occurred here. And, no matter what happened, or how difficult life seemed to become, this impenetrable core held steady). But now there is no centre here, within this space of awareness. There is only 'this', the being behind what I call 'me', looking out, but nevertheless continuing to experience the external world just as before.

Also, whilst I see objects around me, I have noticed that it is as if the space between 'me' and the objects is

318

actually solid. There is a sense that the 'empty space' is energetically 'present' and full.

The second, and perhaps biggest change, is the 'peace', but I would like to qualify this further (whilst acknowledging entirely that as I write this it is still early days. No doubt there will be more to say later):

Over the last couple of days I have been considering how I will write this: what I will say and how best to describe it. The following analogy occurred to me as being perhaps quite a good way to describe the entire process:

The Reluctant Passenger

Initially, when I was struggling, long before I knew anything about the (so-called) spiritual life, I was like a reluctant passenger in the backseat of a car. The car is not going where I want it to go; the driver will not listen to me, and no amount of shouting, screaming, wailing and whining seem to make the slightest difference. It is frustrating, terrifying, shocking, and finally, full of desperation, I begin to give up, and want to know what is going on. I suggest this is the start of the (conscious) spiritual life...

Still in the backseat, I try to stay more aware and in control of my actions and reactions, and more aware of the car, the driver, and where we seem to be going. It is as if I am possessed and have little control over what I am feeling but, bit by bit, my efforts are rewarded with glimpses into what is really going on... I begin to see that I am actually the one driving the car! And eventually I find I am no longer sitting in the backseat, struggling, shouting, but I am actually in the front, holding the steering wheel, driving. Thank God!

But, what is this? I still hear the wailing and the crying from the backseat. Sure, it is no longer 'me', but whatever it is, the creature in the backseat is still most unhappy and demands that I listen to it and that I take it where it wants to go!

I drive on, following the signs and the road, ignoring my reluctant passenger, and apparently knowing where to drive but with no real knowledge of where we are going – of the final destination. I wonder what will make the creature go away, as it is making the driving experience rather unpleasant. I could handle the driving, queuing, getting in the right lane, avoiding the road-hog cutting me off without incident, if only the creature would just shut up and let me drive.

Every so often I get some respite, as the creature seems to have either fallen asleep or has actually found a part of the journey quite enjoyable. But I am always aware that it's not far away, and soon it returns to its deranged state, and lets me know it.

And of course the creature doesn't have a choice. Occasionally I think back and remember what it was like to be there, trapped, imprisoned against my will, consumed with fear and with no-one telling me where we are going or what they want with me. But now, to me, it's just a nuisance!

To me, this is God-Realisation.

Suddenly, having been driving around for quite some time, I notice something has changed. The creature in the backseat seems to have been quiet for longer than usual. Has it gone? Is it dead? In truth, I don't know. All I know is the backseat is quiet and all is well. I can get on with driving and enjoying the journey...

...Ah, that's better... quickly our little friend is forgotten.

With no sense of a passenger, this quiet becomes the norm, the ordinary, as if this is how things should be. Just me and the car, taking the road where it leads...

***

During the first couple of days of this new phase I asked myself:

1) Do I have a Self?
2) Where is my centre?

This is what I wrote:

The answer to the first is that I do not know for sure. I think the Self is still here, but it is now everything. It is as if it is aligned with what is, so cannot be experienced as it is no longer separate or contrary to what is. Whether this is the same as No-self as described by Bernadette Roberts and others in the Advaita teaching, at this point I cannot guarantee, but it is only a few days into the process.

With regards to the second question, if I allow my sight to focus on a particular object, my centre would seem to be the middle point between what is doing the looking and the object being looked at. No longer is my centre in the body.

By way of further explanation: it is a bit like watching a movie in the first person, and therefore self-consideration is minimal as it is not 'me'. 'I' (whatever 'I' am) have no reality here. There is just 'this' being experienced; but I have not changed 'who' I am. I am just not concerned with what is happening to this body or where I am right now.

I also noticed a series of coincidences 'helping' make the physical journey during those few days much more pleasant. As if offering some sort of external indication that all was well and as it should be.

***

The final journey

I have called this section 'The final journey' because it seems as good a name as any, but it is really still mostly speculative to me.

Bernadette describes this stage (which has been termed 'No-self') as there being nothing more for the 'self' to learn, hence its absence. Whether or not it has really gone, or whether it has just given up and is 'going with the flow', I do not know, but the result is the same: no more 'self-consideration'. All is quiet.

She however describes a later level where the mind no longer focuses on specific objects – a state she has termed 'No-where'. I cannot comment further on this at present, except to say that my own insights (in our book *Essays in Truth*) describe how the need for the dream of existence will eventually be lived out, and the dream will evaporate. But I am not in a hurry for this to happen. Just let me drive around for a while and see the sights, without my little gremlin in the backseat screaming at me.

Self-avoidance/Self-denial

I wanted to touch on something here briefly: the teaching of there being 'nobody here'.

I have to say that I still cannot see how it is useful to deny the existence of the self in one's attempt to go beyond it (a point Bernadette Roberts also states repeatedly). It may only be my own path, but the realising of God (for want of a better term) was an important step in the journey. And taking the (above) car analogy further, I do not see how one can hope to have the 'self' that is screaming in the backseat disappear until they have first realised that they are not it (as I see it). Simply repeating, 'There is nobody here!' (as so many seem to do) is delusional, and may serve only to prolong the time spent in the hypothetical backseat. In fact, it could be said that it is the creature itself that has adopted the mantra, hoping in vain that if it repeats it enough, one day it will come true – it will disappear. And of course, one day it will be true, but only after it accepts that it does exist and begins to confront the situation with presence and intelligence. I suggest self-denial or self-avoidance should not be confused with the experience of No-self, and furthermore are probably not the best means by which to realise it.

As I see it (and teach it), the path is first to see, and then to realise, that you are not the self (the emotional monster). You are the space within and behind what you thought was you. Here you find the knowledge that everything comes from this space, and in this you are alone, and yet are complete. Whatever 'you' are, 'this' is all that is – this space that you call 'I'. And eventually, when you have lived enough in this state, 'No-self' will come looking for you. There is nowhere to hide.

***

It is only the next day after I wrote the piece above. Here I will begin listing a few new things in me:

1) **Nature walks** – I have found that I am drawn to spend more time out walking amongst nature, along the canal, in the park, in the woods. It feels as if nature is the external representation, or perhaps it's more of a celebration, of what I am feeling within, and it feels like home when I am amongst it. (However, I am also aware that Bernadette Roberts stated she was moved to spend more time in nature during this

period, so I am conscious of the possibility that I'm doing it as she did and it seemed like a good idea.)

2) **Animals are less afraid** – It may only be a coincidence, but not only have I noticed more wildlife when I am out and about, but animals seem less wary of me than I would usually expect.

3) **'Appearance' has changed** – I was at work today, and a number of people, independently of each other, commented on how well I looked: a couple made reference to my top suiting me (a bright red polo shirt which I had to wear for a community event – the same one I wore two weeks ago, and have many times previously, when no-one mentioned it). And another said I looked like I had been on holiday or something! I mentioned this to Sally later, as it seemed a bit strange to me; it wasn't as if I had developed a suntan. She said I did seem different, somehow lighter, as if a weight had been lifted off me.

4) **Awoke into stillness** – Last night there was an interesting experience: I awoke with a jolt, to be staring into an amazing solid peace (I would say with my eyes closed, but my eyes did not occur to me at the time). It was warm, complete and safe. Not 'intense', as that would imply force of some sort, but I was wide awake, totally aware. Then I began to understand what had happened: my hand had slipped off the edge of the bed and knocked the bedside cabinet. This had caused a bit of a noise and a hard knock on my hand, waking me up suddenly, into conscious dreamless sleep...

As I continued to look into it, moments later the newness of the feeling had evaporated into the norm, as is the way. But what struck me was the contrast between this 'new' awakened state and the sleeping unconscious state that I had been in only a moment previously, without the usual transition of the waking process. This may be nothing important, but perhaps worth a mention.

5) **New 'Being'** – It has occurred to me on a few occasions recently that in any moment of looking, it is as if I am not 'me'. It is as if Nick Roach (or what was identified as being Nick previously, be it his essence or whatever) has gone, and this new energy or persona has moved into Nick's body, still with Nick's memories and of course his appearance, but it's no longer Nick as he was. I seem to recall Bernadette Roberts (BR) describing this in one of her books as feeling like being reborn, and this is as good a description as any. It is like I am experiencing some things for the first time as this new person, and can remember the previous occasions as part of Nick's memories, but they are not my own.

6) **No fear** – One of the characteristics of this state has been described by others as 'no emotional disturbance'. I have been waiting to be able to comment on this because, although I could sense a change, 'feelings' were still here in some form. As BR's works have been my main point of reference in navigating this new phase, I will say that she noticed that the emotions for her did not disappear instantly. Anyway, here it is for now:

Last weekend I noticed, when out walking, that I was aware of an ongoing, painfully drawn out situation at work which I believe is all but resolved now. But unlike previously, there was not the strength of feeling attached to it. It was still there, but only when it occurred to me, and was more of a subtle disturbance rather than the stubborn ogre that I would usually face and dissolve. I likened it at the time to the midges (small flying insects) which seemed to be following me along the path as I walked round the lake. Sometimes they seemed to be gone, at others I would look past them and forget about them, and then there were the times when I would be careful of my breathing out of concern for inhaling one.

A couple of days into this week, as I was driving at about midday, it occurred to me that it was gone: all disturbance about the situation (which had not changed externally at that point since the weekend) had evaporated, leaving a void. I tested it, trying to imagine the problem, but could not. It had gone!

But I was not going to get off that lightly, even in these new times. After a couple more days another major hiccup occurred at work, and I was aware that this, on top of all else that has gone before, could have been crushing, but not this time. This is new...

All fear had gone ('fear' being the centre of an emotional response). I had to respond still, as the issues had to be addressed physically, but the thought process was clear. In fact, I commented to Sally that it was as if this latest event had fallen into our laps. It enabled me to highlight to the people that needed to know how awful the ongoing situation has been, with this latest event being the final nudge, the 'last straw', and all in an extremely direct and yet unemotional manner. Had I known that the last seven years with this single enduring hardship would be the driving force behind my entering this 'final' (so it is said) phase, then it may have made it easier to cope with – but perhaps that's the point! The seemingly never-ending aspect of it combined with it having no apparent meaning made it all the more powerful.

So, I have to assume from everything, and accepting the correlation described above, that the final death of the emotional continuation here will occur within the next few days (if it has not already occurred). If I was pushed to describe what is here now, I may say a phrase I've never used: 'All is going swimmingly!' (In case other people are even less familiar with the phrase than I am, to me, here, it is as if I am supported, all around, floating, swimming relatively effortlessly, going with the flow.)

326

7) There is only 'This' – Another common phrase amongst 'spiritual seekers' is 'There is only THIS', or 'This is only awareness experiencing itself'. I have never quite grasped these phrases experientially. Sure, I could say it is ultimately true, but the experience of 'being here' was still a fact and could not be denied. But now I understand...

The problem to me was that the above phrases can give the impression that in such a state there is nothing of what was here previously still remaining to identify with anything. This (to me) sounded as if it may as well be an inanimate object, a robot going through the motions of existing with no sense of Being – no 'self' awareness. However, this is not the case as I am experiencing it here, and would like to try to describe it further as I see it:

First we have the 'awareness'. This looks through the mind which encompasses the self and out on to the world of physical experiences. The self identifies with the body, with being separate, and carries the emotional history of the person. Every moment the self is driving the imagination to think about what hurts it, as well as what it likes and doesn't like, and even when sitting quietly in the physical world there is little or no peace from its interference in some guise or another. And all the time the awareness is just watching, untouched, unencumbered. With each physical interaction the self is interpreting it, acting as a filter so the awareness receives, not necessarily a watered-down version, but more likely a hyped-up, 'improved' (to the self) and modified version.

So, as we start to see from the above, if one removes the filter – the self – it is true that only the awareness is left, but it is the SAME awareness as before, and that is the point I wanted to make (if only for my own sake). The experience of the world is now direct. It is clean, clear, simple – like a crystal glass in the dishwasher adverts, after it has been through a wash with the newest detergent: my 'self' may have gone (or maybe at this point is still in the transition process), but the awareness that remains is still the same awareness that has always been here, looking out through the eyes and experiencing what is here to be experienced.

To summarise, there is no need to be confused about the saying 'There is only THIS' or 'There is only awareness experiencing itself', and to wonder what it means. The space you feel inside where you are aware that you exist, *that* is what remains, still aware, still watching.

***

(April 2011)

8) **Emotional mist** – It is now mid-April and the journey is still ongoing. The work situation has dragged on and I am taking it as a reflection of the ongoing situation within. What I have noticed is that unlike previously when something occurred that would cause an emotional disturbance and I would hold on to the feeling until it dissolved, now there is nothing to grab hold of. Now, only the thought of the situation will occur to me, and staying 'aware' (not going into the imagination) results in it quickly evaporating. BR commented on the emotions losing their power prior to their final demise, and that would fit with this experience.

To elaborate, during past weeks I did permit myself to imagine the situation (in the knowledge that I still remain conscious now), and what happened was a sort of whirlwind effect: starting with an emotional 'mist' within my internal awareness, and then proceeding to swirl around, building up in strength as it did so, but in this case swirling around a still and quiet centre – like a tornado. Here there is nothing to grab hold of and nothing to fight against. Whilst the imagination keeps going, so does the swirling. Hence, dropping the imagination at the first hint of a thought denies the initial creation of the emotion, even before the first traces of the mist can arise. This has been my own experience and teaching from the beginning, but usually there has been a time delay between holding the mind still and the emotion evaporating. Now the correlation is all but instantaneous.

9) **New teaching** – In this strange unfolding, a major change seems to be the lack of anything new to share, but more than that is the removal of any need to do so.

The elimination of the sense of being anything (e.g. having no centre) means partly that there is a sense of having nothing to give or to offer, but also that there is no-one to take ownership of anything either. That is to say, I (Nick Roach) used to say that I am Enlightened or God-Realised and taught from there about what it is, and that was the Truth.

However, take away the sense of 'Being', and it is as if 'I' have nothing 'to hang my hat on' – and then I notice I no longer have a hat. There really is nothing to teach and no-one to teach it, and yet here I sit, writing this! How peculiar!

BR said one thought that occurred to her is that people may as well keep their self, as in the end it is all they have! (I understand this.)

10) **Living in the moment** – It is said that the experience of No-self is of truly living in the moment, so I have been waiting to write something on this. In the last couple of days, I have asked myself how mindful (in the moment) I currently am, and I am not quite sure...

It seems a bit strange actually, and I think it's because I am on the cusp (or still in the transition process). I will explain...

Here it's been about a month so far, and certainly there has been a big change, but it's difficult to remember sometimes what it was like before. Also, thoughts do still occur every so often, and it's as if I still 'dip my toe' of thinking/imagination into them, as if to test the water, and then quickly withdraw it as if remembering that I have been there and didn't like it. All is good.

However, Bernadette Roberts described the process taking several months to complete once the centre had evaporated for her, so I expect the experience to continue to unfold.

***

Two weeks have passed since I wrote the last part on 'living in the moment', and I now have more to write. I would say the process is almost complete with regards specifically to 'being in the moment' (as it is said) and I would like to say a bit about this:

When I have heard or read about this element of 'Enlightenment' (No-self) there was always a small question in me as to what really meant and what it was like. And why would there not be? Until one has experienced what is being described, it is largely theoretical.

As with much of the information that has come to me as insights into how this existence works, this new phase has also been interpreted for me in relation to this behaving like (or more precisely, actually being) a dream existence. When it has occurred to me over the last few days to reflect on what I am experiencing here and how best to describe it, this is what has been offered:

The phrase 'living in the moment' for some reason always gave me the impression of a fixed, structured, Now! Now! Now! sort of experience, where one would be totally aware that there is only now and where 'I' am. However, this is not how it has come to me...

As I looked, I likened it to when I am asleep in bed, dreaming: although I may have a thought, such as 'Where is so-and-so?' or 'What is that?', there is no drifting off into the imagination ('daydreaming'). I am totally 'in the moment' (in the dream). But also I noticed that this is not through any effort (and this may be a new connection). In the dream, the idea of past and future does not really arise in the usual

330

sense; I simply deal with whatever is in front of me at the time. And that's not to say there is no emotion in the dream. It can occur (as we all know). It is just that it lacks permanence...

And this is how I experience this 'living in the moment' here, whilst 'awake'. There is no effort, and most of the time I am not even aware that I am in the moment. Again, the notion of past and future simply does not occur. All 'time' is part of the unending moment now!

Another way of explaining it may be to liken the 'normal' way of thinking and living to navigating a fast-flowing river with its twists and turns, where one must watch out and allow for the oncoming rapids whilst bailing water out of the boat and patching up any damage from the last stretch. But living 'the moment' is more like floating, bobbing up and down in the open ocean, with no sight of land and little sense of time. It is as if there is no past or future, and certainly no way to know from which direction one has come or where one is heading, if one is indeed heading anywhere.

('Enlightenment', my previous state, I suggest, is somewhere in between the two – perhaps still in the river, but it has widened and slowed considerably. There are still rocks and turns to navigate around, but no more rapids and no more having to bail out water or repair the boat to prevent it sinking.)

***

(May 2011)

11) **Liberation** – It occurred to me to contact our good friend Dr Nitin Trasi as I recalled him writing about 'Liberation' occurring after Enlightenment. Then I remembered that I too wrote an essay about this experience back in 2004. This was initially published on the website and later was put into our second book *Essays in Truth, Glimpses into Reality*. At that time the writing was based on a combination of insight and

logic (from what I had already gone through), and once written it was soon forgotten. (This is another example of the time delay which will often exist between seeing a truth and fully realising it.)

As I go further into this experience, I am beginning to see that I prefer the term 'Liberation' to 'No-self'. This is because there is so much confusion as to what the word 'self' means (complicated further still by the use of the capital 'S' to indicate the 'other'), that if one has to go to considerable lengths to define what one means by self before one even gets to what it is to have 'no self', the whole subject can become confusing. However, the term 'Liberation' is descriptive in itself (and quite accurate), and thus requires far less explanation to the layperson when trying to at least give an idea as to what is meant. (To make the point, Bernadette Roberts has written a book entitled (and investigating) *What is Self?*)

And in pretty much the same way, the state of Enlightenment or Self-Realisation has also been described as the 'No-ego' experience. But we have a seemingly never-ending debate, spanning history across the globe, regarding the reality or exact nature of the 'ego'. Hence I have always avoided this term too.

12) **Liberation continued** – A few days have passed since I wrote the above piece on Liberation, in which I related it to being in a boat on the ocean, and as I was writing it an image came to me: it was of a person seated in a single-person dinghy in the middle of the ocean, with no land or indeed anything in sight besides the water. (It has just occurred to me that I don't think I even noticed any horizon.) There was no sense of fear, or indeed any emotion, or movement of any sort from this lone person. The boat had no means of propulsion and there was no intention within this person to go anywhere – just floating, watching...

332

I write this now because this image has stuck with me ever since. Every so often it has occurred to me to look at it, but it is as if it is always there. (I suspect it is simply reflecting, in image form, the phase I am entering, but it is new to me.)

What I had not appreciated until earlier today is that the person, the boat and the ocean all still exist. As peaceful, amazing, and even 'alien' this new state of being may be, it is still 'Being' nonetheless. There is no denying that 'I' still am. There is no sense of time, no wanting to get anywhere and no sense of having been anywhere. There may be only 'Being', but 'Being' there is.

And I felt moved to add the following:

While the word 'Liberation' remains, in whatever sense – in fact, while any word remains...

...and then, perhaps meaningfully, here the sentence ends without words! But the meaning is clear...

This then reminds me of the quote from the Bible: 'In the beginning was The Word'. (I am not totally sure what the relevance of the last paragraph is, but it felt right to record it. It perhaps feels like being back at the beginning.)

***

(July 2011)

13) **Life changes** – The external life has now changed, enabling me to have more time away from work. Time will see how this goes, but I feel I desperately need it.

***

(August 2011)

14) **Cheyenne** – The extended time away from work has given me a feeling of space within, and with it came a new experience:

333

Becoming Cheyenne

A little over a week ago, after work, as we were driving to go away for the weekend (Sally was driving on this occasion; I was playing the role of the relaxing passenger), I was relaying to her how the lady who was coming in to 'help' me with being dyslexic had said it was perhaps time that I relaxed and became more of a 'cool dude', and had even suggested that perhaps I should grow my hair long or something...?

I said I was not sure about growing my hair specifically, but I could see, with the strict parental upbringing and the intense discipline that I had imposed on myself for most of my life, there really isn't a 'me' in any external sense. By this I mean, for example, I have no sense of fashion or specific character, and have never really tried to have. I am always smart, clean, 'neat', 'middle of the road', and apart from the energy someone may pick up on from me, there is nothing to identify me as anything at all. I just look from the outside as 'straight', 'nice', even uptight and rigid. And these descriptions would be quite accurate. (It was many years into my 'journey' before I finally relaxed enough to even ruffle up my hair a little – as I said, everything has always been 'neat' and controlled...)

Also, it may be worth mentioning that the strict upbringing during my childhood and schooling instilled in me an insecurity, and this was further nurtured throughout my working life as I repeatedly found myself in situations where the manager at the time was over-controlling and critical, deceitful, or an outright bully. My enduring 'neat' appearance has possibly been a combination of a wish to please, combined with the fear that 'stepping out of the norm' would draw unnecessary negative attention to myself from those in authority which I really did not need, as well as it feeding my own need to be in control of something. Anyway, back to the point of the story:

As I told Sally about this, agreeing that I was indeed open to exploring this new, more relaxed and chilled out 'me', and feeling a little strange about it, suddenly I had the image of a Native American Indian's head in my mind. It was not a chief, nor a painted warrior, but a relaxed-looking male Indian brave, with long black hair and two feathers hanging loosely at the side of his head (possibly through a headband, but I did not notice this).

As I looked at this image, it remained motionless (lifeless), left side on (so not looking at me), just 'being', and with a great inner-strength which was communicated to me as the essence and purpose behind what I was being shown. I did not know why I was being shown this specifically, but I could feel myself seemingly absorbing the strength from this image.

For the next few days it was there, prominent and at pride of place in my mind, whatever I was doing; and even now, as I write this over a week later, if I am reminded to look, there it is.

I wanted to find out more about this Indian aspect and did a few searches online. There were many Native American Indian tribes, but from the pictures I found and from what I read, the tribe known as the Cheyenne was the one that stood out, and for some deeper reason felt 'right' to me. I was cautious, but have since accepted and adopted this as being my Indian tribe.

There is a great deal of information online about this tribe, as well as many others, but I would like to share here a few of the more prominent points (to me) that I picked up:

About the Cheyenne

Interestingly, the name 'Cheyenne' was not the name they gave themselves. One of the most common theories behind the name Cheyenne is that it means 'a bit like the [people of an] alien speech' (literally, 'red-talker'), i.e. 'those who speak a foreign language'. Apparently this was given to them by another tribe who met with the westerners and described the different tribes to them.

1) The Cheyenne Nation is composed of two united tribes, the Só'taeo'o (more commonly as Sutaio) and the Tsétsêhéstâhese (more commonly as Tsitsistas), which translates to 'those like us' or 'human beings'.

2) The Cheyenne were a peaceful people, never looking for a fight. However, their warriors were the 'Dog Soldiers' and were reportedly amongst the most feared of all the Indian tribes.

3) The Cheyenne were highly adaptable, and over the years spent time as hunters, fishermen, farmers and nomads.

4) They had rules, and these were strict, but the rules only existed where necessary for the absolute good of the tribe; the people were mindful not to squash the individual's need for self-expression.

5) They thought very highly of the women.

6) During their time they affiliated with many other tribes, and some of the members of these joined them. There is even a story that during a battle with the Sioux, many Sioux were captured and these soon were absorbed into the Cheyenne tribe.

7) Being highly adaptable, their Dog Soldiers fought with the USA in the World War, and to this day the Cheyenne are one of the few tribes existing in the

reserves in the US (though not surprisingly, the Dog Soldiers found it harder to adapt to reserve life).

The above points struck a chord with me; the qualities and values are ones which I can relate to, and the culture as described is one which I believe I would have fitted into well.

Reason for the image?

The above is all very well, but I was still a little bemused as to what it really meant. I had this image of an Indian brave within me, and I was feeling stronger apparently due to this, and on investigation had found I liked their approach to life and living, but I was still not sure why I was being shown this...

At first I wondered whether this was something to do with one's (so-called) Spirit Guide. I have never had reason to explore this subject, but it occurred to me, if I do have what someone else would refer to as a Spirit Guide (these are often associated with some Native Indian-type figure), it has to be an aspect of my own Being. So, perhaps there comes a point in one's personal development at which they take on or absorb the attributes of their guide – the point at which the guide is no longer needed as there is nothing left to learn, i.e. the guide was really the person's true nature, and having taken on some sort of separate form then assists them on the journey to realise the guide as an aspect of themselves?

Whilst the above was not impossible, it did not seem to ring true for me. This was partly because I have never had any dealings with this area and the only way to confirm this theory would be to go to a psychic who has. The trouble with this is that it would mean relying on second-hand information, which was not something I had had to do on my journey so far and did not wish to start then, right at the end when it most mattered (let's say). Also, what if two psychics said different things? How would I know which one was 'correct'? Should I just pick the one that suited my theory?

Then I asked myself whether this could be some sort of past life connection, where I was recovering (or uncovering) memories from before. But this also did not fit right because, however many past lives I may or may not have had, they are all past, and as such have no greater reality than this one here now. Therefore, it did not seem logical that at that point, having come so far, that the highest level would be to re-realise an aspect of my past. (However noble or spiritual that guise may have been, it was still past and part of the dream!)

So, I had to keep looking for a reason behind this image I was seeing and for what I was experiencing as a result of it. (Or was the image as a result of the internal experience? Either way, they were connected.)

Looking back, I remembered as a child playing cowboys and Indians, or on my own playing only Indians. Regardless, whilst all my little friends were arguing over who would NOT be the Indians, as they all wanted to be cowboys, I would have already kitted myself up in my own Indian outfit. It never occurred to me to be a cowboy; why would I want to be? As an Indian I was closer to nature, more free and easy, more subtle, more creative; and yet I was only five or so years old. Where did this come from? Whatever it was that stirred me to be the Indian then, that has been my driving force throughout my life. I have lived a fairly 'normal' Western lifestyle, but have struggled every step of the way. None of it has seemed natural to me. I play the game but don't really fit in, a bit like an Indian living an imposed and sterile half-existence in a reserve allocated to them by a greater force (e.g. the Cheyenne specifically make it their way to adapt and survive, but that does not make it easy or ideal).

As I have looked at this over the last few days, I then remembered that Bernadette Roberts talked about her No-self experience being that of Christ permanently possessing her body as her own self fell away; thus was revealed to her the truth behind Christ's reincarnation, free from the physical structure and limitations. Her entire journey had been one of Christian contemplation, always travelling closer to God, with the knowledge that the end somehow related in some way to Christ. I had the experience a couple of months ago of 'me' falling away and of a new energy moving in, with my memories but seemingly experiencing everything for the first time through 'my' eyes, but it was not connected with Christ, nor indeed any spiritual or religious figure. It was just something new: whatever remained when 'I' was gone. It has come to me only in the last day or so that what Bernadette Roberts experienced as Christ is very likely my Native American Indian brave...

To further illustrate the point: there have been studies with people who have had near-death experiences, some of whom describe meeting a religious figure, usually Christ himself. Apparently he did not need to introduce himself to these people; they just knew intuitively who he was. I do not believe that a devout Muslim, Hindu or Buddhist (for example) would also be met at the 'Pearly Gates' by Jesus Christ, as he does not have the same power for them. If such a figure was to meet them, it would have to be someone who symbolised or represented the same energy that Christ does for a Christian. (Funny to consider it: can you imagine a person refusing to accept Jesus Christ and having an argument with him about how they will wait for someone else? No, it would not − indeed it could not happen.) We know everything is connected, 'One', and it is one's own self or Being that creates their existence, and as such it is their own Being that determines and creates their death and what is experienced as they pass from one 'reality' to the next...

So, with the above in mind, it seems clear that one's own mind creates the image or personality that most represents the deity required to assist in the process, and it follows that this should happen both at death and indeed in the (so-called) spiritual life before death. (In fact, it has been said by many authoritative spiritual figures that the spiritual life, when taken to the ultimate, involves dying – psychologically – whilst still alive.)

Accepting the reasoning above – as Christ holds little power for me (as I am not particularly religious), but the Native American Indians and their way of life did (and subconsciously always have) – it is perhaps fitting that my end personality or figure would reflect this aspect!

What does this mean?

Not much really, at least not to anybody else. This section (as well as the website, and to a large extent our work generally) has been written as a record of my own journey and serves mostly to assist me in solidifying the experience and knowledge here. If others benefit from my sharing it, then that's great.

However, I hope the point is gained throughout my story and teaching that the journey varies from person to person.

If I could, I might make myself an Honorary Cheyenne, if only to acknowledge what I have gained from them and their power recently (or, more specifically, the link between my own spiritual development and what the image represented for me; I am not planning to plait my hair or wear moccasins).

But, as we know, for Bernadette Roberts the 'deity' she made way for was Christ. For another person it could be someone or something else, or even nothing at all as they pass through it without incident. By all means read others' works if you like, but don't try to live another's life. It cannot work and is likely to result in unnecessary frustration.

Running Bear
(only kidding)

340

(Note: A little while later I got my first, and currently only, tattoo. On the back of my left forearm I have my two Indian feathers, tied together, with a small dream catcher at the top (just to give them something to hang from; but it too is probably highly appropriate, in hindsight). The feathers, as per the image in my mind, are white with black tips, which I later learnt are from the bald eagle – the Indians regarded the large birds such as the bald and golden eagles to be the closest creatures to heaven, as they flew so high and for so long.

I also got my ear pierced and learnt to ride a motorbike, as part of this new and relaxed 'me' I was uncovering.)

***

(Note: A couple of years later something similar happened, but this time not with a Native American influence. This is how I described it to Nitin Trasi at the time:)

> *...As you know, I learnt to ride a motorbike the other year (which was part of the 'new me'), and a few months ago I started my IAM training (Institute of Advanced Motorcyclists). My test was last Monday, and I passed.*
>
> *However, I was apprehensive during my training, as I expected I would be very nervous in my test (I tend to not do well in tests). But suddenly, two weeks before my test, something started to change. I was on the penultimate lesson before my test, and suddenly I was relaxed during the ride; and I had never been relaxed in any of my lessons before (with someone watching and critiquing me). And this relaxed 'feel' stayed with me during the days up to my test.*

Then, the night before the test (last Sunday), in my mind I had the image of a small table with items on it, related to a Japanese ceremony, and 'I' was kneeling before it. I was not sure what this was at the time, but this image stayed with me leading up to, during, and after the test, lasting several days in total. And it seemed to communicate, or reflect, a feeling of being relaxed but focussed (on the job at hand).

Later I was describing this to Sally, as I was seeing it, and suddenly remembered where this image came from. A couple of weeks earlier we had watched the film The 47 Ronin, and this was from the scene where the warriors committed hara-kiri, kneeling calmly before a small table, gently laying out a few items in front of them, lowering their robes and plunging a dagger into the stomach, cutting across, then leaning forward for their 'second' to decapitate them. All without any display of fear, or indeed pain.

At this moment it seems a bit vague to explain, but at the time when it was with me, there seemed to be a very definite correlation between what I was seeing in my mind's eye (which was 'me' preparing to 'do what had to be done') and my committing myself to the IAM test (up to ninety minutes of being followed and assessed by a police motorcycle rider). During the test, I was totally calm (which is unheard of for me during a test). I knew what had to be done. I knew it could go wrong (if circumstances turned against me), but I knew also that I could only do what I could, and that is what I did. I knew what was expected of me, and it was carried out calmly and decisively, without fear or apprehension (as with hara-kiri)... Interesting.

I even recognised the hara-kiri scene in the film, with a rolled manuscript (which a look online informed me was the Death Poem), and the wooden-sheathed knife. And it coincided with (and seemed directly connected to) my no longer being afraid of what was to come; all made sense...

(NB. By being in the moment and fully present, and in the 'right' frame of mind, the samurai warrior was expected to accept death without fear or regret. And while my motorcycling test was possibly a poor comparison (with committing hara-kiri), at the time it felt like I was facing a death of some sort: putting myself through a challenging situation, willingly and without fear.)

***

(October 2011)

15) **The new phase** – It has been a while since I wrote anything, and the other week I looked back at some of what I had written before and saw this from April: 'No Fear: So, I have to assume from everything, and accepting the correlation described above, that the final death of the emotional continuation here will occur within the next few days (if it has not already occurred).'

Reading the above, I had to ask myself, Has the emotion 'died'? Am I now free? And as I looked, the first response was No, nothing has changed! Sure everything is OK and I have no problems and life is going well, but nothing has actually changed!

So, I brushed this aside as not being worth recording, but over the next few days it dawned on me the implications of what I had seen: externally the circumstances of life had

343

changed to allow me more time outside the working environment (which I knew I desperately needed), and since then internally and emotionally everything had changed – but only in so much as there are no problems...

I had to wonder if that meant something had actually changed within, or was it simply that the issue causing the problems had been removed, and hence I was now feeling better...?

Then something else happened:

The new additional time away from work has allowed me to slow down. The momentum which has been going for so long is now transforming into more of a pause, even in action. That is to say, whilst the pause used to be present between action (and this was all it was), I have noticed that even in the midst of action a pause is developing. And more so, this pause has information in it! And thus we get to the point (and it may be only a passing point, as experiences change and I can only write what I experience as I do).

16) **Enlightenment vs. Liberation** – It is often the case that it is only once one has gone beyond something, all the way through and out the other side, that one can see it for what it was. A truly 'Enlightened' person may be able to describe perfectly their experience of Enlightenment, but they are missing one major aspect or perspective. Sure, they know what it is like both before Enlightenment and during it, but they still lack the ability to look back on it from the other side. It is this new phase that I am entering here, and I would like to write a little about it.

Looking back, I would now describe the experience of my Enlightenment (and I say it like that because people will experience it in different ways) as being Self-Aware or conscious all the time. But that only means to be aware of oneself all the time. The centre of my 'Being' was always present, regardless of what else was happening around me,

344

regardless of how difficult the circumstances of life were and regardless of how painful life got – my centre was strong and constant. And, if I was replying to an email or giving a talk, or indeed at any other point during the day that I was reminded, the knowledge that this is all a dream (more so, (to me) *my* own dream) would be there, immediate and unquestionable. However, even in this state, this brief and occasional reminder was not enough to break through the disturbance which I was facing in my day-to-day living. Thus difficult times continued and I had to persevere...

The new change, which is only days old as I write this, is that every few minutes the Self-Knowledge comes to me that this is indeed a dream, my own dream, and that I am alone. But more than being a knowledge, this is a real experience – the same one it seems that I had nine years ago when sitting on that bench in Australia, and is what I have always described as my initial entrance into Enlightenment: it was as if I was truly awake in the dream, rather than just intuitively knowing it was a dream...

But at that time the experience faded leaving only the knowledge that was available at any time that I looked: 'I am This' or 'I am alone'. However, this new phase seems to be the becoming of the constant experience (with the knowledge) that this is indeed a dream.

I suspect this is going to be the major aspect of the Liberation state for me: to never again be engulfed in emotion as a result of an external situation. Time will tell...

***

17) **The Dream goes on...** – This new phase is a little strange. As I described above, the information is not new – I first had the insight that this is a dream about seventeen years ago, and this knowledge was further cemented nearly nine years ago with the experience of 'Becoming it', but that quickly passed and left only the inner knowledge – a sort of

345

intuition. As undeniable as it was, it was only knowing it, not being it. Here, the experience is back...

It still comes and goes throughout the day. But to further describe what it is like: imagine if you can that you are at work, in the usual office (assuming you work in an office), and you are aware that you are 'awake' but walking around in your own dream: the office, the building and indeed the task you are currently carrying out, are all within your dream. What would you do?

Many would suggest that in the situation described above, if they were absolutely sure it was a dream, they would walk out of the office, possibly pausing only to tell someone what they really thought of them, and off they would go for good, very likely to indulge in a series of other 'reckless' activities on their way home – or possibly just leave their life behind and not go home at all (i.e. no fear of consequences).

But hold on a moment... What if there are consequences, not because it is not a dream, but because the dream keeps going? Whatever you do 'today', whether 'today' is real or not, will affect what is dreamt tomorrow. As per the words that came to me when I first had the insight all those years ago: 'A Dream it may be, but the Dream goes on!' There is no escape. (Another relevant saying is 'You reap what you sow'.)

Another 'What if...?'

Most of us have seen the film *The Matrix*. Perhaps you too would be tempted to 'take the red pill' – to end the Dream and to see what is beyond it. BUT, what if there is nothing beyond it? Or worse still, what if another Dream is created and you start again, but without the knowledge that it is a dream? Would you rather live with the knowledge, which awards a certain detachment and a relative end to the day-to-day emotional struggle, or end this Dream and risk jumping straight back into another without it? (I am referring to the suggestion that a person may feel like killing themselves: to end this dream and wake up, if they knew this was not real.)

Another thing to consider (even if you 'know' this to be a dream) is the people you interact with and the daily living that you may currently enjoy, and all that you might 'miss'...

You see, just because you are 'awake', the Dream does not change. Only the way you perceive it has changed. So, I suggest that since one has struggled so long to get to this point and to now be free – 'Liberated' – it is easier to carry on, and begin to enjoy the Dream – to go with the flow.

***

18) **Finding the Truth** – So, you are awake in the Dream (following on from the above scenario):

Question: What do you know?
Answer: Well, not much really!

You know you are here, but not what you are, or even where 'here' is. And you know (as much as anything can be 'known') that this is a dream (taking the meaning from our common understanding of the word 'dream') and yet, except for the regular respite from it when you appear to go to sleep here, each time you return to the Dream the circumstances continue where you last left it...

(Imagine for a moment the above happening every time you went to sleep each night: you 'awoke' back in the same dream, night after night, each time with the memories of previous nights. Sure, time had moved on a bit – say eight hours since you last were there – but nothing to raise any questions. How easy would it be to become emotionally attached to the dream, whether pleasant or extremely painful? We are affected emotionally by our dreams, as they are real to us whilst we are in them (just like here). But what if the same dream was continued night after night, week after week, year after year? That is what this is like.)

We have always assumed this 'physical environment' was reality, and when we 'sleep' we let go of it for a while. But now, what we call 'deep dreamless sleep' seems to adopt the mantle of being the nearest to 'true' reality that we can get, as this is when the Dream ends – when all dreaming ends!?

So, to find The Truth, where should one look? Your whole reality is dreamt after all. Experience has shown that the more you look within, at your sense of 'Being', the more the illusion of the Dream is seen through and the less 'important' it becomes. Reasoning suggests that eventually the Dream will simply evaporate and there will be nothing (no-one) left to either know anything or to be known; so only here, in the illusory existence, can anything be known to any extent, whilst it is here.

And yet, how do you dissect a dream? This is a truly amazing place. Scientists are trying to understand this reality in so many ways, and have made wonderful progress, but will there ever be a point when the true nature of this place will be undeniable, or will we always simply find more stuff to measure, more 'Dream'? (Maybe the nearest we can currently get to science finding 'The Truth' here is something like the theoretical 'Dark Matter', or even more so 'Dark Energy': it cannot be seen, so it is 'non-physical', and yet its effects are (apparently) there. But in saying that, I am by no means a scientist, so I am only speculating here. The point is, whatever is measured here is measured within the dream of existence. 'Truth' cannot be measured.)

***

19) **New implications** – Another week has passed and we are now at the end of October 2011. The experience is almost uninterrupted now, in my 'waking state' (and that can be taken

both ways). I wanted to make note of a few observations I have made:

First, again I will say that there is no new information in this for me. I had the initial insight (as a glimpse into true Self-Knowledge and not just an intellectual understanding) when I was about twenty-one years old, and nine years later I had the experience of becoming what I had known all those years. This latter experience passed and left only the knowledge which has been growing ever since...

Now that the experience has returned, the implications of the information also return: the questions and the new perceptions.

For example, I was reminded of the TV series and films *Highlander*, where the main character is immortal (unless his head is cut off), going through his long life having to change his name every so often, taking on the identity of someone who has passed away. That story always seemed quite cool to me, but not anymore; once one is 'awake' in their own Dream, the idea of the Dream lasting forever seems to lose its sparkle to some degree.

And likewise, watching the TV series *X Factor* which is on at the moment, and seeing how hollow it now seems, if one was to be idolised and one's attention craved, when everybody else is known to be figments in one's own dream.

Being successful at anything carries the same feeling: nothing is really achieved – like kids fighting over who has built the best sandcastle on the beach as the tide comes in to wash it all away.

And having said all that, this must still be lived; the game must still be played and one must still get up and do what needs to be done each day. As I said above, a Dream it may be, but the Dream goes on. There are still consequences, nonetheless.

However, another aspect worth noting is that this transition is still emotionally unsettling for me, if only a little.

349

Even though none of it is new, clearly there is an emotional death going on.

A phrase which has occurred to me is what the Buddha is supposed to have said to the men who noticed he was 'different' in some way and had asked if he was a magician (amongst other things). Eventually the Buddha replied simply, 'I am awake!'

***

20) **Buddha poem** –
Quoted from:
(http://www.religionfacts.com/afterlife/buddhism - 1)

The Buddha said of death:
Life is a journey.
Death is a return to earth.
The universe is like an inn.
The passing years are like dust.

Regard this phantom world
As a star at dawn, a bubble in a stream,
A flash of lightning in a summer cloud,
A flickering lamp - a phantom - and a dream.

One word common in Buddhist philosophies and teachings is 'Nirvana': a term frequently used to describe the ultimate state of Being.

> Nirvana is the state of final liberation from the cycle of death and rebirth. It is also therefore the end of suffering. The literal meaning of the word is "to extinguish," in the way that a fire goes out when it runs out of fuel. In the Surangama, the Buddha describes Nirvana as the place in which:

> '...it is recognized that there is nothing but what is seen of the mind itself; where, recognizing the nature of the self-mind, one no longer cherishes the

dualisms of discrimination; where there is no more thirst nor grasping; where there is no more attachment to external things.'

(http://www.religionfacts.com/afterlife/buddhism - 1)

***

(January 2012)

It has been several weeks since I updated the website and it seemed time to do so. Below I will list the main points:

First, since writing above that the knowledge that this is a dream is now constant, this has since changed to be more a gentle coming and going of the awareness of the knowledge. Not a major point perhaps, but for the sake of accuracy I wanted to include it.

Second, possibly in keeping with Barry Long's teaching regarding one's relationship being a vital part of the (so-called) 'spiritual journey' (Barry's main teaching was largely focused on how to love 'rightly' in order to grow in love and consciousness), as close as Sally and I have been over the eight or so years since we met, suddenly things have entered a new phase in recent weeks and we are much closer and more in tune than ever before.

Another small point: last week I received an email from a visitor to the website asking whether the page describing my 'three requirements for lasting contentment' should be updated following the developments over the last few months, so update it I have. Not much has changed, but there may be an interesting addition:

I have received contact from a number of people regarding various teachers who, invariably having had some kind of spontaneous awakening, teach with bold phrases like: '*This is just happening; there is no "path" and no "spiritual journey"!*' – 'You are

351

already Enlightened; you just don't know it!' – 'There is nobody here to be, or to not be, Enlightened.' – 'Just surrender and be here now; there is nowhere else to be as nothing is real!'

After considering the above for a little while (not for the first time) and how different my approach is from theirs, I eventually came to the conclusion that the reason these teachers do not teach a 'path' or process to 'spiritual' development (such as the facing and dissolving of emotion) is simply (and this seems obvious really) because they did not follow a path themselves...

I was taught by Barry Long about the cause and effect of this emotional temporary existence, and have watched the domino effect of the circumstances of my life every day for the last twenty plus years, and to me it is obvious.

And yet these teachers insist there is no cause and effect: everything just is! All I can say to that is, if you really are able to simply 'be' like that, then great. But for the rest of us who have to play the game, I can teach you the rules.

***

21) **Dream: Dying in a car crash** – A few days ago I had a dream: I was the passenger in the front seat of a car driving up some steep and winding roads on the side of a mountain. Soon the driver pulled into a gravel car park, swung the car around and parked so that I was looking out of the side window over the valley, about eighteen inches from the edge and the steep drop below.

352

Only a moment later the driver said, 'Hold on, I will pull forward a bit,' and he started the engine and drove forward, closer to the edge... From this moment the dream was in three stages, each one being a moment frozen in time, allowing my mind to consider what was occurring...

1) In my mind's eye, I saw the outside of the car, like a camera zoomed in on the front wheel next to me, and I watched as it tipped over the edge and small rocks fell away; and for a second the image froze... As I looked at the wheel and saw the extreme drop below, down the several-storey-high vertical cliff to the rocky surface at the bottom, a few thoughts quickly went through me: *Is this real? Is this a set-up, some sort of* You've Been Framed *TV show?*

2) Then, my view of the edge of the cliff disappeared underneath as the car lunged forward, and the entire front end of the car was over the edge and starting to fall. At this point I knew this was real... Again, here the scene froze, and I had time to ask a few more questions: *Why is this happening? What will dying now achieve? I have come so far... What will I possibly learn from dying, now, like this? What is the point?!*

3) Then the scene jumped forward again, and I was staring out of the front window only yards before we hit the bottom. The rocky surface filled the entire windscreen. During the fall the car had begun to flip head over heels, and the landing was going to be partly nose-first with a heavy crash on the roof, flattening the car...

As I looked, I knew this was going to be all but certain death, and at the very least I would be left in a hell of a mess if I was to survive. Because of this knowledge (and this is the point for me), the words that actually came out of my mouth (in the dream) were surprising in that they were humorous. I said simply, 'Oh fucking hell; this is not going to be good!'

Then it went black, and I woke up.

Meaning...?

I can usually glean some sort of message or lesson from a vivid dream such as this, as my dreams tend to follow the same pattern as in my daily life and relate to some sort of emotional attachment. The scenario itself probably came from a combination of watching the *Ice Road Truckers' Deadliest Roads* recently, and likewise an episode of *Top Gear* where they were on the same type of roads: teetering on the edge of a sheer drop with two cars trying to pass where there was only room for one and a half cars...

But as for the lesson itself, so far I have just been intrigued by my attitude at the time. There was no fear, just a questioning as to the reason, and then a feeling of total 'surrender' to 'what is', and indeed what was to be, where I was powerless to affect the outcome in any way. This is probably the meaning: my acceptance of the worst possible situation, and with humour no less!

***

(March 2012)

22) **'Awake' when asleep: Lucid dreaming** – So far, my being 'awake' has been in this 'real' world (where everybody thinks they are awake, but that is because they don't know they are dreaming).

Well, within the last couple of weeks I have had two additional meaningful dreams:

1) I was in a house with the occupants. They were being very pleasant and were about to show me around, and suddenly I was awake and aware that I was dreaming. A moment later it occurred to me, as this was a dream, that nothing can go wrong, so I decided to see what would happen if I was to take off all my clothes (please forgive the mental image if you are easily offended).

354

As I stood there, naked, the occupants did not flinch. They continued to act as if nothing had happened, and we spoke normally.

A few minutes passed, and still unsure as to whether their lack of reaction was due to them not noticing, or being too polite to say anything (in the dream), it occurred to me that actually I was being very rude. Dream or not, I was showing no respect to these people who were being very nice to me.

With that I began to get dressed. (I remember having a little trouble locating my underpants and picking up and studying a pair that did not look like mine.)

2) The second dream I cannot remember in any detail. All I recall was that I was awake again, aware that I was dreaming, and this time I chose to carry on as if nothing had changed (as one must do here). The dream was uneventful, but that shift was relevant.

***

(14.03.12) It has been a year since this process began and this diary was started. A lot has changed:

Environmentally, my life is now very comfortable (thank you); it's been a long time coming. Work is good, and home life (specifically my relationship) is great. It's an amazing change.

Personally, I am more relaxed, and yet I have also been moved to break down a few of the mental barriers that have existed in me all my life with regards to how I perceive and present myself (namely: I got my ear pierced; got my first tattoo; my goatee has become a fuller (but still quite neat) beard; I am learning to ride a motorbike; I have gone back to the gym; and I have given up coffee and gone on to herbal tea. Quite a list – I am not quite becoming a hippy though, if that's how it sounds).

Spiritually (for want of a better word), being 'Awake' is increasingly becoming the norm. Again, this is not as an intuitive knowledge that this is a dream, but as a real experience.

I will add though that this does not mean in a day-to-day sense that living has changed. By that I mean, being 'Awake' does not mean I can walk through walls or fly, or move mountains with a single thought (years ago I read some of the old stories about Eastern Masters who apparently did these things). However, blatant coincidences do occur regularly, making living (at present, at least) relatively effortless.

I don't know how things will progress from here, or whether there will just be more of the same, but I will update this page in future if anything spectacular does change.

***

(November 2012)

Living with Liberation

It has been several months since I updated the website. At various times I have thought to myself *I really should write about that*, but time passed and things happened, and the website took a bit of a backseat to actually living...

So, I will now try to summarise where, or perhaps 'how', I now find myself (no pun intended).

1) I am still 'me'. The space that was previously here, within, is still the same space. It is just that it is always here (instead of being obscured by my awareness of it by other emotions and thoughts).

2) Despite the above, I still get enveloped in the activities of day-to-day living. But several times a day (possibly many times, but I don't actually pay much attention to the frequency), depending on what I am doing, I find I am 'awake' again and aware that I am dreaming (as an experience of

actually being awake, rather than an intuitive knowledge); but this is not constant, and it is also not a big deal. It is a gentle wave of extra awareness, drifting in and out effortlessly. There is no need for me to do anything – unlike previously when I would have been fighting all the time to stay conscious. It is just a reassurance that all is well. And the less busy I am, the more it is there. It is the activity of the moment that seems to consume the knowledge. (It would be so much easier, living on a hillside.)

3) 'As within, so without' is not a new saying; it is commonly quoted in spiritual teachings. And it occurred to me to have a look, finally, at what this could mean in relation to my difficulties at work and specifically the problems with the managers.

So I asked myself what they represented to me, and I found myself creating a list of the following words: overpowering, judgmental, demanding, hypercritical, controlling, micromanaging, bullying. And as I looked at the list of words, I noticed these words also described how I treated myself: I always expect a lot and really give myself no leeway. (After all, that is how I had got so far with this teaching of facing and dissolving emotion within.) And then it hit me: these managers, and indeed every overpowering personality throughout my life, both past and present, have been my self externalised! They were treating me physically – outside – the same way as I was treating myself internally. The same energy was creating them both! Hence, 'as within, so without'.

As I saw this, I hoped this realisation would mean it was nearing the end now.

4) Work: Using the above logic, I then asked myself why I was still in the same job. What did I still have to learn from working for a local government authority? Why could I not

withdraw from it and just enjoy relaxing a bit, possibly writing and teaching more?

As I looked at what working for the council meant to me, I found that again an interesting list of words unfolded and all became clearer. These included the following: structure, formality, routine, discipline, responsibility. And as I looked at the list of words, I noticed that they also reflected aspects of my own personality. These very characteristics that had been my driving force to grow in Self-Knowledge and which had enabled me to uncover so much with regards to how this existence works, were the same aspects of myself that are creating my work environment.

And when pointed out, it is obvious really: we know all is one, and that this existence is within the one Being – one's own being. So it follows that one's personal inner traits would create the outer...

The other interesting aspect therefore is that there really is no escape. I will always be 'me'. If I was to force a change and resign from my job, I wouldn't go far; my life would not change much: my 'inner' self would still create the outer world and it would continue as before. A different name above the door perhaps, but I would still be me, and my life would still be my life, whatever I found myself doing.

Then for a moment I had a clearer view into what we call Karma: one's 'self' will always create its environment. That is the natural law. The only way it can be. Whatever one's inner nature, their external reality will be reflected in that. (That is not to say that people choose their lives, or even deserve their lives so to speak. There is one Being here, and that is what is creating this place. Every religion (let's say) states this as a fact, so it is not new. The scary bit is coming to terms with the implications of there being only one Being: if there is only One, then who else could it be?)

So it's nice to think that perhaps, having seen this, the energetic movement is already set in motion to address this aspect too. There can be a time delay between seeing something and one's external environment changing. But maybe I'll be able to leave work soon. We'll see.

23) **Stopping situations in their tracks** – Over the years I have become quicker and quicker at 'waking up' when faced with a difficult situation. Originally I would have been lost for hours in the emotion, going round and round in the imagination until finally, when I had endured it long enough that I could see it for what it was and be able to step back, I began to dissolve it. As the years passed, when I found myself in a difficult situation I would wake up earlier. Eventually, very soon after a 'problem' developed I would begin to dissolve it within, and it would be resolved quickly without. But this is a new area.

On repeated occasions I have had an idea or been made aware of the potential for something to go 'wrong'. In that moment I would feel a pang of emotion and often have a short time to face and dissolve the emotion prior to the situation actually manifesting here. Remaining conscious and facing the emotion in the moment dissolves the origin of the situation even before it occurs (as the energy of it is created inside and it only manifests 'outside' afterwards), and what could have been never happens...

This is not to say difficult situations never happen at all, but when they actually do come to fruition, their level of difficulty seems to be minimal and they are resolved quickly (both within and without).

***

Final stages
Wow, doesn't time fly...?! It has now been over a year since I updated the site, not because nothing has happened but because it has – lots. But where to start?

A major aspect has been the frequent correspondence via email with Nitin Trasi, author of the book *The Science of Enlightenment*. Nitin's book was published in 1999, seven years before our first, but I suspect he had been in the state for a while prior to that. And regardless of how long he has been Enlightened, Nitin has been in close communication over the years with some of the greatest Eastern gurus of this age, so his general knowledge and experience in these and related matters are extensive.

So, what happened?

Well, first, we (actually I; it was all 'me') got a little stuck: Nitin and I were talking via email, and he finished one with the statement that there is nobody here now (in me).

Those of you who have followed my story will know I object to this approach, that there is nobody here, and we had to of course explore this further between ourselves. I have huge respect for Nitin, for his experience, his state of Being, and his vast knowledge and learning, so I was not going to discount what he was saying. And yet, I could not agree... 'I' was still here!

Emails went back and forth, in which I explained that 'I' still am, and Nitin showed me that a number of the most famous gurus (such as Nisargadatta Maharaj and Ramana Maharshi) had, like myself, followed a method which required total dedication to the experience 'I am'; and specifically that Alan Watts (another very famous Western teacher) and Ramana Maharshi had expressed teachings very similar to my own with regards to this being a Dream, so I was in good company.

(Note: Despite Barry confirming my original insight for me, on a number of occasions when asked whether this was an illusion, he would reply saying that he did not like the terms 'illusion nor dream', when describing this place, as these words do not speak to the deeper reality that is occurring. He

said it is NOT an illusion (or dream); it's a projection!
Nevertheless, this is how it came to me, and I do actually
agree with Barry regarding the term 'illusion', and do of
course acknowledge the greater reality that is occurring which
does not seem to be represented in this word. However, I
regard a dream as a projection also, of the unconscious or
emotions on to the screen of awareness, just as with this
place. So while those who are familiar with Barry's teaching
may have wondered about this point, there is no contradiction
here, as I see it.)

Example: In the eighteenth paragraph of *Nan Yar?* (Who Am
I?) Sri Ramana says:

> Except that waking is [long lasting] and dream is
> [momentary or lasting for only a short while], there is
> no other difference [between these two imaginary
> states of mental activity]. To the extent to which all
> the [activities or occurrences] that happen in waking
> appear [at this present moment] to be real, to that
> [same] extent even the [activities or occurrences] that
> happen in dream appear at that time to be real. In
> dream [our] mind takes another body [to be itself].

> *(Quoted   from:*
> *www.happinessofbeing.blogspot.co.uk)*

This was very interesting to me. But I still really wanted to at
least understand this 'There's nobody here' teaching. It had
been bad enough having to 'discuss' it with people online,
and then meeting that teacher in London who stated the
same thing; but my good friend Nitin, who I not only knew to
be Enlightened and indeed Liberated but whom I also trusted
implicitly, also said that he was in 'experience' of 'not being

361

here' (and perhaps now more so, that I was). So there had to be more to it.

In an early response to Nitin I wrote the following:

(August 2013)

I cannot say there is 'Nothing' or 'no one' here, as 'I' am still here, and it does feel 'solid'.

I think I am probably still in the settling down of this last phase though. While it is indeed 'solid', it is still new here, in the sense that this blatant (I almost want to say 'fierceness', but that is clearly wrong. It is more unapologetic, substantial, like a sledge hammer wrapped in cotton wool), has not been as obvious before. It's a bit like walking indoors from outside, where it was a little chilly, but not too bad. But here the heating is on, and I sit down in front of an open fire, sinking into a large, soft and amazingly comfortable armchair, with a hot drink of whatever; and all is well. Outside wasn't bad at all, but this is lovely. But, it's almost not in a positive way, because there is no excitement, no activity – it's just extremely comfortable. I am sure you know what I mean, Nitin.

Then things began to change: first was this email (below). And I have included it 'as is' in case it helps others. It shows the level of our communication and the depth of my questioning, despite arguably already having all the knowledge (I have been teaching for ten years to date). However, it also shows the thought process and how the 'Truth' (for want of a better term) presented itself. I have not posted Nitin's replies, not because he would mind as I don't think he would at all, but because this story is about my growth and as such it did not seem necessary.

362

In this email, I am challenging how 'everything is already done', or 'nothing can be done', or the like.

14/11/13

Hi Nitin,

As ever, thank you.

And yes, I think I am getting there...

My hesitancy has in the first instance been in understanding the path of the Advaita. For me, when faced with a difficult (emotional) situation, I came to know well that the unhappy or distressed emotion that 'I' was feeling was the very thing responsible for the situation outside. Thus, facing this consciously and steadfastly within directly addressed the problem outside (as the saying goes: As within, so without...)

It is therefore well-ingrained into my life experience that 'my' emotion creates the external circumstances of my life, and when the emotion has gone, so too will the physical manifestation – as there will be nothing left to create it.

So, trying to imagine another path, one that does not include this, one where it all just happens without 'me' having a direct impact, is alien to me.

However, with regards to how to see it now and my little struggle with the two views, I was going to say that I see two possible reasons for my current apparent (minor) dilemma:

1) My history and life experience being hard to deny (i.e. I learnt that 'I may be suffering, but 'I' am doing it and only I can change it').

2) The idea of the 'I' now being so subtle that I can't even see it (i.e. it's gone, but I don't know it).

Then, prior to actually writing the above, I had a little shift, and began to see the two options as one and the same, in the sense that:

The (my) path and history have served to reinforce the idea of 'I' and 'me' (not erase it), even though the actual experience of it has possibly since gone.

And while this idea remains, that is all it is, an idea. And as it is only an idea and not an experience per se, and this idea has intertwined itself with the experience of 'Being', as you say, there is nothing of it left to dissolve (which has been my path…)

So how does one dissolve a concept?

It's fascinating really…

It just occurred to me that it's perhaps like building a boat to escape a desert island, and having spent years at sea fighting to survive, refusing to get out of the boat when safely beached on another shore: the very thing that has been my friend and saviour now must be abandoned as false and out of date.

Hee hee.

I am just not sure how to do it… How to get out. How to dissolve an idea!

But then again, if there is no one to do anything, and nothing to do, then of course I can't do it!!!

…Oh dear!!!

364

And then the next day I sent this:

15/11/13

Ok, I did it... I got out of the boat!!!

Thank you... When I read your reply first thing this morning (saying it can't be done – in the sense of a conscious action), I thought to myself, if that is the case, then it's the first step or stage that I have met where there is nothing I can do. (Everything else has followed a set procedure and routine, albeit one that took years...)

Suddenly I was reminded about the initial Liberation experience, and how I read the interview with Bernadette Roberts where she described a major part of the stage was the centre of her 'Being' evaporating...

And while I knew intuitively that I was at this new stage, I did not know at the time how to make the centre point disappear...

But then it had occurred to me, what would happen if I simply let go of it and directed my full attention to the rest of the 'space'? And in that moment it was gone, as quickly as that, never to return!!!

With this in mind, I wondered what would happen if I did the same here...

So I 'forced' myself to let go of the knowledge 'I am' by directing 100% of my attention outside, to what was around (I was having a shower), and as before, the 'I am' was gone!!!

It makes sense really: there is only so much attention-energy. I did not have to try to forget the 'I am'; instead, I just had to turn all my attention away from the idea of it.

So, how is it now...?

There is only what is experienced, what is seen or heard, but no one who is doing the seeing or listening. (Darn it; I sound like one of the 'There's nobody here' types who I have come to dislike fairly strongly.)

(smile)

And again, 'Being' is still here, but no one is actually doing the 'being' or even experiencing it. The experience is complete.

I will keep looking at it, but it looks like we (I) are there.

Thank you for your patience Nitin. I know I must have almost driven you to despair with this one.

So, that was it, as it is said: there indeed was no one here...

***

But then a few days later I wrote the following:

20/11/13

Hi Nitin

Looking at this still, it seems nothing actually changed, as such... (But the fact is still the fact.)

It is (was) a bit like I imagine losing one's leg, and one may continue to have sensations from where the leg used to be, even though it has clearly gone...

It seems the 'I am' had gone a while back, in the way that it is usually felt, but the idea of the 'I am' had become such an established part of my experience of living that even after it had been dissolved, the area that I associated with it still remained and this was identified as still being it...

It is of course fitting that the 'I am' should be the last thing to go.

And it was a battle. No amount of anyone telling me that 'I' had gone was going to convince me, as the 'awareness' was all that was left, and I 'knew' I was that. (What else could I be...? There was nothing else here...)

Very subtle.

Looking at it here, it is actually more like the 'I am' has gone, but the 'I' remains...

There is the experience, and it is being experienced without a doubt; but not by anybody or anyone, as that would imply separation where there isn't any. There is only the experience...

As the saying goes 'The perceiver and the perceived become one'.

And I don't really like the phrase that I have often read online 'This is just awareness experiencing itself' (though it may be true), as it implies (to me) a separation from 'I'. It always gave me the impression that the person was talking in the third person about something 'else' that was operating their body and experiencing their life (that the 'I' had gone too), and that confused me...

367

Now it makes sense.

Anyway, thank you again Nitin.

Nitin replied to the last email pointing out that Ramana Maharshi said or wrote something almost identical to my 'I' vs. 'I am' conclusion:

Quote taken from Wikipedia 'Questioning "Who am I?"':

Ramana Maharshi:

In response to questions on self-liberation and the classic texts on Yoga and Vedanta, Ramana recommended self-enquiry as the means to awaken to the 'I-I' and the Self-enquiry in the form 'Who am I?' alone is the principal means. To make the mind subside, there is no adequate means other than self-enquiry. If controlled by other means, mind will remain as if subsided, but will rise again.

'...Basically "self-enquiry" is the constant attention to the inner awareness of "I" or "I am".' Sri Ramana Maharshi frequently recommended it as the most efficient and direct way of discovering the unreality of the 'I'-thought.

Enquiring the 'I'-thought, one realises that it raises in the hṛdayam (heart). *'The "I"-thought will disappear and only "I-I" or Self-awareness remains, which is Self-realization or liberation*:

'What is finally realized as a result of such enquiry into the source of Aham-vritti ("I"-thought) is verily the Heart as the undifferentiated Light of Pure Consciousness, into which the reflected light of the mind is completely absorbed.'

Ramana warned against considering self-enquiry as an intellectual exercise. Properly done, it involves fixing the attention firmly and intensely on the feeling of 'I', without thinking. Attention must be fixed on the 'I' until the sense of 'I' disappears and the Self is realised.

'Verse thirty of *Ulladu Narpadu*:

'Questioning *"Who am I?"* within one's mind, when one reaches the Heart, the individual *"I"* sinks crestfallen, and at once reality manifests itself as *"I-I"*. Though it reveals itself thus, it is not the ego *"I"* but the perfect being, the Self Absolute.'

Verses nineteen and twenty of *Upadesa Undiyar* describe the same process in almost identical terms:

19. *'Whence does the "I" arise? Seek this within. The "I" then vanishes. This is the pursuit of wisdom.'*

20. *'Where the "I" vanished, there appears an "I-I" by itself. This is the infinite.'*

And as I write this page, 'I' (with a big 'I', or 'I-I', as above) still is. I can't even say 'still is here' as even the word 'here' is no longer accurate, but the witness remains nevertheless.

And perhaps amazingly, I still object to the 'There's nobody here' teaching. Because whilst the witness remains, and remains 'in' a body, I consider it to be misleading to tell people who are not in the state that there is nobody here, because the mind of the other is likely to imagine one is saying that the witness has gone, and that is of course not the case.

***

There's nobody here
I later saw, finally, what I believe to be the answer to my longstanding confusion, and I'd been dancing around it all this

time; sometimes even stating it, but not truly seeing it: whether someone says they are all that is left and identify as being the very awareness itself, or whether they say they are gone and there is nothing left, would appear to be determined simply by the path they took. If they always identified with being the emotional self, then when it has gone, of course they will say they are gone and there is nothing left. But if their path involved facing and dissolving the emotional self, in the belief (or knowledge?) that they are not that – they are the awareness behind it – then when the emotional self has gone and only the awareness remains, then they may say they (as 'I') remain. It seems obvious really, now I actually see it.

***

Back at the beginning
So, more time passed and the emails continued, sometimes daily, and then one very early morning in January something new happened. This is the email I wrote to Nitin:

16/01/14

5.26 a.m.

Hello Nitin... I have just been moved to get out of bed, sit in the bathroom so as not to disturb Sally, and write this...

Wow...

It is 4.55 a.m. as I write this, and I am stunned; but then 'I' am not, because that is the point...

Last night we watched the final episode of a TV series ('Dexter', for those who know it), and we were extremely disappointed. We even looked online and found most people felt the same way...

I mention this only because on waking a few

moments ago, it felt like the end of my own TV series, the end of a book of my life, in which on the last page the final revelation turns everything on its head...!

I saw, clearly, that 'I' see nothing. There are two components here: there is the apparent existence, which means everything from the sky and mountains, to my body and even my thoughts and feelings; and then there is the 'I', the constant but passive observer. 'I' don't even have my own thoughts...! (But I knew that, didn't I? I wrote that many years ago, and it is published in my first book in the article entitled 'Free Will' – but that was an abstract and veiled insight. Here, 'I' am seeing it, becoming it!)

But what am I seeing? And which 'I' is seeing it...?

'I' am seeing it, but 'I' lack the capacity to do anything about it, to even think anything about it. 'I' see all but do nothing...

And this means (so it would appear as I write this), that the whole journey has been a farce. There is no journey. The method I have followed, of facing and dissolving emotions to become more conscious, actually was not me doing it at all. This body (and mind) is just a robot in which I am the intelligence looking out, experiencing what it experiences, convinced that it is 'me' because that is what the robot has been programmed to think! Of myself, 'I' can't even think!!!

And yet, the robot mind and body are 'thinking' this, and feeling the indignation (if that is the right word) for me. 'I' can't 'feel' anything. 'I' just watch...

...Who or what is doing this?!!

Very strange...

I (one of me, anyway) is/am stunned...

And how can I (either one) ever understand this place? The intelligence, 'I' cannot even think, let alone understand anything. And the robot-I cannot do anything without an observer (me/'I') to observe it. The robot-I cannot even ask its own questions, as they are created for it along with everything else...

And the thought has just occurred, am I sure I am the observer...? Am I actually the robot...?

And I see almost immediately that I am both. Without either, there is no experience, no self-awareness.

It is now 5.25 a.m., it is still very dark but the birds are singing outside. I am not due to get up for a while so will go back to bed.

Again, as I said in the email above, none of it was really new, but it felt very new. Just as when the Enlightenment occurred here, and at the time I had the experience that everything around me was my own reflection, and it was another ten years before that experience returned and became constant (this new phase), the knowledge that 'I' only exist because 'that' is over 'there' (for the awareness to reflect off) was written years ago, but actually becoming the experience was very different.

***

372

Inevitability?

Then Nitin and I began discussing the question of inevitability and the teachings that there is nothing one can do and all is already done, etc., and I struggled with these ideas for a little while, having followed a definite path to get here which involved facing and dissolving emotion as I went, seemingly 'doing' something to aid progression.

And then a few weeks later I wrote the following pieces in an email:

26/01/14

...Ok, next bit: last night again, it occurred to me that it doesn't actually matter what happens to this body and personality, as it is all part of the story.

In a week or so now I have a meeting at work re an on-going situation; it has been on and off my mind for a few weeks (pushing me deeper).

But last night I saw that the outcome is irrelevant, not because it's already done so much, as because what has to be will be. Nick's story must be told, and told accurately. 'I' just happen to be in Nick, witnessing it from his perspective...

***

The Big Bang Theory – The origin of existence

Later, when I was considering further how the whole physical universe comes to be, I wrote this in summary:

07/02/14

...So, we simply have (from what I am seeing here), the Mind. Within it erupts some emotion which creates forms, but is itself unconscious. The Mind watches on as scenarios are played out. The

meeting of these two creates Self-Awareness – 'I am' (ego?) – but neither the Mind, the unconscious emotion, nor the newly created but temporary 'I am' can actually change what is occurring. It is experienced and then is gone; that is, once all the emotion/unconscious is again conscious.

As I said yesterday, I can see this as the true origin of the Big Bang Theory (and Barry said that the most exciting part of the journey is seeing where the Truth is represented here in physical form).

It would also fit with the Advaita description of Brahman breathing existence in and out. I can see it as if watching a movie internally: out of a single point within of 'nothing' spills existence, expanding outwards, like a volcano erupting; until withdrawing again, back into itself, eternally, timelessly, like the tide going in and out, in and out, in and out... (Actually, the Brahman story seems to fit pretty well with what I am seeing.)

I feel quite content with this (though you of course may see it differently). It feels here as if the questions have indeed gone. It's quite strange. Barry used to say there are no answers, and I have said that too as I understood it intellectually and perhaps intuitively, but seeing it as described above has left a feeling as if I have indeed hit a solid wall and the end of all answers (but strangely in a comfortable, reassuring way): the end of the road yes, but more importantly, I am back at The Beginning?!

***

It is now 28 February 2014, and all seems to have settled down since the above experiences, exactly three weeks ago now. But then again, what else could there be left to see or realise? I still have the mental vision (if I am reminded to look) of the universe emerging from a centre point, expanding outwards, later to withdraw again, back to nothing...

Summary

The Big Bang Theory describing how the universe came to be is no longer a theory to me. It is indeed the truth of the origin and creation of the universe. It is presented here in the physical existence as a theory for how the universe came to be, and it is correct. I assumed, perhaps unconsciously, that it was just science trying to make sense of something that cannot be understood, and that the true origin, if I was ever to see it, would have to be something else. But here, the last insight (for now at least) which shows to me the origin of everything that is, is the very same one that we have always been shown. It was never a secret. And it feels as if it has united the two worlds together for me (the physical with the spiritual) and is indeed both the beginning and the end!

...And that is how it should be... It's truly amazing (to me)!

Thank you for reading.

PS. When I first wrote the last section above (and the email to Nitin), re. The Big Bang Theory and my seeing it as the origin of everything, in error I wrote 'Black Hole Theory'. I share this here only because, as I see it in my mind, the image looks the same as a black hole from the movies, but in reverse with everything coming out, and then being drawn back in again as one sleeps...

***

375

The Ultimate – Freedom from problems

> A popular concept is that after, say, God-Realisation ('Self-Realisation' in the East), the whole life is instant bliss. This, like all assumptions, is not true... what is not commonly known is that there then follows an external testing of the inner equilibrium... This may take many years. The deeper the realisation, the more provoking or demanding the circumstances are likely to be...
>
> (Long, B. 2013. *My Life of Love & Truth: A Spiritual Autobiography*: Barry Long Books, p. 1)

The above is a quote from the second paragraph on page one of Barry Long's autobiography; the book was finally published in 2013, ten years after Barry's death, and this section spoke directly to this latest phase which has been deepening in me over the last two years.

I will add here that I named this section 'The Ultimate' because of the nature of this latest phase. However, to allow for yet further development, I wished to stop short of using the other well-known expression when speaking about the deeper levels of Enlightenment: 'The Absolute'.

What is also worth noting is that Barry (who was kind and replied to my letters on several occasions over the years when I was following his teaching) extremely generously replied at the time when he was very near the end of his life, and his letter included the following:

> ...It seems to me, your qualifications to serve by teaching the people are solid or well-founded. It is true at 30 there is still much living to do, as J. Krishnamurti found. But that did not stop him. At that age - & I suppose at every age - one must face

the testing circumstances of the realisations of truth / and or love. At 30 however, with profound knowledge already realised, there's a lot of living to do...

I see now that these two quotes are making the same point:

After 'Enlightenment' occurred here, about eleven years ago now, I was surprised life did not seem to get easier; at least, not in the way I expected. Sure, I knew why things were happening, in the broad sense that 'I' was creating them to teach me (something?), and there was a solid 'strength' inside which was always there, even when things got tough and I was really struggling, but I *was* still struggling.

And this would have surprised others too, had they known what I was going through when I was giving the talks and writing the books, etc.: 'Here is a teacher of Enlightenment, talking about life and death, saying he is God-Realised or Self-Realised and teaching people how to consciously face and dissolve emotional situations, and yet his life is still difficult. How come?'

Now it makes sense to me, and as per another quote from a later paragraph in the same section of Barry's autobiography:

Finally, the inner state is known to have been perfected; and the perfection (which has nothing to do with the man or woman) is reflected in the harmony of the external life. All is solved; all is provided. The life is free of problematical circumstances...

(Long, B. 2013. *My Life of Love & Truth: A Spiritual Autobiography*: Barry Long Books, p. 2)

Here, now, life and day-to-day living are enjoyable, easy even. Life still has to be lived, and circumstances or situations can and do arise that require attention and action, but these tend to be quickly and easily resolved. Thus, some ten years after Barry wrote me his last letter and stated in it the fairly cryptic prediction (at the time, to me) that there would still be testing circumstances, now it all makes sense. The amazing part is that I was 'allowed' to struggle for the ten years, not really knowing why, or when it would end, and it was only when it did finally begin to come to an end that Barry's autobiography was published stating that this is how it has to be...

Perhaps interestingly, my whole journey has revolved around Barry in one way or another: first, at about eighteen years old, when I was seated on the sofa at home after college, having already begun to practise self-observation and questioning and analysing all my thoughts and their origin, when I felt intuitively that I had got as far as I could with that system. I paused, and suddenly said out loud to the four walls the words 'I need a Master!' And in that very moment I remembered a book (of Barry's) that I had purchased a year beforehand but never opened. That was my introduction to his teaching. I ran to my collection of unopened books and began reading.

A few years later, Barry replied to a letter from me in which he confirmed my insight that there is only one dreamer here, and said to keep going. That was a massive step for me and everything else built on this point. Later I learnt that very few seekers ever realise this; even some who claim to be Enlightened have argued with me over this since I began teaching. (It seems it is common to accept everything as 'One', but the idea of being that One is another matter entirely.)

A further ten years passed, during which I followed Barry's teaching as diligently as I was able, fighting all day, every day to remain conscious, through the hell of emotions that plagued me. Numerous insights, experiences and realisations came and went over the years, several times leading me to wonder whether this was it, only to find it was not. Finally, Barry replied to another letter in which I stated I thought I was 'there', and by then I had already recently begun teaching.

And then here we are, a further ten years since the last letter from Barry. His autobiography is finally published, and its opening section reiterates and actually explains what he said in the last letter he wrote to me, and in doing so, explains the last ten years of my life. (My own self-knowledge did that too, but as is often the way, someone or something 'outside' will often appear to confirm one's insights.)

So (and as I have said before), thank you Barry.

**

Final thought: there are many levels of Enlightenment, in the same way that there are many 'levels' as one travels up a hill. But as with a hill, there are also infinite (let's say) routes one may take to reach the top, and various means of travel one may use. As a result, it can be very difficult to know how 'advanced' another is, especially when they are on the opposite side of the hill from you and proceeding via a completely different path. Thus we have all the debates as to which route or method is best. In the end, it is irrelevant how one got 'there', to the top. One will arrive just the same, via their own route and in their own time...

However, as I write this, and see in my mind's eye the symbolic hill and the individual reaching the summit, it occurs to me that once there, they will probably stand and face the way they came, or look 'up' or 'out', or simply enjoy where they are now. They will not look 'down' and all around and suddenly become knowledgeable of everybody else's path. They will be experts in their *own* journey, whatever that may be, and will indeed be able to talk to others coming up from their own experience. They will also be able to describe the summit perfectly to all who would listen, and amongst all those on the summit their descriptions of the top itself will be nearly identical. However, each will not be able to speak or teach with real authority to those who are still on the way up but whose journey is totally different from theirs, as they do not know the path.

***

(December 2015)
Freedom
Again, it's been a little while since I had anything to add. The occasional new page has been posted on the website, but nothing personal from my own journey.

That was, until last week:

It was at night, and I was lying in bed, in the dark, waiting to go to sleep, when I noticed an irritation in me. And when I looked closer I saw it was a frustration at feeling trapped, but not trapped as most people may understand it, as there was nothing on my mind – but trapped in the body. It was a little strange. But then I saw it wasn't actually strange at all. Whilst I know intuitively that the body is only dreamt as part of this temporary existence, and I have had experiences related to this, at that moment the sensations of the body, such as where it touched the bed, were very much present and the focus of my awareness was on this. It WAS me, and yet I knew it was not. So the question in that moment was what to do about it; what would I need to do so as to no longer feel trapped inside the body, whilst still having it?

Almost immediately I was reminded of the process I have had to go through in recent years, in similar situations. My entire journey, since I was eighteen years old, had been of being conscious and dissolving anything that exists: all (emotional) feeling survives in unconsciousness, and being conscious and holding on to it will dissolve it.

380

But then this new phase brought with it (i.e. forced) a new approach. No longer could I hold on to something to dissolve it, because what was left was part of 'Being' (of being alive in a body). Having dissolved everything emotional – everything which arose as a result of my attitude or interpretation of an event, and all mental structures related to ideas of what I am had to be dismantled – what was left were the foundations: the origin and basis of 'Me'.

So, several years ago now (at the start of this new phase), the centre of 'Me', which I had held on to for so long and which had become the rock of my existence, had to be let go of. Then later, the sense of 'I am' which had been my constant companion for so long, also had to be let go of. And now this: my body...

As with the previous instances, this time lying in the dark and being aware of the body, I forced my attention away from what I could feel and into the blackness, almost imagining I was out 'there'. In a flash it was as if I disappeared, and then in the same instant, in shock, I was back again. I did this several times before I did fall asleep.

I awoke the next morning with this knowledge and continued the exercise. Throughout the day, all day (at work, mostly driving from one task to the next), I held on to or projected my awareness to a point some distance in front of me, forcing it away from the body. It was surprisingly easy. And by the end of the day it made no difference whether I held the point in front, to the side or behind – it felt equally comfortable. And by the evening it was as if 'I', the awareness, was all around (all around the body), extending outwards indefinitely in all directions (and yet, at the same time evaporating into nothing). I was no longer trapped in the body!

***

As I write this, New Year's Eve (day) 2015, there is no obvious sensation. But that's how it always is. Anything new is only felt whilst it is new. Then it becomes the norm and is no longer experienced.

There is what is seen and.... as I write this and look... it seems that is all there is (what is seen...) Oh, there is also what is felt, as part of the sensual reality. But it seems 'I' really am disappearing (as One must).

***

(February 2016)
Living in the Moment
This is a term we have all heard many times throughout our lives, whether we are interested in the so-called spiritual life or not. Personally I have had little to say about this so far. My journey has been one of struggling to be free of the emotional elements that one must deal with, whilst having a 'normal' job in the 'real' world. But I knew one day it would come.

I write this mid-February 2016. I have had a few weeks off work, away from the hustle and bustle, and have focussed my efforts on slowing down. The increasing challenges of work meant I have always been busy. I've been conscious, sure, but still busy, in the knowledge that I must get through the jobs today as there would be more tomorrow (no doubt many will recognise this). But this 'time out' has been invaluable, as well as timely.

It's been a few weeks since I wrote the last section entitled 'Freedom', about letting go of the body. I write here now about 'Living in the Moment', as I let go of business (i.e. busyness).

The latest shift occurred only yesterday evening. I was sitting at home watching television, doing my best to slow the mind (after so many years of rushing everything, conscious effort has been required for this part recently. One can still be conscious when one is busy; just as one can be unconscious when one is not). I was again feeling the sensation of having a body, but not actually feeling the body, per se. It was the energy I was feeling rather than bodily parts. Nonetheless, I found this energy intrusive. And wanted to let go of it, be free of it.

So again I let go of holding on to it and directed my attention away, to the 'screen'. Not just the television screen, but the entire visual appearance in front of me: the walls, curtains, etc. And instantly the sensation was gone. 'I' was gone. There was only what was seen!

This is not entirely new to me. I wrote about an earlier experience in our first book, in the section 'The Disappearing "I"' (and is described in a previous chapter of this book). That experience, which occurred perhaps fifteen years ago, was in the entertainment club of a holiday park in West Sussex whilst I was watching a band. Suddenly it was as if 'I' disappeared; there was only what was being seen. It was as if there was no perceiver. The perceiver and the perceived did indeed become One; not because they merged, but because the perceiver disappeared. The experience lasted a few moments only, but the memory of it has stayed with me ever since... Now it was back – this time to stay (?)

I like to be original in my descriptions of my experiences and insights, but as very little will be totally new (it's a well-trodden road), there will inevitably be some overlap. And I here have to refer to a description I have heard before. Not because I remember it as such, but because it came to me, and then I recognised my insight as something I had come across previously:

As I look at the screen of perception in front of me (the world of apparent objects), it is as if there is no interruption. There is a purity, a clarity between the perceiver and what is perceived. And the explanation or description of it came to me as follows:

The pure consciousness or awareness looks 'out', through the person and into the world of the senses. Whilst the person may not feel like s/he is thinking or feeling anything at that particular moment in time, the person is there all the same. The person (call it 'ego', or 'self') acts as a filter, and thus there is a sense of separation – *that is over there; I am here!*

So, if we liken the person to a piece of glass (and this is the bit I've heard before), the light of perception is dulled somewhat by passing through the dirty pane. But of course it doesn't know it; 'light' (perception) doesn't know anything. And the person doesn't know it either – doesn't see it, the obstruction, as it *is* it – the person is the dirty glass.

The so-called spiritual life is simply the process of cleaning the glass: dissolving the person as a person-al entity so as to leave only what is looking and what is being seen. And as what is looking has no attributes, only what is seen remains. Beautiful!

***

(March 2016)

Further Disintegration of the Self

It's now the beginning of March 2016 and a further two weeks have passed since I wrote the above piece. There have been a couple of items worth noting since, but they seem to dissipate so fast: what in one minute is quite a profound experience is only a faint memory a few days later.

Nearly two weeks ago, when seated in a local coffee shop, reading, with the book on my lap and my hand supporting it underneath, as I looked down at the page I noticed my arm ended at the edge of the book, as my hand was covered. And the strange bit was that, although I could feel my hand underneath, the information was that there was no hand. There was only what could be seen... Much like a very young child who is so new to the world, and takes much

384

enjoyment playing 'peekaboo': the adult hides their face behind their hands (for example) and then emerges again, as if by magic (to the child). As time passes, this wonder is lost into the world of experience. Now it was back, for me. There is only what is seen.

A few days later, when in bed at night lying in the darkness 'trying' to go to sleep, I noticed I was not trying at all. I was wide awake, and was actually fine about it. This may have been helped by it being a Thursday so there was only one day of work remaining (and I would not spend the rest of the week suffering with tiredness from having not slept). But certainly this seemed to be a new experience. There was just no urgency, no pressure, no time... (just 'being'.)

And since then, it is as if whatever I am doing is part of a larger picture. I am never 'just doing' something which in a while will be over. There is a greater experience (or reality, or even 'truth') behind whatever is occurring. The 'doing' is still 'being done', but perhaps not by 'me'.

Both the above have apparently become part of everyday experience. But this means they cannot be felt or experienced anymore (at least, not with the same impact). They do however appear to be part of the continuing detachment from the physical, of being the slave to the never-ending 'time' and 'doing'.

***

It seems this part of the journey is coming to an end. I have been advised that I may leave work, taking voluntary redundancy at the end of June. It has been a difficult period spanning thirteen years in total – since I started with the council, at least. My working life was difficult long before that. As is the way, now that I have learnt all I can, and have been conscious throughout (as much as I was able), the emotion, indeed the *need* for the (work) situation to exist has been dissolved. It is now time to move on!

In the following weeks at the council I was able to work at a more sensible pace and cover a more manageable area. The job was still done, and done well, but without the stress and the rushing about. A few days before I left I was asked how I felt about leaving. When I looked I saw that I felt like I was 'abandoning my post', leaving my colleagues to 'continue the good fight'. And this probably sums it up pretty well. But I was neither sad to be leaving nor excited to be going. I was not relieved it was over, nor was I looking forward to the new start. It had served its purpose and now it was coming to an end. As a result, my exit was as low-key as I was able to get away with, all things considered.

***

So I left. And within weeks had got out my bag of files and handwritten notes spanning the last twenty plus years, purchased a microphone and began to use the speech-to-text software which enabled me to create this book with far less effort that I would ever have deemed possible. (I was writing – or perhaps that should be 'dictating' – between five thousand and eight thousand words per day!)

And as the latest phase of my life and living settles down, and I am again the 'Being' that was lost and smothered under all the emotion for so long, what now...?

Well, as per those simple words with which the journey began:

...A Dream it may be,

But the Dream goes on!

So what is next?

Actually that is a tricky question to answer, 'What is next?' To offer any sort of answer requires that one use a combination of logic, speculation and resourcing the experiences of others who have gone before.

But having said that, with regards to the latter, not very many have gone before; and of those that have, a large proportion tended to have been entrenched in Eastern teachings and philosophies and their descriptions relate to this background. As a result, whilst they might be interesting and can suggest an idea as to what may happen next, these cannot be relied upon as any sort of road map.

What we can be fairly sure of is that the experience will become finer, both within and without (in myself, and my experience physically in the world). And as the sense of 'Being' deepens, there will most likely be new experiences related to this.

By way of a few brief examples that have happened just in the last few months since I left work: 1) On several consecutive days I found myself stating out loud that it felt to me as if I could remain in that specific location indefinitely (regardless of where I actually was at that moment). 2) My memory has never been good, but it seems hopeless now for me to even try to retain any information (though thoughts may arise in the moment, and often these are perfectly relevant to the situation at hand). 3) It has become near impossible for me to make a choice in some situations; especially, it appears, with regards to food. (I don't eat meat if I can avoid it, but besides that, I'll enjoy whatever is put in front of me.) 4) When faced with an emotional situation, it occurred to me that I was now like a pebble skimming across the surface of a pond, lightly touching the emotion but not becoming immersed in it. 5) It is as if I no longer 'do' anything. Things are 'done', but there is nothing of 'me' invested in the doing. 6) When I see people working, it is as if I intuitively see or recognise the emotion in that body that is being lived through the duties. (After all, this world is made *of* emotion, *for* emotion, as we know.) *And last, but by no means least: 7)* After noticing one evening that the sense of 'Being' felt like it was 'silky smooth', this quickly faded and I was left with the phrase (though I'm not sure where I have heard it before), [I am] 'residing in Self'.

I have no doubt that new experiences will continue to unfold over the coming weeks, months and years, and I would love to be able to include them all in this book. But of course that would mean delaying publication until the end of my journey – which could mean the end of my life – and that would seem to be a shame as the rest of it might be worth reading before then.

***

Looking at the question 'what is next?' regarding Nick and Sally physically, that is perhaps another story entirely. And one, it could be said, that began thousands of years ago as depicted in the Bible in the chapter Genesis, of Adam and Eve in the Garden of Eden:

The story says that God warned them that while they could eat the fruit of any tree they wished, they were not to eat from the 'Tree of Knowledge', for they would be doomed to die if they did so!

And as we know, the story says they ate the fruit and were therefore expelled from the garden to suffer in the world.

What is perhaps not so well known or appreciated is that the 'Tree of Knowledge' is further described specifically as giving the knowledge of good and bad. And this 'knowledge' is of course to make a mental and/or emotional judgment about something.

So what we have is God warning them not to create an emotional self, a self-ish, unhappy and wanting

390

personality. Because they would lose their conscious connection with the 'One'; thus the self, the person(ality) would inevitability one day die (as the 'One' must be made whole again).

So, back to Sally and Nick: Nick has finished work; Sally is due to finish in a few weeks (mid December 2016), and after that they have few if any real plans. But they have returned home – home to the experience described as the original Garden of Eden, and here they are once again united in love, both within and without.

So I will close the book here, in the knowledge that the journey will continue in one way or another; that is, at least, until all emotion, all need to exist has been dissolved and the dream evaporates. Until then,

...A Dream it may be, but the Dream goes on!

Acknowledgments

First I would like to thank The Barry Long Foundation for their kind permission for Barry's letters to be published in full.

Besides the above, these acknowledgments are probably best phrased so as to encompass absolutely everything that has affected my spiritual journey. In a story such as this, it is perhaps noticeable that the most difficult parts, the most emotionally painful and challenging experiences, are when the biggest strides are taken towards self-growth. And in that sense, absolutely everything which has had an effect on one's emotional state of mind becomes not only relevant, but positive as well.

With the above in mind, I would like the reader to regard this entire book from start to finish as a long list and description of acknowledgments which have assisted me on my journey.

Thank you,

Nick Roach

Also by Nick Roach: *Enlightenment, the Simple Path*
                        NR Publishing, 2010

                        Essays in Truth, Glimpses into
                        Reality. NR Publishing 2010

For information on Nick's talks, teaching classes, one-to-ones and other publications:

Please visit: www.nickroach.uk
Email: info@nickroach.uk